MAINSTREAM of AMERICA

Mainstream of America Series ★

EDITED BY LEWIS GANNETT

THE LONESOME ROAD

books by Saunders Redding

THE LONESOME ROAD

AN AMERICAN IN INDIA

ON BEING NEGRO IN AMERICA

THEY CAME IN CHAINS

STRANGER AND ALONE (Fiction)

NO DAY OF TRIUMPH

TO MAKE A POET BLACK

THE LONESOME ROAD

The Story of the Negro's
Part in America

BY SAUNDERS REDDING

Doubleday & Company, Inc., Garden City, New York.

Library of Congress Catalog Card Number 58-6647

Copyright © 1958 by Saunders Redding

Printed in the United States of America

To My Father

Contents

PART ONE: GLORY ENOUGH FOR A DAY

CHAPTER I: Bombs Bursting in Air   13
   1. *Death in the Dark*   13
   2. *A Question of Identity*   21

CHAPTER II: Born Free   25
   1. *Charleston Child*   25
   2. *And "Every Distinction"*   31
   3. *Preceptor's Farewell*   32

CHAPTER III: Born Slave   39
   1. *To Be Free*   39
   2. *Runaway*   44
   3. *North Star*   47
   4. *Days of the Martyr*   57

PART TWO: ALL GLORY GONE

CHAPTER IV: Faith   65
   1. *Isabella No-Name*   65
   2. *Bathed in Holiness*   67
   3. *Sojourner*   72
   4. *God's Pilgrim*   75
   5. *"Frederick, Is God Dead?"*   80

CHAPTER V: Mississippi Delta   83
    1. *Crusade in Cuba*   83
    2. *Santiago*   86
    3. *Rope and Faggot*   91
    4. *"Keep Powerful Friends"*   93
    5. *No North: No South*   100
    6. *Black Man's Place*   105
    7. *The Boss*   113
    8. *Patience Is the Pay-Off*   121

CHAPTER VI: A Doctor's Dilemma   127
    1. *My People*   127
    2. *Mixed Heritage*   128
    3. *Doctor in Chicago*   133
    4. *Our People*   142
    5. *Song of Love*   148
    6. *The Nadir*   151
    7. *Freedmen's Own*   154
    8. *Conflict in Cow Town*   157
    9. *Washington, Farewell*   162
   10. *Dirty Work*   165
   11. *Resignation*   174
   12. *Resignation Rescinded*   177

PART THREE: MEN IN MOTION

CHAPTER VII: Paths to the Future   181
    1. *"Nigger Demus"*   181
    2. *Less Than Enough*   183
    3. *Mixed Blood*   188
    4. *"Everybody Always Picked on Him"*   191
    5. *Race War*   197
    6. *Moods of Despair*   204
    7. *Exodus*   208
    8. *Walk Together, Children*   215

CHAPTER VIII: African Fantasy   220
    1. *Les Enfants Perdus*   220
    2. *Black Star's Zenith*   227
    3. *"Oh, Kinsmen!"*   229
    4. *Black Star's Decline*   234
    5. *Jazz Age*   240

CHAPTER IX: American Chapter   246
    1. *Bust*   246
    2. *Apostle*   249
    3. *Victory?*   260
    4. *Untrod Path*   266
    5. *A Big Man Goes Far*   275
    6. *The Better Man Wins*   286
    7. *Folk Epic*   288
    8. *"Ain't Fightin' for Nothin'"*   300

PART FOUR: AND LONG ENDURE

CHAPTER X: "You Can't Tell Which of Them Joes"   305

CHAPTER XI: Morning Fair   313
    1. *Strategy*   313
    2. *Nobody's Fool*   315
    3. *Bridgeheads*   321
    4. *The Conscience of the Country*   326

CHAPTER XII: Mr. Smith Goes to Washington   330

BIBLIOGRAPHY   335

INDEX   341

PART ONE

Glory Enough
for a Day

CHAPTER ONE

Bombs Bursting in Air

1. DEATH IN THE DARK

EVERYTHING WAS quiet except the sea, and that—ebbing as the purple dusk congealed to darkness—sucked back through the marshes and hissed along the narrow strip of beach with the sound of ravening mouths. The air was acrid, partly from the odor of the marsh, partly from the brine of the sea, but mostly from the sting of burned gunpowder and cordite. Though the bombardment of forty-one guns, aided by the cannons of six warships riding a stone's throw offshore, had ceased three hours ago, no breeze had risen to dispel the hot scent of the cannonade. It had lasted eleven hours, but Fort Wagner remained—slope-sided, parapeted and silent, as impregnable as ever, it seemed, in the thickening twilight. It would have to be stormed.

Shortly before seven o'clock a fog-laden breeze drifted in from the sea, and the men of the 54th Massachusetts Regiment tried to relax. It was impossible. They were raw troops, having had only a skirmish on James Island the previous day to learn from. For two years, while the battles of the Seven Days, second Bull Run, Fredericksburg, and Chancellorsville were fought and lost, certain leaders and champions

of freedom had urged, pressed, harangued President Lincoln to re-
cruit black men for war. "With every reverse to the national arms,
with every exulting shout of victory raised by the slave-holding rebels,
I have implored the imperilled nation to unchain against her foes her
powerful black hand," cried Frederick Douglass. Charles Sumner and
Samuel Pomeroy echoed him in the Senate, and Horace Greeley in
the press. Carl Schurz, minister to Spain, came across the ocean:
"Mr. President, all Europe is looking. . . ." And now at last that
black hand was unchained, a thousand pairs of black hands. But
they could not relax.

In this battle, and in what was left of the war, they would have
much to contradict and more to affirm. They would have to contradict all those charges made against them: that they would not fight,
for "at a crack of Old Master's whip" they would flee the field in
abject terror; that even were they endowed with courage they were
too ignorant to learn the arts of combat; that this was, after all, "the
white man's country and the white man's war"—charges that Lincoln
himself seemed to believe sufficiently to keep black men from battle.
Now by their conduct in this engagement they would have to prove
that they possessed all those qualities—confidence, resolution, and
valor—summed up in the word "manhood." They would have to
affirm their faith that the ultimate mission of this war was not only
to save the Union but to free the slaves. They would have to vindi-
cate their belief that "liberty won only by white men would lose half
its lustre."

Gathered squatting and sitting in little knots to themselves, some
distance from the seasoned white troops that had occupied the southern end of Morris Island for several days and that were also to be
committed to this battle, the men of the 54th were not aware of the
approach of their brigade commander. But suddenly a low-pitched
voice called out, "Men! Men of the 54th!" They scrambled up
quickly, tensely, snatching rifles and fixing bayonets, and pressed together just as General Strong, flanked by aides and orderlies, rode up.
The lights of federal warships, bobbing at anchor in the channel,
pulsated dimly through the drifting fog. The general clapped his

white-gauntleted hands, making a sound like a pistol shot, but his voice was quiet when he spoke.

"Men of the 54th—free men. We will attack." He paused dramatically, and for a moment there was a silence as palpable as a knife thrust. His gaze swept the disordered press of men. "You will lead it," the general said. Then a cheer rose uncertainly, gathered strength, but never really swelled to the full, and years later a man of the regiment was to say that they were choked up with emotion.

With the barest gesture of salute, General Strong cantered away.

The emotion that choked up the cheers of the 54th may have been gratitude; it may have been pride; it may have been fear. It may have been all these and more, so many feelings so compacted that they could not be defined. The heart too often ravaged cannot defend itself. "I remember how it was," wrote a young man of the regiment to his father, and in the moment of knowing how it was he had wondered how many black men would have to purchase dignity with death. For he remembered also the mocks and taunts, the gibes of certain Northern Negroes grown cynical and bitter. "Sure *they* want you. They want you dead, sacrificial blacks on the altar of Union!" He remembered the jeers of not always hooligan whites, set to the cadence of a march, *the* march from camp in Massachusetts to Boston Harbor, thence shrilling to the hammering of an engine vessel, the *De Molay*, chugging past a thousand miles of terror-blasted shores:

> In battle's wild commotion
> I won't at all object
> If a nigger should stop a bullet
> Coming for me direct.

> A nigger's just an ape-thing,
> A thing of no respect.
> If he should stop a Minié ball
> I shan't at all object.

Lewis Douglass—the younger son of the Negro abolitionist Frederick Douglass, who with his brother Charles had been the first in the state of New York to enlist—remembered. But also he remembered his father's answer to those jeers. "Better even die than to live slaves. . . . The day dawns; the morning star is bright upon the horizon! The iron gate of our prison stands half open. One gallant rush . . . will fling it wide, and four millions of our brothers and sisters will march out to liberty." Lewis wrote to his sweetheart in faraway Syracuse, "I thought of it and felt better." But this was afterward.

Now, as the troops formed and moved forward over the hard-packed sand of the narrow causeway, no one felt good, and especially none of the men of the 54th. They had arrived on Morris Island only a couple of hours before sundown. They had had neither rest nor refreshment for two days. Moreover, a sudden severe thunderstorm had drenched them, and as they moved to the van their steaming uniforms weighed heavy as lead. There were six regiments in the 1st Brigade, commanded by General Strong, but since the plan was to commit them a regiment at a time the 54th was ordered up on the double so as to widen the distance between it and the supporting 6th Connecticut.

There was an air of suspense as they advanced the depth of a regiment. No gun spoke and no light shone from the fort less than four hundred yards ahead. Had Wagner been knocked out by the bombardment and evacuated? Soon they were almost within musket range, an excellent massed target against the fading sky and the tawny beach. Still nothing from the fort. Perhaps the rumor that went whispering sibilantly through the ranks was true. Perhaps in that hour of blackening rain and thunder the Confederates had scampered down the hidden sea face of the fort and escaped in small boats to Sumter.

But, indeed, the opposite had happened. Wagner had been heavily reinforced.

All at once the cry "Heads up!" rang out from the rear, and the column of moving men on the left pressed inward against their companions as a horseman went tearing by. There was no room for dispersion on the road between the sea and the marsh. Two more mounted men galloped past. The first was General George C. Strong. He was easily recognized by his white-gauntleted hands, with which he held the reins high and loose. It was not certain who the others were, but word came back that one was General Gilmore himself. A moment or two more and the troops were ordered to halt. They did not have long to wait. General Strong's voice spoke out. The forward men could hear well enough, but the breeze, blowing stiffly now, whipped the voice before it reached the rear, and the men back there caught only drifting tatters of it.

"Free men . . . 54th . . ." The general first expressed his regret for sending them into battle without food or rest, but ". . . hour has struck. Men . . . tonight for freedom . . ." It was the kind of pre-battle address fashionable since the days of the Caesars. It was the siren voice of glory "luring them to the bloody and inhospitable trenches" of Wagner. A little more of this and then the three horsemen, General Strong the last, rode back down the line, but slowly, fixing the troops with steady gaze, and all three holding salute, their horses sidling with their heads toward the ranks.

But speechmaking was not yet over. Colonel Shaw, the regimental commander, stepped forward. He had been until recently a captain in the 2nd Massachusetts, and had fought at Winchester and Antietam. The commission for his new command had been carried to him like a votive offering by his father from Boston to Virginia. Ordinarily Shaw's manner was uncommonly impressive, but in the dusk before the battle, survivors said later, the man shone with "angelic light." And even if this was merely the normal glorification of the heroic dead, all sources are agreed that Robert Gould Shaw was an exceptional human being. Between him and his men flowed a strong tide of feeling. He gave them his patrician-bred understanding and sympathy; they gave him gratitude and their implicit faith. He was for them a symbol of what men—and black men too—could be; of what perhaps this war was fought to prove they could become once it was over. He was a talisman. As if to prove it, the skies, lowering and threatening since the storm, cleared and a few stars winked as Shaw stepped forth. A quite spontaneous cheer went up. The men leaned to hear him. They did not need to, for the breeze that had torn General Strong's voice to tatters had no power over Shaw's. It was bugle-clear and beautiful.

It took him only a minute to make his speech. He told them that much depended on this night's work. He reminded them that an act of the Confederate Congress made the Union's Negro soldiers outlaws, denied them the protection of the captured, and that as prisoners they might be sold into slavery, summarily shot, or hanged. The military design of the assault, he said, was to breach the defenses of Charleston. But was this all, or even the main? Not by any means. Lifting his drawn sword, the colonel pointed to the emblematic pennon, which none could read in the gloam. But they did not need to do this either, for they knew what that oblong of white silk bore—the figure of Liberty. The simple command "Forward!" rang out, and the mass took stride on the shelterless narrow strip of the flat.

Before they had gone forty paces, being now within musket range, the bastion front lit up from end to end with a sheet of running flame. It was a terrific shock, for the men half believed and half hoped that the bombardment had permanently silenced the Rebel guns, sealed up the approaches to the bombproof, and sent Taliaferro's forces skedaddling for the relative safety of Cumming's Point.

With that first blast, this was proved a delusion. Men dropped like ripened fruit in a windstorm. But in that instant glow of sulphurous light before the smoke and dust rolled out, Colonel Shaw saw his first objective—a place forward where the gourd-shaped island flared out before it narrowed to a neck of land on the tip of which blazed Wagner. Urging his men to it, Shaw loosened his ranks and charged them into that murderous hail of canister, grape, and musket ball. The screams of the wounded pierced the frightful din, but as if in eerie counterpoint the voice of a corporal named Payne kept shouting, "Liberty, boys!" and a moment later from farther down the line, "Freedom, boys!" Corporal Payne was everywhere at once. The ramparts of Wagner crackled and roared, spurting the blue flames of small arms and the reddish-yellow blasts of cannon. And as if this were not enough, a crash of artillery and a storm of solid shot thundered in from the left. The Confederate batteries on Sullivan's Island had opened up, and it was like sweeping a corridor with a broom of fire. Men fell in swaths: others pushed ahead.

Indeed, there was nothing else to do and no place else to go but ahead. For now the Rebel guns at Cumming's Point and Sumter were lobbing shells onto the sandspit, plowing up the ground in the rear of the 54th and pinning down, at least temporarily, the supporting regiments. The wider ground on which Shaw had deployed his troops was completely plastered. Somewhere off on the seaward flank, but apparently in the path of fire, General Strong realized what the situation was and ordered a double-quick charge. He did not live to see it executed; nor could it have been executed. All the 54th could do was creep into a musketry fire that was as solid as a wall of steel. The rest of the 1st Brigade, consisting of five regiments, staggered in behind.

Almost every step produced confusion. No one knew the terrain in the dark. The regiments backing up the 54th got scrambled like eggs. Colonel Barton of the New Yorkers found himself in the midst of troops from Maine. His own men had gone on ahead, where they briefly occupied some rifle pits hastily dug for the assault of seven days before. When he did find his men they were coming back with their wounded. Meantime a company of Connecticut men had got bogged down in the marshes of Vincent's Creek off to the left and, caught in the heaviest fire from Sullivan's Island, were churned to bloody mincemeat in the mud. The 2nd Brigade came in under Colonel Putnam, who kept shouting, "Forward! Forward!" and, losing his men, himself advanced so swiftly as to overtake the rear of the 54th. The hailstorm did not slacken. The din was "like a million locomotives straining on a grade." There were now three thousand men caught on a spot of land three hundred yards at its widest. Two thousand more were to come. But none of them, except those who died, stayed for long.

It seems impossible that no one on the Union side knew about the ditch. Eight days before, on July 10, the Union landing on Morris Island had been effected, and that same day an attack was pushed within six hundred yards of the fort, but the position was untenable.

On July 11, General Gilmore's dispatch to General Halleck noted: "We now hold all the Island except about one mile on the north end, which includes Fort Wagner, and a battery at Cumming's Point. . . ." On the twelfth a parallel was commenced for the emplacement of siege guns a thousand yards from Wagner, and other measures were taken preliminary to the assault, timed for six days later. Since it is impossible to conceive that among these measures was none for scouting and reconnoitering the terrain, it must be supposed that in the furious, milling confusion of the infantry attack the ditch was forgotten.

There it was, several feet wide and filled with four feet of water. The glacis of the fort sloped down to it, and the glacis was Colonel Shaw's next objective. Only the musketry and grenades of the enemy could reach here. But the going was tough. The sandy slope was pitted from the bombardment, and it was dark, and darkness was the doom of this attack. With Shaw at its crest, the first wave of the 54th plunged headlong into the unseen ditch. A few men panicked and drowned, but most scrambled out, shouted warnings to those who followed, and started up the glacis. Musket fire hissed into them. Grenades screamed down. Beyond the ditch, and halted by it in utmost confusion, a company of Maine men began firing on the slope, and Captain Luis Emilio, bringing up the rear of the Negro columns, shouted out, "Don't fire on us! We're the 54th!" But his shouts were ineffective. He ordered a retreat, and some of his men slid down the scarp and waded back across the ditch.

Meanwhile the brave or reckless Colonel Shaw and about ninety men, Corporal Payne and Sergeants Lewis Douglass and John Wall among them, had clawed their way to the top. A sudden blaze of calcium light revealed them mounted on the parapet. For a shocked moment the Confederates who saw them there stopped firing as if in awe, or in tribute to such daring. How could they have come up the glacis slope through that savage storm? Yet there they were, plainly to be seen in the blaze of light, their colonel waving his sword, and next to him the color sergeant, John Wall, carrying the flag. Both were hit at the instant Lewis Douglass' sword sheath was blown off him and he, uninjured, blasted back down the scarp. Wall staggered and dropped the flag, but the wounded Sergeant Carney caught it and slid away. Colonel Shaw, however, toppled inside the fort, and some eighty of his "reckless and insane men," said General Taliaferro's report, "who seemed to insist upon immolation," jumped in after him. There they fought hand to hand around Shaw's lifeless body until every man of them was killed.

The assault on Fort Wagner was totally repulsed and over in an hour, but the Union forces did not retire completely. Captain Emilio gathered what was left of the 1st Brigade, dug in on a line seven hundred yards from the fort, and kept up a desultory and useless fire through half the night. Scattered elements of the 2nd Brigade fronted the enemy at other points. Until two o'clock in the morning they waited for the order to renew the attack, but it never came. The sand had drunk its fill of blood. In the morning, "as the sun rose and revealed our terrible losses, what a rich harvest Death had gathered during the short struggle!" Two thousand men had fallen. Five hundred and fifty-eight of these were officers and men of the first Negro regiment recruited in the free states. When in the morning a request was made for the body of Colonel Shaw, a Rebel officer sent back the reply, "We have buried him with his niggers."

2. A QUESTION OF IDENTITY

A little while earlier a good many people, and perhaps a majority even in the North, would have snickered with gratification at this reply. Save only the abolitionists, few felt sympathy for the Negro, and even a considerable group of abolitionists led by William Lloyd Garrison had not wanted a war to free the slaves.

> To the flag we are pledged, all its foes we abhor,
> And we ain't for the nigger, but we are for the war.

But, indeed, enthusiasm for the flag and "union forever" soon drained off in the defeats of Bull Run, Fredericksburg, and Chancellorsville. Before the winter of 1861 ran out some Northern newspapers, like the Philadelphia *Age*, were complaining that the government had "plunged the country into a costly war to help the undeserving Negro." Horatio Seymour, governor of New York, Franklin Pierce, New England-born and -bred ex-President of the United States, and James Gordon Bennett, editor of the New York *Herald*, expressed— and heatedly, too—the opinion that the North had committed a "crime" against the South and that it should be expiated by a peace that left undisturbed all the prerogatives of the slave power.

In short, the great body of Northerners did not care to fight for the freedom of Negroes. When the Emancipation Proclamation made it clear that the issue of freedom was joined with the issue of union, a crisis developed. It was especially acute among the working-class whites, who, already in competition with free Negroes in the Northern labor market, saw emancipation as the start of a tidal wave of black men that would wash them out of the labor market entirely. The crisis swelled and burst in the spring of the Proclamation year, when Lincoln signed a draft law whose provisions made it virtually impossible for the common run of white men to escape war service. Infuriated, they turned upon Negroes. They destroyed Negro property. They murdered a hundred Negroes in Cleveland. At the very time when black soldiers were dying in droves at Wagner, black men, women, and children were lying butchered, shot, and roasted in the ashes of an orphanage in New York.

The Negro's recruitment into the Union Army seems to have increased the hostility. This was irony and paradox. Negroes had fought and several thousands of them had died in the war for American independence, and when the victory in that war seemed about to be undone they fought again and died in the War of 1812, when they were invited by the hot-eyed General Andrew Jackson "to share in the perils and divide the glory" with their "white countrymen." But their feeble identification both as Americans and as men had been destroyed in the years between the wars. It had been destroyed quite relentlessly by the economic and social imperatives of slavery, which, combining with an abstruse metaphysic, made the declaration, "Negroes, sir, are brute beasts," sound reasonable. No one except Negroes themselves and a few abolitionists seriously argued against this opinion, based as it was on the "scientific calculation" that the Negro was only three-fifths human. Thus as a matter of course he was excluded from the dispensation of the natural rights of man. Thus it seemed an abomination that his freedom should be a cause of war and a defilement of humanity that he himself should fight for it, or want to.

The same reasoning had produced in the South, the place of its origin, quite other results. It created the anachronistic spectacle of masters riding off to war with black body servants to squire them. It led to the impressment of slaves to do service for the Confederate cause in arsenal, mill, and factory; as cooks, teamsters, and ambulance attendants; as builders of roads, bridges, and fortifications. It produced legislative authorization (Tennessee, 1861) to enlist free Negroes in the Army of the Confederacy. And finally it led to the adoption of a resolution by the governors of North and South Carolina, Georgia, Alabama, and Mississippi to arm the slaves to fight for the perpetuation of their own slavery.

No Southerner pretended that this resolution failed of implementation because of a revulsion of Confederate sensibilities. The evidence is that it failed under the weight of a practical consideration. "God forbid that this Trojan horse should be introduced among us!" cried a member of the Confederate Congress. But in the last grim days of the war the Trojan horse was less fearful to contemplate than total defeat, and one no longer shilly-shallied over the meaning of a foggy passage in President Davis' message (1864) to Congress: "Should the alternative ever be presented of subjugation or the employment of the slave as soldier, there seems no reason to doubt what should then be our decision." The alternative presented itself, and there was no doubt, and on March 13, 1865, Davis signed an enactment to enlist slaves in the Rebel army.

In the established pattern of thinking and feeling about the Negro, this too was logical. And having come to this decision, if the South then wooed the slave, or tried to, with wine and song, parade and drum, to fight for the continuance of his vassalage, this was no more aberrant to Southern minds than the hostility to the Negro's fighting for union and freedom was to Northern minds. That is to say, not at all. Indeed, Northern and Southern minds were one in the pattern of reason—a pattern that, operating with equal effectiveness in both sections of the country, could not have been better devised to destroy the Negro's last thin ties to humanity and drive him to the verge of madness had this been the conscious intention.

It is no wonder that in their convention of 1863 free Negroes revived and debated in gloomy wretchedness the once damned question of immigration to Africa and South America. It is no wonder that one of their leaders cried out in weary anguish, "Who am I, God? And what?"

CHAPTER TWO

Born Free

1. CHARLESTON CHILD

THERE WERE those of his contemporaries who said that Daniel Payne was always crying out to God. It was a habit that he had acquired early, even perhaps by inheritance from that Grandfather *Paine* who had fought at Bunker Hill, whose twisted, thickened, gray-black likeness can be seen in Trumbull's painting of that battle, and who had a reputation for eccentricity—"he walked and talked with God"—as well as character. The reputation was not unearned. Dismayed or angered by the order of General Gates discharging black men from the Continental Army, Paine, a free man, shipped for Virginia in the 1780s. Here he changed the spelling of his name, married a free woman, and begot a son called London.

By this time there were two hundred thousand slaves in Virginia, and the state was a notorious slave-trading center. But from the beginning slavery there had created problems and raised grave questions of control, and the consciences of the best men of the land were never at peace with it. Negro rebellion flared with terrifying regularity. Miscegenation was producing a "mongrel race, unamenable to reason and

proper rearing alike." In the 1750s heavy duties had been imposed
upon slave importation, but the furious greed of traders would not
be denied, and the duties were overridden. The liberalism for which
Virginia colonial life was said to be distinguished dried up, and aristocratic sensibilities hardened under the scab of economic necessity.
But they were set in flux again by the humanistic ardor that boiled
up in the 1770s. Virginia aristocrats took the lead in the revolutionary struggle. They framed the state constitution of 1776: ". . . all
men are by nature equally free and independent, and have certain
inherent rights . . . namely, the enjoyment of life and liberty. . . ."

This was not all hollow sentiment. Anti-slavery societies had
sprung up and were active everywhere during and just after the Revolution. In Virginia alone ten thousand slaves were emancipated, and
Patrick Henry was moved to write a friend: "Is it not amazing, that
at a time when the rights of Humanity are defined and understood
with precision in a Country above all others fond of Liberty: that in
such an Age and such a Country, we find Men, professing a Religion
the most humane, mild, meek, gentle and generous, adopting a Principle as repugnant to humanity. . . . Would anyone believe that I
am Master of Slaves of my own purchase!"

Like Henry, other liberal aristocrats were stung by the inconsist-
ency—stung sufficiently hard to put through a law prohibiting the
slave trade in Virginia. But slave traders were resourceful enough to
get around the law. They bought slaves directly from trim "Maryland
runners, the fastest vessels that ever sailed the African coast," and,
posing as "gentlemen removing with their slaves to other parts,"
brought them into Virginia without molestation and sold them
south. They bred slaves too, but this took time and money. And
what was a nigger good for if he was not a slave? The question was
not rhetorical. Traders kidnaped free Negroes, among them London
Payne.

There is not much of a record of London Payne: cloudy dates haze
over what there is, and the secondhand memory of a four-year-old
across a span of sixty years is necessarily taken on trust. But Daniel
Payne's testimony is that his father was still a "child" when he was

kidnaped and sold south to Charleston—to a house and sign painter who was probably a "kindly" man. For though the sign painter's professional interest may have made it expedient for him to teach London to read and letter, mere expediency cannot account for letting London join an association of free Negroes called the Brown Fellowship Society and attend the midweek meetings in the newly founded African Methodist Church, where, as often as not after 1809–10, a bitter, burning ex-slave named Denmark Vesey identified the Negro race with the ancient Israelites and turned Holy Scripture to the purposes of rebellion. Expediency did not require that London Payne be let to hire out his spare time, so that his savings mounted year by year. Or perhaps he was helped by the free half-Indian woman—the mother-to-be of Daniel—he met and married. At any rate London bought his freedom for a thousand dollars the year he came of age.

So Daniel was born free on February 24, 1811, and the date was duly recorded in the metal-clasped family Bible. He was only four when his father died, and just turning eight when his mother also passed away. His memory was of having learned his letters before their deaths. His memory was of being carried on his father's shoulders from the house on Swinton Lane and along the purpling evening streets to church. He remembered his mother striding just a half a step behind, the better to hum in London's ear and help him carry the tune of the hymn he would be singing. Daniel himself could never sing a note, but in later years he was to compose religious verse, bring instrumental music and robed choirs to the services of the African Methodist Episcopal Church, and to write the lyrics for sacred hymns, some of which the Church still sings today.

After the death of his parents the days grew grim in Charleston, as everywhere in the Southern seaboard states. The economic crisis brought on by the Embargo and Non-Importation acts and the new war with Britain in 1812 had just appreciably lessened when natural disasters aggravated it again. Drought one year, rain and flood the next marched in implacable alternation through the seaboard states from 1815 to 1819. In South Carolina indigo plantations failed. Rice fields reverted to swamps. Cotton had all but exhausted the soil. The day was fast approaching when Robert Hayne, a South Carolina senator, would testify, "If we fly from the city to the country, what do we behold? Fields abandoned; agriculture drooping; our slaves . . . working harder and faring worse; the planter striving with unavailing efforts to avert the ruin which is before him."

Ruin had already overcome many. In 1820 depression rode Charleston itself like an incubus. Merchants went bankrupt. Crop loans were foreclosed. Shipyards shut down. A noticeable number of the sea-front houses that used to sing and purl with music and the gaiety of guests were boarded up and silent, and their mortgaged owners gone to live permanently in the country, there to brood over the sterile fields and the thinning ranks of slaves, and to breed into a new generation of their kind that passionate pride and contempt and resistless will to domination that, grown desperate, carried it gleefully into a hopeless war. Whites of another sort turned their faces west.

Meantime slaves were restless and defiant too, as ever in periods of economic distress, when their provisions were cut to the "scurvy sickness" level, or they were "run off," or leased out, or—fate most dreaded—sold down the river—when, in short, the master's only other option was to "be ruined to save the wretches." In the decade 1810–20 and for some time thereafter not many masters in the seaboard states could save the "wretches," whose subterranean discontent broke the surface here and there like so many erupting volcanoes: Maryland in 1811; Virginia in 1810, '11, '13; North Carolina in 1814, '15; South Carolina in 1817 and again in 1819.

This last was the year Daniel Payne, age eight, was taken to live with a Mrs. Elizabeth Holloway, who very shortly besought the Brown Fellowship Society "for aid for the helpless orphan." Aid came and was later supplemented from another source. The Minor Moralist Society was a group of free Negroes organized to provide for the material needs of colored orphans. It also ran a school, and Daniel went to it. He acquired reading, writing, and arithmetic, as well as the hunger for a knowledge no man has ever found in books alone—"Who am I, God?" Payne was past fifty when he thus addressed the Almighty, but even later he declared that he was still seeking knowledge of himself, "which, next to knowledge of God, is hardest to acquire."

But Payne's book learning was interrupted early. It was interrupted by one of those rebellious incidents in consequence of which slaveholders "never lay down to sleep without a brace of pistols at their side," and in consequence of which the South Carolina Supreme Court held that "A free African population is a curse. . . . this race, however conducive they may be in a state of slavery, in a state of freedom and in the midst of a civilized community . . . become corruptors of slaves." And by 1822 hundreds of slaves in Charleston and the surrounding forty miles had been corrupted by Denmark Vesey. If rebellion was a spreading disease—and it seemed to be— Payne's youth alone saved him from infection. He knew Vesey well, and Morris Brown, then Payne's "spiritual guardian" and later his devoted friend, was Vesey's "secret counsellor."

But secret counsel was not enough to insure the success of Vesey's ambitious plan. It had been preparing in his head for twenty years and outside it for two. Six companies of slaves, each under carefully selected leaders, were to be formed. One company was to seize the arsenal in Meeting Street, another the guardhouse, another the post at Cannon's Bridge, another Bennett's Mill, a fifth Bulkley's farm, and the sixth was to be on orders at Vesey's house. The day was to be a Sunday in the summer, for Sunday crowds of Negroes on the streets of Charleston were no unusual sight, and in the summer many whites left the city for resorts. About five thousand Negroes, slave and free, were involved. A few had guns, but mostly they were armed with pikes and bayonets and daggers, which Mingo Harth, a blacksmith co-conspirator, had forged in many midnights. As Vesey paraphrased it from Holy Writ, the purpose was to destroy "utterly all that was in the city, both man and woman, young and old . . . with the edge of the sword." Letters had been sent to the black President of the new black republic, Santo Domingo, describing the sufferings of Negro slaves and asking aid in the enterprise.

The operation was to begin at midnight, June 16. In mid-May the leaders began passing the word down to subleaders. One of the latter, a William Paul, had more will than wit. He was anxious to swell his corps of men. Unaware of Vesey's interdiction against house slaves, whom he distrusted more than "drunkards and loose-tongues," Paul spoke to one Devany, the cook in the Prioleau household. Devany's genius was "culinary, not revolutionary," and he promptly informed his master. This was on May 25. Moving furtively so as to arouse neither the alarm of the whites nor the suspicions of the uncaught insurgents, the authorities arrested Devany and Paul. Devany knew little, and for two weeks Paul refused to talk. But red-hot copper wires driven under the nails of hand and foot will draw words from any mouth. By June 14, carried forward with all the secrecy circumstances allowed, "extensive and efficient preparations had been made for the safety and protection of the city," reported Governor Bennet, three of whose slaves were among the rebels shortly to be hanged.

Informed by grapevine of what was afoot, the companies did not rendezvous—nor, strangely, did their leaders take advantage of the avenues of escape still open to them, though they knew that arrests were being made with little discrimination. A fit of petulance, a muttered word, a sullen look, a fancied discourtesy remembered from five years before was enough to bring arrest. On June 28, though the authorities were not sure that all the rebel leaders were in their hands, trials were begun. They were over by July 9. Thirty-seven Negroes were executed, forty-three transported, and forty-eight, found guilty of being privy, were publicly lashed and discharged. If this was all, a reporter for the New York *Commercial Advertiser* did not believe it. After commenting that Charleston was getting rid of its free black population "without the aid of the Colonization Society," he reported on August 5 that "there are about fifty more in confinement . . . who will probably be strung up with as little ceremony as they string up fish in the Fulton Market."

2. AND "EVERY DISTINCTION"

It was not necessary for the full extent of the conspiracy to be revealed to obtain the results that followed. Events
had always given substance to the fear of slave conspiracies, and the
specifics against fear were the very stuff of which revolts were made.
Now more specifics were proposed. They make a catalogue that
sounds, but was not, fantastic. It was proposed that itinerant
preachers, those "apostolic vagabonds who, with the sacred volume
of God in one hand, breathing peace to the whole family of man,
scatter at the same time with the other the firebrands of discord and
destruction . . . among our Negroes," be found out and dispersed.
It was proposed that Negroes not be allowed to "wear any silks,
satins, crepes, lace, or muslin," for "every distinction should be created among whites and Negroes, calculated to make the latter feel
the superiority of the former." It was proposed that the number of
Negro mechanics be limited, since many of the leaders of the conspiracy were mechanics, and that the hiring out of free time should
end. It was proposed that the prohibitions against slaves owning
property be erected against free Negroes also. It was observed that
many of the late leaders of the conspiracy could read and write,
and it was concluded that literate Negroes were dangerous. Negroes,
therefore, slave and free, should be prevented from learning to read
and write.

But proposals were not enough. Portentous logic said that laws
must follow, and they did—immediately. Hereafter conspiracy to
rebel was punishable by "death without benefit of clergy." It was
decreed that slaves could no longer hire out in spare time. The Negro
Seaman's Act provided that sailors entering Charleston Harbor be
arrested and held until their vessels sailed again. All other free Negroes entering Charleston did so under penalty of prison or the
auction block. To supplement an older statute that taxed free nonnative Negroes fifty dollars a year, a new law required all free Negroes above fifteen years of age to have some respectable white

person as guardian, and any who failed to maintain the reputation vouched for by his guardian would be sold forthwith into slavery. Negroes were denied the right of assembly, and this drove their churches underground. It was ruled a felony to teach, or permit to be taught, reading and writing to any Negro, and this closed down Negro schools.

And to enforce these laws? By the winter of 1823, Charleston had become an armed camp. Frederick Olmsted, later to journey there, wrote: "Police machinery such as you never find in towns under free government: citadels, sentries, passports, grapeshotted cannon, and daily public whipping of the subjects for accidental infractions of police ceremonies. I happened myself to see more direct expression of tyranny in a single day and night in Charleston, than at Naples for a week . . . there is . . . an armed force, with a military organization, which is invested with more arbitrary and cruel power than any police state in Europe."

3. PRECEPTOR'S FAREWELL

Daniel Payne, still short of his teens, did not understand all that was going on in 1822–23. The lot of a free Negro orphan child was somewhat harder than the lot of a slave child separated from his parents. Without blood relatives, cut loose from the ties that normally belong to childhood, Payne was projected into a dark, disorganized, and complicated world of fear and violence. The woman to whom he had first been sent, Mrs. Holloway, was dead. So too was Mrs. Sarah Bordeaux, an "aunt" more by courtesy than kin. Among other adults of his acquaintance, Vesey, Gullah Jack, and Monday Gell were dead by hanging. Thomas Bonneau, who had taught Payne the first two books of Euclid, was unaccounted for, simply vanished without a trace. Thinking it best to get out before it was discovered that he had encouraged the conspirators, the leader of the congregation of free blacks, "Elder" Morris Brown, fled north to Philadelphia, there shortly to become a bishop in the infant African Methodist Episcopal Church. The Church, the

Brown Fellowship Society, and the Minor Moralist Society were disrupted or suppressed. The free Negroes of Charleston—collectively "a curse to any country" and an "evil exactly proportional to the numbers of such population"—lived in a wilderness of laws and regulations to which no light of hope or reason seemed able to penetrate.

In this violent disorganization of his life, and as much from natural inclination as from imitative habit, young Payne turned to God with an intensity of religious passion most unusual in a boy of twelve. It was a period of seeking, he said later. The group worship—the singing, the prayers, and the testimonies—and the formalisms of the Church, however erratically practiced, had been a smooth and well-trod highway direct to heaven, and most of the people he had known marched along it. But now the road had disappeared overnight, by terrifying magic, and he was alone in a trackless desolation, he must find his way alone. He made solitary prayers. From his seventh or eighth year, sitting with his elders in weekly religious meetings, he had "sometimes felt the spirit of God moving" through his heart. Now he implored the spirit to take up permanent residence there.

At this time he was apprenticed to a carpenter and had a tiny back room on the ground floor of a house just off Swinton Lane. His room gave onto a patch of garden, ragged with a few flowers, grassless under a great magnolia tree, and here at night he used to pray. But nothing happened for a long time. When at last something did happen, it was not in the garden, or at night. "Between twelve and one o'clock one day, I was in my humble chamber pouring out my prayers to the listening ears of my Saviour, when I felt as if the hands of a man were pressing my two shoulders and a voice speaking within my soul saying, 'I have set thee apart to educate thyself that thou might be an educator to thy people.'"

If this was a mystical experience, Payne nowhere records having another. Perhaps he did not need another. This one he took for truth and, God's voice or not, Payne gave it an obedience that, except in one moment of extreme discouragement, never slackened. For the next six years, until he was eighteen, he lived like the ascetic he basically was. Now and then he found a teacher courageous enough to risk prison to help him, but mostly he taught himself. He had advanced far enough in the carpenter's trade to make simple things such as clotheshorses, benches, and stools, and these he peddled from door to door on Saturday afternoons. Other days he had fairly regular employment as a carpenter's helper. Nights after a supper of roasted sweet potato, or perhaps "a dish of black-eye peas boiled to a mush with a piece of fat," or, on a good night, "a scrap of ham or chicken" pilfered from the white folks' table by a slave woman who befriended him, Payne studied until midnight, slept until four, and studied again until six. He committed *Murray's Primary Grammar* to memory. He studied the *Columbian Orator*, as Frederick Douglass was to do in a few years, and pored over the *Self-Interpretating Bible*, whose Scotch author, the Reverend John Brown, noted in the preface his unaided conquest of Latin and Greek. Payne also studied Latin and Greek. Books were hard to come by legitimately: Payne "found" some and "borrowed" others. He studied geography, botany, zoology.

Meantime the lid of repression clamped on the brisk boiling up of slavery in 1822–23 was eased off a little. Another pot was on the fire. The tariff question of 1816 and 1824 began to simmer again in 1827. It gave off a smell offensive to Southerners, and particularly to John C. Calhoun, the most influential South Carolinian. For the better protection of his political career, he had recently abandoned his federalist views. Tariff was now a national issue, and slavery—not yet raised to that "bad eminence" by the organized agitation of "crack-brained abolitionists" and the presidential ambitions of Calhoun—was nothing compared to it. In 1828, when the "Tariff of Abominations" was passed, the North-South seam running down the back of the nation was strained almost to splitting.

Vice-President Calhoun represented the extremist view. He was for nullification and secession. Other men, including the governor of South Carolina, spoke more loudly about "the alarming extent to which the Federal Judiciary and Congress have gone toward establishing a great and consolidated government subversive of the rights of the States," but none had Calhoun's steely ambition. Senator George McDuffie might shout about resorting to arms to restore the "dignity of the South," but he did not have Calhoun's dogged, calculating, though disingenuous hate. And Charles Pinckney might declare that "the Constitution is degraded [by the tariff] to destroy one [the South] and support the other [the North]," but only Calhoun's tongue and only Calhoun's ambition and hatred were equal to annealing South Carolina, and with it the whole South, to the issue of secession.

If slavery was made an element in this issue by virtue of the first move to petition Congress to abolish it in the District of Columbia in 1828, the fact was temporarily overlooked. And so too were the slaves.

Thus it was no wonder that the Methodists also should be ignored, and that they should take advantage of it. Though the high fever of abolition had abated in them since the death of Wesley, they were still subject to "fits of the humanitarian sickness," and they still had their proselytizing zeal. They believed and said—and very persuasively, too—that the neglect of the spiritual needs of the slaves was a reflection on slaveholders. What a nuisance they made of themselves deploring the absence of suitable opportunities for giving their "inferior brethren" a Christian education and improving thereby their souls! In the midst of the congressional uproar upon which most Southern attentions were focused, one of these Methodists went quietly about his ordained business of "adapting and teaching Christian truth to the condition of persons having a humble intellect and a limited range of knowledge."

But Bishop William Capers was no emancipationist. It was no part of his idea to teach Negroes to read and write. Though he set up missions and persuaded some masters to send their slaves to them, he made it very clear that instruction would be oral, "by constant and patient reiteration," and based on biblical injunction: "Our heavenly Father commands that you, who are servants, should 'be obedient to them that are your masters according to the flesh.'

. . . As you ought to understand well what is the will of God respecting you, I will read to you again this part of the Bible. 'Servants, be obedient . . .' "

Bishop Capers' mission class did not promise much, but it allowed for a certain freedom of social intercourse that Payne needed. It brought him in contact with Samuel Weston, who gave more and other instruction than the bishop intended. Weston was the sort of Southern white man who was apotheosized in John G. Fee, who, disowned by his slaveholding family and mobbed twenty-two times for his anti-slavery views, went on to found Berea College for the education of both whites and Negroes.

Bishop Capers' dedication to his mission classes and their "beneficent" Christian influence contributed to a relaxation of the whites' fear and vigilance and made it possible for the free Negroes of Charleston to mend and patch their torn group life. For two or three years Daniel Payne attended the Cumberland Church mission class. Then at eighteen he opened a school of his own and started the work he believed God had called him to do.

It was not easy then, or ever. The first year his pupils were three freeborn children and three adult slaves. The schoolroom was in a building owned by a prosperous freeman on Tradd Street, and though Caesar Wright gave the use of it rent-free, the fifty cents a month Payne charged each pupil was scarcely enough to keep the place warm in winter. The teacher was constantly pressed for subsistence. He dressed in castoff clothing. A slave pupil brought food as often as she could manage to steal it. When Payne closed the term in May, he was tempted by an opportunity to go to the West Indies with a white man who wanted a free, intelligent Negro servant.

There's the proposition. Well, boy, damnit, what do you say?
I would like to pray, sir.
Pray if you must, but, damnit, the experience will be worth more than wages. Goddamnit, boy——
You are too profane, sir.

Payne had sixty pupils, mostly freeborn children, when he opened for the second term in the autumn of 1830. Wright's room was now too small, and Robert Howard, another free Negro, built a suitable shed in the rear of his yard on Anson Street. Here Payne kept school for the next five years. He taught grammar, arithmetic, geography, and the elements of zoology. He studied. He purchased books from friendly itinerant canvassers and, sub rosa, through Samuel Weston. Local bookstores would sell Negroes nothing. He picked herbs, shrubs, and flowers and studied them. He caught small animals, fish, and insects, examined their structures, and afterward frequently cooked and ate them. Worms, toads, and snakes he refused to eat. Much of what he did he recorded in a journal he kept from time to time.

"I bought a live alligator, made one of my pupils provoke him to bite, and whenever he opened his mouth, I discharged a load of shot from a small pistol down his throat. As soon as he was stunned, I threw him on his back, cut his throat, ripped his chest, hung him up, and studied his viscera till they ceased to move."

But an end to all this, never more than an arm's length away, was now at hand, and the hand grew tight with apprehension. Every wind brought the clamor of new alarms. In 1830 there appeared almost simultaneously in a half dozen places in the South copies of an inflammatory pamphlet addressed to "the colored citizens of the world, but in particular and very expressly to those of the United States," by a free Negro named David Walker. The following summer in Virginia Nat Turner's rebellion, thought to have been touched off by Walker's *Appeal*, raged through two bloody nights and days and brought "death in the most horrid forms" to sixty white men, women, and children. It required the mobilized military of three states to put it down. William L. Garrison founded the *Liberator* in Boston in 1831. The next year he declared that "no truth is more self-evident than that moral power, like physical, must be consolidated to be efficient." Issues of the *Liberator* mysteriously turned up in the South.

Aroused, and indeed already leaping to the first pitch of madness, the citizens of Charleston broke into the local post office to search for anti-slavery propaganda. "It will fall into the hands of niggers!" and too many Negroes could read and write. But hereafter the new South Carolina law of 1835 said, "If any free person of color or slave shall keep any school or other place of instruction for teaching any slave or free person to read or write, such free person of color shall be liable to the same fine, imprisonment, and corporal punishment as is by this act imposed and inflicted. . . ."

The long night had come. Payne closed his school. He was twenty-four, and old beyond his years. His yellow-brown, cadaverous face, under the taut skin of which the skeleton showed like brittle filigree, and his wasted-looking frame gave him the appearance of a graveyard thing. But behind his steel-rimmed glasses his eyes burned. He was full of obscure intricacies. To his students he addressed a poem, *Preceptor's Farewell.*

> Hate sin; love God; religion be your prize;
> Her laws obeyed will surely make you wise,
> Secure you from the ruin of the vain,
> And save your souls from everlasting pain.
> O, fare you well for whom my bosom glows
> With ardent love, which Christ my Saviour knows!
> 'Twas for your good I labored night and day;
> For you I wept and now for you I pray.
>
> And I! O whither shall your tutor fly?
> Guide thou my feet, great Sovereign of the sky.
> A useful life by sacred wisdom crowned,
> Is all I ask, let weal or woe abound!

Whither indeed?

CHAPTER THREE

Born Slave

1. TO BE FREE

THE VERY presence of free Negroes was anathema
to the slaveholding South, where, on the word of
Charles Van Evrie, "Free negroism [is] not a condition . . . which
the higher law of nature grants. . . . There are then only two possible conditions for the Negro—isolation or juxtaposition with the
white man—African heathenism or subordination to a master. . . ."
Free Negroes were "a dangerous anomaly," a "threat to the established and natural order of our society," and "an incubus upon the
land." And an incubus must be exorcised by the mighty conjurations
of *lex scripta, non scripta,* and *talionis.*

Thus in South Carolina, as elsewhere in the South, the free Negro was allowed very little initiative. He could not move into the
next county, where, haply, there might be work. In his own county
he could not engage in any occupation that required reading and
writing. He could not learn or engage in certain trades, such as
brewing. He could not buy or sell brew made by others. He could
purchase nothing on credit. He could not vote. Free Negroes could
not testify against white men or protect themselves by carrying or

possessing firearms. In conformity to the opinion expressed (in 1832) by the South Carolina Court of Appeals that free Negroes "ought by law be compelled to demean themselves as inferiors, from whom submission and respect to the whites . . . is demanded," they could not even carry canes. On the other hand, the colored freeman had to carry a certificate of freedom or risk being taken up and sold, though his certificate did not permit him to join "lyceums, lodges, fire companies, or literary, moral or charitable societies." Indeed, the distinction between slave and black freeman was sometimes so slight as to be indiscernible.

But if free Negroes seemed a dangerous anomaly to many in the South, they also seemed to some in the North a threat to society. A contributor to *Niles' Register* was not alone in believing that free Negroes were "a species of population not acceptable" to the people of Indiana, "nor indeed to any other, whether free or slave-holding, for they cannot rise and become like other men . . . but must always remain a degraded and inferior class of persons without the hope of much bettering their conditions."

That was written in 1818, when the number of free Negroes in the North was relatively small. By the 1830s the number had grown to two hundred thousand, an increase of 82 per cent, and there were highly visible concentrations of Negroes in Philadelphia, New York, and Boston, and west in Cincinnati. Here the English actress Fanny Kemble, embittered and grown restless on her husband's Georgia plantation, saw them and reported in her journal: "They are not slaves indeed, but they are pariahs, debarred from every fellowship save with their own despised race, scorned by the lowest ruffians. . . . They are free, certainly, but they are also degraded, the off-scum and the off-scouring of the very dregs of your society."

It was a society—in the late thirties and all through the forties— daily burdened with new problems. The industrial revolution was happening to America. Immigration was happening. Urbanization was happening. Migration westward was happening. Touched off by the flaming words of Garrison and blown upon by the timeless winds of social reform, abolition fires were roaring to a blaze. That abstraction known, then and now, as the "American way of life" was suffering changes of such profundity that the American mind could not fathom them. Having subconsciously adopted the German philosopher Herder's rosy conception that a nationality is "a plant of nature . . . one nationality with one national character," Americans had achieved by the 1830s a fancied homogeneity of character as stable as England's. It was a character molded and supported by three extrinsics: the Protestant faith, the designation Caucasian, and political freedom. Combined, these made "Anglo-Americans" who, in subliminal expectation of the fulfillment of De Tocqueville's prophecy, "alone will cover the immense space . . . extending from the coasts of the Atlantic to those of the Pacific."

But that homogeneity, as well as the prophecy, was threatened, and if this was for the metaphysicists and the population theorists to worry about, the fabled man in the street had his worries too. What worried and alarmed him was the threat to his economic well-being. This was personal, this was real. In the face of it there began to develop one of those periodic blights of Northern grass-roots idealism that, temporarily, made the poet Bryant's words sound ironic:

> There's freedom at thy gates and rest
> For Earth's down-trodden and oppressed,
> A shelter for the hunted head,
> For the starved laborer toil and bread.

Native-born Americans in the North resented the black freemen, who were certainly among the "Earth's down-trodden and oppressed." Thus in 1834 the *American Sentinel*, a New Jersey paper, declared that the state was "literally overrun with blacks, driven by the violence of an infuriated mob from their homes and property in Philadelphia . . . the first indication of a permanent residence [here] should, and we feel confident will, call forth rigid enforcement of the statute against admission of blacks into our boundaries." But this was far from the only statute. Across the river in

Pennsylvania, and in Ohio, Illinois, Indiana, and Michigan, Negroes were denied the free franchise, were ruled vagrants on the slightest pretext, and were subject to penalties, in some cases even enslavement, "harsher than those imposed upon white people guilty of the same crimes." Up in Massachusetts itself the abolitionists grew mute with suspense and confusion while the state legislature debated a bill forbidding admission and residence to Negroes.

But neither council chamber nor court of law was the arena in which the common native-born Northern workman chose to fight his battles. He chose the labor hiring hall. He chose the street. In one he waged a war of attrition; in the other, battles of blood. Trade unions, which since the 1790s had been slowly gaining effectiveness, proscribed Negroes for the silliest of reasons: Negroes depressed wages. They could not find apprenticeships in industry. The carpenters of Philadelphia, the shoemakers of Boston, and the ship caulkers of New Bedford and New York said, "No work for niggers," and when this was ineffectual, as it sometimes was in a labor market beginning to grow cheap from oversupply, Northern workmen went into the streets with club and torch and gun. They did this in Philadelphia in 1834, as we have seen, and that same year in New York, and again in '35, '36, and '39, and in Boston, as in the West, periodically. Whereas in Philadelphia in 1820 a decided majority of the artisans were Negroes, fifteen years later only 350 of the 11,500 Negroes were employed in the skilled trades. In New York, 2386 of 3237 were common laborers or domestic servants. In Boston in 1850, when the working Negro population numbered 935, all save 46 "barbers and hairdressers" were laborers and house servants.

And even these jobs were hard to find and harder to keep when the Irish, and to a lesser degree the Germans, started coming in the 1830s. Mostly peasants who had grown weary of peasantry, the Irish swarmed in the Northern cities, where they too met opposition from the native-born. Though "street fights between natives and foreigners were common occurrences," and "Catholic convents and churches, and German *Turnverein* headquarters were sometimes attacked and destroyed," the enmity was not altogether cultural.

It was also—and principally—economic. The Irish and German workers competed with native mechanics who employed against them the weapons already proved against the Negro. The immigrants were left out of labor unions. Natives refused to work with the "dirty foreigners." Forced into digging, ditching, and docking, while their women went into "service," the Irish accepted lower wages than even the Negroes and in many places forced the latter out of jobs.

In these circumstances, without any place in the economic and political order, and without any dependable means of support, Negroes in the North began to be credited with those attributes of character that the white South was busily fashioning for the defense of slavery everywhere—namely, cunning and ignorance, laziness and prodigality, mendacity and lechery, rowdyism and criminality: in short, beasts. These attributes were to constitute a race concept of such durability that a century of time and change would not entirely obliterate it. If the concept was embraced by the mind in the performance of its simplest function, rationalization, it must nevertheless be remarked that even the simplest minds do not rationalize from nothing.

And there were the Negroes, many of them fugitives from slavery, used to dependence, drained of initiative by the meagerness of rewards, public charges. There they were, proliferating in slums spreading through the waterfront districts of Cincinnati and Philadelphia, crowding each other in the fetid alleys and dead-end streets of lower east side New York, and dying (as Phillis Wheatley, the first poet among them, died) of poverty, disease, and exposure in the teeming courts of Boston. And an undue proportion turned mean and vicious, creating problems for the police and shame for their upright brothers. They attracted attention. The jails, the poorhouses, and the prisons were crowded with them, and in 1836 a Senate committee predicted that the disparity of "Negro crime would be absolutely intolerable" within a few years. The very next year, with regard to Philadelphia, the committee seemed right.

Thirty-six per cent of Philadelphia crime was committed by the colored 9 per cent of her population.

2. RUNAWAY

Nevertheless, freedom was North, and when Frederick Augustus Washington Bailey escaped in 1838 he headed straight for it. He went boldly by train, pretending to be a sailor and flashing an official-looking paper with the American eagle engraved on it. Arriving in New York with scarcely money enough to feed him for a week, he found refuge with David Ruggles, secretary of the New York Vigilance Committee, and the first Negro to edit an anti-slavery magazine. New York was not heaven, Ruggles warned him—and no man knew better than Ruggles—for slave catchers were everywhere. It would be wiser for Frederick to move on. But first he had better change his name: he had too much of it. So Bailey became Johnson, Frederick Johnson; and a few days later, when Anna Murray, the free woman he had met in Baltimore, joined him, this was the name he gave her as his wife.

But New Bedford, Massachusetts, where Ruggles sent them, had a superfluity of colored Johnsons, and Frederick soon discovered that there was much confusion in those very situations where confusion was most ruinous. Prospective employers sometimes could not tell one Johnson from another. The police were not always discriminating either. On one occasion an innocent Negro had been jailed in place of another bearing the same name. If all Negroes looked alike, as the popular expression had it, at least they did not have to sound alike. Frederick began to cultivate his speech very carefully and to increase his reading skill. After a few weeks he again changed his name, adopting Frederick Douglass. Sooner than anyone dreamed, the name was to acquire a special meaning.

Not even Douglass himself suspected that he was about to begin a career that would make his name one to be conjured with in the highest councils of the country, that would bring him scorn and hatred, but also great honor and high place and international fame.

It started modestly enough, for his simple wish was to fulfill the "sweet responsibilities" of freeman, husband, and father. There were proscriptions, but he took them in stride. Pro-slavery, anti-Negro doctrine had long since reached the shipyards and docks of coastal New England, where the slave trade once had thrived, and the section had its share of slavery sympathizers. Unable to get employment at his trade of ship caulking, Douglass did odd jobs. He "sawed wood, shoveled coal, dug cellars, moved rubbish from back yards," and worked as a stevedore. But already he had heard Garrison lecture in New Bedford, had subscribed to the *Liberator*, had become a member of an informal Negro group to discuss the issues of slavery. Already he had begun to "whisper into every sympathetic white ear" that all men must be free.

What he whispered to whites he spoke out bold and clear to Negroes when they gathered in their little church and schoolhouse on Second Street. They gathered rather often, for the little brotherhood of black men was close-knit, sensitive, and probably afraid. It embraced Douglass warmly. Douglass could read, he could write and, it was soon apparent, he could speak with force, logic, and clarity; could speak so well, indeed, that the African Methodist Church wanted to license him as a preacher.

Word of such a man got around quickly in New Bedford, and when it came to the ear of William Coffin, a white abolitionist, he knew what to do with it. In 1841, Douglass was asked to address an anti-slavery convention in Nantucket. His stomach quivered and his voice quaked, but Douglass made a better speech than he thought. Moreover, he was impressive to look at. A massive mulatto, he had a strong rather than a handsome face that, seasoned by only twenty-four years, was already so deeply lined as to excuse the beard he later felt constrained to wear. His hair was as long and coarse as a lion's mane and swept back from a broad forehead. He spoke that day without gestures, without oratorical flair, "simply, yet with deep feeling." John Collins, general agent of the Massachusetts Anti-Slavery Society, had advised him, "Give us the facts; we will take care of the philosophy."

And for a time, while he gained valuable experience as a full-time lecturer for the Anti-Slavery Society, Douglass let them take care of the philosophy. He saw no reason to question it. He had no intellectual sophistication by which to test the philosophy's beguiling simplicity. Indeed, it was for him much less a philosophy than a program, and the program was also simplicity itself: immediate emancipation. How this was to be accomplished and leave undisturbed the tangled growth of legal, economic, and social relationships that, million-rooted, burrowed into every area of Southern life he completely ignored. It did not occur to him to question Garrison's artless expedient of dissolving the constitutional Union. Slavery was an unmitigated evil, the Boston abolitionist had no doubt, and Douglass' job was to depict and portray that evil. "Tell your story, Frederick," Garrison admonished him. The story was argument enough, and if it were not, then "the very look and bearing of Douglass," James Russell Lowell said, was "an irresistible logic against the oppression of his race."

Perhaps it was. But it was exactly this that caused Douglass embarrassment. As he developed ease of manner, people began to doubt that he had ever been a slave. He did not look like the well-advertised notion of one. The habit of plantation speech being now entirely gone, he did not talk like one. He did not act like one. A shrewd Yankee listener summed up the general disbelief: "He don't tell us where he came from, what his master's name was, nor how he got away. Besides, he is educated and is in this a contradiction of all the facts we have concerning the ignorance of slaves."

Add to this the fact that Douglass himself was beginning to be bored with repeating his story. He was no longer a "brand-new" and curious fact. The time had come when he could not narrate the wrongs of slavery without denouncing them. And, finally, he was beginning to harbor cautious doubts of Garrison's absolute wisdom. "New views of the subject [of slavery]," he wrote later, "were being presented to my mind." Already he had been, though unwittingly, in one political campaign over the Dorr constitution in Rhode Island and found that he liked the passion and the sound, the intellectual thrust and parry. He was beginning to think that politics had its uses in the fight against slavery. His study of the federal Constitution led him to question whether that instrument was quite the "agreement with hell" that Garrison contended, and whether it *was* part of his duty as an abolitionist to advocate its destruction.

But if these were signs pointing a new direction, Douglass tried to ignore them. He liked Garrison, even revered him, and he was grateful to the Massachusetts Anti-Slavery Society. He did not want to invite a break. What appeared to him to be of immediate moment was the re-establishment of his credibility as a bona fide escaped slave. After all, there were charlatans abroad. Although Douglass did not know it, some of his abolitionist friends connived in the publication of spurious narratives of "escaped slaves." Douglass was scrupulous to a fault, and he was also farsighted enough to see that lies, half-truths, and fraudulent claims could destroy the abolition movement. He determined to tell his whole story; to give dates and to name people and places, and to do this in writing. It was a risky decision, for it would mark him as "Bailey, runaway slave of Thomas Auld," and expose him to recapture by any slave catcher. His friends warned against it. But the *Narrative of the Life of Frederick Douglass* was published in May 1845. Three months later, partly to escape the consequences of his confession, Douglass sailed for England.

3. NORTH STAR

The signs Douglass tried not to read in 1843 could not be ignored when he returned to America in 1847. They blazed brighter, more legible, and more demanding all the time. The British Isles had given him the "room" he complained of lacking in the United States, and his experiences there had broadened his thinking and deepened his insights. His speeches in England, a London critic said, had revealed him as "the master of extraordinary information" on such topics as world peace, universal manhood suffrage, women's rights, and labor. Still he was first and foremost an abolitionist. George Thompson, an English friend, chided him time and again, saying that merely to preach Negro emancipation was not enough. And, anyway, how was it to be achieved?

The appetite for politics that Douglass had not satisfied in 1841 grew to a lust for political action while, on the other hand, Garrison's position was the exact one he had taken almost ten years before in organizing the New England Non-Resistance Society. Garrison and his followers would "voluntarily exclude themselves from every legislative and judicial body, and repudiate all human politics, worldly honors, and stations and authority." Garrison condemned servile rebellions as a moral abomination. Douglass was moving toward the opposite conviction, and in 1849, galvanized by the currents already shooting from John Brown's "divine madness," was able to say that he would "welcome the intelligence tomorrow, should it come, that the slaves had risen in the South, and the sable arms which had been engaged in beautifying and adorning the South were engaged in spreading death and destruction there."

Back in Massachusetts, Douglass again suffered from lack of scope, and it was more acute now. English friends had raised twenty-five hundred dollars for him to start his own paper, and he wanted to get on with it. George Thompson had made him aware of more than the need of emancipation for slaves, and Douglass began to talk of the day when the "school-house, the workshop, the church, the college" would be as freely accessible to Negro children "as to the children of other members of the community." He thought his work as an editor might hasten that day. For a decade he had been at least one remove from "the people with whom I had suffered . . . as a slave." Now he wanted to identify himself with all phases of Negro life; to address Negro audiences, to join Negro organizations. Starting a paper for his people was a challenge he could not bolt.

Still he held off for weeks, while Garrison and Wendell Phillips bombarded him with arguments. Such a paper was not needed, they said. He, Douglass, was especially endowed as a lecturer, they said, and he should stick to it. He had no proven editorial gifts, and Phillips predicted the exhaustion of his resources and failure within three years if he started a paper. Douglass "brooded," Garrison wrote his wife, " 'like the black storm cloud over the capes' upon the future."

But Douglass, though he was "under the influence of something like slavish adoration of these good people," determined to go ahead. Late in 1847 he moved from Lynn, Massachusetts, to Rochester, New York, and in the first week of December of that year he issued the first number of the *North Star*. From then until the emancipation was an accomplished fact and the union of the states assured, the *North Star*, later known as *Frederick Douglass's Paper*, was published weekly.

Nevertheless, Douglass was reluctant to cut the ideological cord that bound him to Garrison's impractical idealism. That idealism had tested brittle against successive onslaughts of the slaveholders, who, battening on a feast of political victories since the Missouri Compromise of 1820, were even then fashioning the strategy by which to accomplish another—the admission of California as a slave state. But even in the face of this threatened overwhelming addition to the South's political force, and through all the testy and sardonic talk of restoring "to the South, through constitutional amendment, the equilibrium of power she once possessed in the Federal government," Garrisonians continued to abjure political action, to remain non-voting abolitionists and non-resisters to the aggressive Southern will. Though he did not say so at the time—and, indeed, continued to support Garrison's philosophy in the *North Star*—Douglass in fact was done with all this.

Moreover, he had to be done with it if he was to work with his own people. *They* had not been patient. They had been angry and urgent, and their frequent conventions had long and loudly proclaimed them committed to political action. As early as 1838 they had served notice that "We take our stand upon the solemn declaration, that to protect inalienable rights 'governments are constituted among men . . .' and proclaim that a government which tears away from us and our posterity the very power of consent is a tyrannical usurpation which we will never cease to oppose." Since the 1840s they had gone further. "If we must bleed, let it all come at once. . . . Brethren, arise, arise! Strike for your lives and liberties!"

Frederick Douglass had some catching up to do. He began by working for the Liberty party in the campaign of 1848. It was not much of a start, for the Liberty party had already grown so anemic on the diet of abolition that the transfusions (recommended, it might be said, by Dr. James Russell Lowell) of the tariff, the public lands, and the Mexican War questions could not bring it back to glowing health. Besides, Douglass found politics a strange forest, and he was lost in it. There were too many parties and too many candidates. The Democrats had nominated Lewis Cass of Michigan, but he was completely cold to the slavery issue and therefore the anti-slavery Democrats were cold to him. These latter, mostly New Yorkers who called themselves Barnburners, wanted Martin Van Buren. So did the anti-slavery Whigs. On this common ground the dissident anti-slavery factions of both parties met in Buffalo in August 1848 and, declaring themselves for "free soil, free speech, free labor and free men," nominated Van Buren.

Perhaps the measure of Douglass' bewilderment was that he was at that convention, addressed it as a "noble step in the right direction," commended its choice of Van Buren and condemned Zachary Taylor, the regular Whig candidate, as a "known robber and assassin," but continued to support John P. Hale, the candidate of the Liberty party.

If there was method in this, it did not become apparent until later, when Gerrit Smith, the enduring spark plug of the Liberty party, proposed that the party's paper and the *North Star* merge, with Douglass as editor. Smith was wealthy, generous, and dedicated. The *North Star* sorely needed financial help. Negroes, for whom it was primarily intended, were too poor to support it. Besides, there were those who would not support it if they could, for some refused to ally themselves with the "race movement." Among Negroes in general there were all shades of opinion, all varieties of interest, and loyalties as diverse and unstable as the fulfillment or the violation

of personal hope and ambitions could make them. But Douglass had
this to learn. Meantime he accepted the help Gerrit Smith offered,
renamed his paper *Frederick Douglass's Paper*, and spent the last
two years of the decade trying to resuscitate the Liberty party.

This was a hopeless endeavor. The party had been swamped in the
political seas of 1848, and the seas, agitated by the storms over the
boundary of Texas, the territories of New Mexico, Utah, and Oregon, and the admission of California, had grown more turbulent.
Danger signals flew. No one could doubt that the leaky ship of states
was at hazard.

Old, ill, and embittered by frustration, John C. Calhoun, who had
threatened secession over the tariff, threatened it again in 1849 if
Congress admitted California as a free state. The North, he declared,
must concede "to the South an equal right to the acquired territory,"
must vigorously enforce the Fugitive Slave Law, the breach of which
was costing the South "millions in human property annually," and
must "cease the agitation of the slave question."

But Calhoun and the South had no monopoly on sectional feelings: there were men of the North who welcomed disunion as
heartily as ever Calhoun did. Perhaps a compromise could save the
situation? Old Henry Clay thought so, and he came out of retirement to propose one. California should be admitted as a free state;
Texas should give up her claim to extend her western boundary;
Congress should give up the right (which had never been granted
in the first place) to control the slave trade within the states and
between states; Utah and New Mexico should become territories in
which the decision on slavery would be left up to the people of the
territories; and a more stringent fugitive slave law should be enacted.
Webster of Massachusetts supported Clay of Kentucky. Flashing
some of the brilliance of twenty years before, Webster spoke for the
"preservation of the Union. Hear me for my cause."

The "cause" was saved, but few approved of the compromise that
saved it. And the compromise itself could not for long hold up to the
battering of sectional pride and prejudice and the moral indignation
that immediately beset it. Southern politicians were quick to see

that the admission of California as a free state upset the balance in Congress. Virginia, South Carolina, Georgia, Alabama, and Mississippi declared for secession. Northern abolitionists were not slow to realize that the new Fugitive Slave Law was a "screaming iniquity," and their cries of outrage rose from all sides. Garrison saw villainy "of an unmitigated type, treachery to the cause of liberty and humanity of the blackest shade." Senator Seward of New York, who was always the politician and whose professed political object was to defend and further the interests of Northern farmers and wage earners, regarded the compromise as a subversion of the "law of God, whence alone the laws of men can derive their sanction." Even Emerson descended from Parnassus to pronounce the compromise "a filthy enactment. . . . I will not obey it, by God!"

Passion took over.

It is not strange that Douglass missed or ignored the political significance of the compromise. Excepting the moderate Whigs, nearly everyone did. For Douglass and other free Negroes, the Fugitive Slave Law was a stunning personal blow. "It broke down," as Whittier said, "all guarantees of their personal liberty." It made it possible for an alleged runaway slave to be arrested without a warrant, taken before a commissioner or a judge who, legally bound to disallow the defendant's testimony, could take the word of the claimant and capturer as proof of the charge. Trial by jury was not required or even permitted. "Free papers" had no more value than a cynical or a venal commissioner cared to place on them. "Even free colored people who had been free all their lives felt very insecure"—insecure enough, in fact, to send whole communities scampering into self-exile in Canada. In Douglass' home town of Rochester all but two of the entire membership of the Colored Baptist Church fled.

Many Negro leaders pulled out. Henry Highland Garnet slipped away to England. Samuel R. Ward, whose "depth of thought, fluency of speech . . . and general intelligence" had impressed the leadership of the Free-Soil party, scuttled into Canada. Martin Delany, who had been associated with Douglass on the *North Star* for a time, took ship for Africa. Soon to be a bishop in the African

Methodist Episcopal Church, Daniel Payne, distressed beyond the solace of religion, lamented to Douglass, "We are whipped, we are whipped! And we might as well retreat in order."

But Frederick Douglass was not whipped. He had courage that, in the instance, amounted to a reckless and foolhardy contempt for danger. For two years his house in Rochester had been the jumping-off place for slaves escaping into Canada. At one time in the early winter of 1850 as many as eleven fugitives had harbored there, and John Brown, on one of his periodic visits of solicitation in the neighborhood, made a speech to them. Now, though the danger of such activity was more than doubled, Douglass did not stop. In the very week in which the Fugitive Slave Law became effective he gave refuge to three runaways who were charged not only as fugitives but as murderers, for in making their escape they had killed a man. "I could not look upon them as murderers," Douglass said. "To me, they were heroic defenders of the rights of man. . . . So I fed them and sheltered them in my house."

Other men—and mostly white men—in Delaware, Pennsylvania, and New York, in Kentucky, Ohio, and Kansas were feeding and sheltering runaways too, and had been for years. More and more runaways required this charity. Though the Underground Railroad ran on a faster schedule after the new Fugitive Slave Law of 1850, it could not run fast enough to satisfy the North's conscience and pride. That conscience was exacerbated by the harshness of the law upon whose "faithful execution . . . depends the preservation of our much-loved Union." Pride was painfully injured by the South's verbal assaults against the North's free society and the unceasing references to Northerners as "mongrels" and "mudsills." So Northerners, each according to his nature, took baleful glee or moral joy in defying the law.

Nor was the satisfaction of conscience and pride their only excuse. Slaveholders and slave catchers had grown aggressive to the point of criminality. In Maryland a white man was lynched for proving the free status of a kidnaped Negro girl. Aprowl in Philadelphia, a Baltimore sheriff shot and killed William Smith, a free Negro, for

saying that he was free. Northerners responded to such acts as these
with equally criminal acts of their own. In Troy, New York, they
seized a recaptured runaway and set him free. A Boston mob rescued
Frederick Jenkins from the United States marshal who was about to
return him to slavery, and Theodore Parker called this the "most
noble deed done in Boston since the destruction of the tea in 1773."
Northern mobs in Philadelphia, New York, and Syracuse matched
this nobility.

With so many Negro leaders gone or grown silent, a man more
self-centered, perceptive, and less scrupulous than Douglass might
have tried to lay hold of authority. But neither acute perception nor
ruthlessness was a quality Douglass could claim. An effort to seize
power over his people was utterly beyond him, though in the circumstances he might easily have done so.

For it is true that white people generally thought of him as the
outstanding Negro leader and spokesman. After 1847, when a deluge of national publicity, some of it scurrilous, swept over him in
connection with his return from England, the purchase of his freedom, and an open letter addressed to his old master in the pages of
Greeley's *Tribune*, he was the man to whom white people turned
with questions about the Negro. Without his willing it, his opinions
were suddenly influential among whites. He was quoted in and out
of context everywhere. He had authority among whites. Since Negroes had little power to implement their own will and sought re-
course in their white friends, it is probable that Douglass could have
influenced substantially the Negro fate. But he believed in discussion. He referred questions about Negroes to Negroes themselves.
He set such questions forth in his paper. He brought them up in
the Negro conventions, where, more often than not, crafty strategists
managed to bring about a repudiation of Douglass' own opinions.

For this was also true: Douglass had some implacable enemies
among both his own people and white Garrisonian abolitionists.
Charles Remond, the first Negro anti-slavery lecturer, was jealous of
Douglass' reputation. Robert Purvis, a quadroon of considerable af-
fluence, clashed with Douglass over Negro freedom as against the

"rights of free Negroes." William Wells Brown accused Douglass of belittling him. Having become a favorite of Garrison, William Nell, the Negro historian, followed his inflexible patron down a tortuous byway to bitter estrangement. Garrison had never forgotten or forgiven the fact that Douglass had established a paper against his advice. He made opportunities to blast his onetime protégé in the press and from the platform. In 1853, when Julia Griffiths, an Englishwoman living in Rochester, was managing the finances of Douglass' paper, Garrison, hinting at sexual immorality, alleged that Miss Griffiths was "one whose influence had caused much unhappiness in his [Douglass'] own household" and that he "could bring a score of unimpeachable witnesses . . . to prove it."

In spite of his enemies Douglass' influence over his own people grew and spread slowly, almost imperceptibly, and in no fixed pattern. Although he gave up profitable lecture engagements to speak gratis to small, impoverished Negro groups and wrote hundreds of private letters to unknown Negroes who asked his advice, other leaders seemed more popular than he and were applauded with greater gusto at Negro meetings. In 1848 he was elected, grudgingly, president of the Colored Convention, which had been meeting sporadically for two decades, but the next year, when he proposed to organize a convention on a national basis the more effectively "to fight slavery, secure interracial cooperation . . . improve the conditions of the Negro people," other Negro leaders refused to indorse the plan. When Douglass, who advocated woman suffrage, became prominent in the feminist movement, William Nell sneered at him as an "Aunt Nancy man." Some Negro leaders were for colonization; Douglass was against it. Entranced by the dream of a "purely educational institution for Negroes," some leaders actively and acrimoniously fought Douglass' idea of "a series of workshops where colored people could learn some of the handicrafts, learn to work in iron, wood and leather, and where a plain English education could also be taught." (This was the idea that an ex-slave named Booker T. Washington was to lift straight from the pages of Douglass' *My Bondage and My Freedom* a quarter of a century later and set forth as his own.) This was the idea that Douglass outlined in great detail to Harriet Beecher Stowe.

The publication of *Uncle Tom's Cabin* in 1852 had catapulted Mrs. Stowe into international fame and given her prestige in councils and controversy far beyond her housewife's capacity and experience to support. In America, where she was backed by all the emotional force of the anti-slavery movement, the general if reluctant acceptance of female reformers such as Lucy Stone, Elizabeth Stanton, and Jane Swisshelm—"those hissing esses," a bawdy-tongued Georgian called them—and the reputation of her thunderous brother, Henry Ward Beecher, it was easy to maintain this prestige. But later in the 1850s she was going abroad to England, and in England the London *Times* had criticized *Uncle Tom* as "unrealistic": "Its effect will be to render slavery more difficult than ever of abolishment." Mrs. Stowe knew that she must be practical and realistic in England, where she had already been pledged "a considerable sum of money . . . for the permanent improvement of the free colored people." What could she offer her audiences there?

She sent for Frederick Douglass. Could he suggest anything? she inquired. He certainly could. Then would he "write out his views in the form of a letter" so that she could take it to England with her that "friends there might see to what their contributions were to be devoted"? He would indeed—and did.

". . . An industrial college—a college to be conducted by the best men, and the best workmen which the mechanic arts can afford . . . where colored youth can be instructed to use their hands. . . . Prejudice against the free colored people in the United States has shown itself nowhere so invincible as among mechanics. . . . Denied the means of learning useful trades, we are pressed into the narrowest limits to obtain a livelihood . . . and even these employments are rapidly passing out of our hands. The fact is (every day begins with the lesson and ends with the lesson) colored men must learn trades. . . ."

It seemed unlikely that Douglass' idea "could . . . be tortured into a cause for hard words" by either the British or the American people, but a segment of the American people found cause for hard words anyway. Mrs. Stowe was virulently attacked, especially by the pro-slavery press. She was accused of "misrepresenting slavery with iniquitous lies," and no one bothered to refute this old canard. But when she was charged with receiving "British gold for her own private use," and was persistently and bitterly attacked by some of the abolitionist press on this score, her brother, the Reverend Henry W. Beecher, came to her defense and very pointedly referred her maligners to Frederick Douglass, "if they would learn what she intended to do with the money." Douglass responded immediately and at length. The attacks on Mrs. Stowe soon ceased.

But Douglass' response did as much for him as for Harriet Stowe. The fortuitous linking of his name with that of the most famous woman in the world in such a way as to reveal that she had taken council with him and with him alone enormously increased his prestige. Even the most jealous and suspicious Negroes paused to take another look at the man whom Garrison had admonished them to ignore. How could they now? Douglass' stock shot up, particularly in the Negro market. By 1855, when many people were beginning to realize that the social ferment of the times was a plexus involving more than abolition and more than a single body of ideas, Douglass was the Negroes' acknowledged leader, and clothed by them with an authority such as no single Negro has since acquired.

4. DAYS OF THE MARTYR

He was to need that authority almost immediately to win his people to a recognition that the policy of "abolition or disunion" was futile. Only by winning them from this Garrisonian nullity could he hope to get their support for a program of political action. What that program would be or what name it would bear Douglass was by no means certain. His own political allegiance had been divided. The Liberty party, which he had joined when it was organized, was split and weakened to the point of collapse by 1852. For a time he flirted with the Free-Soil party, but its principal candidates, George W. Julian and John P. Hale, ignored two direct and pertinent questions: whether a political party should regard it a duty to secure equal rights for all; and whether "slavery, so far as capable of legislation, is a naked piracy, around which there can be no legal covering." Douglass felt that he could not support the Free-Soil party. Politically he did not know where to go, but by 1854 he knew he must go somewhere and take his people with him.

For in that year it became evident that the skillful machinations of the South were increasing the power of that section out of all proportion to political equity. Stephen A. Douglas, the senator from Illinois, introduced a bill to organize the central plains into a territory, and won the support of the most radical pro-slavery sympathizers by agreeing to have the measure provide for the repeal of the Compromise of 1850. Having made this concession, he was forced to make a further one: so that the principle of popular sovereignty could work to the advantage of the slaveholders, the senator agreed to a provision that divided the territory into Kansas and Nebraska. Now the political strength of the South stood out in naked arrogance.

Though the North desperately mustered its own strength, it could not prevail against the power of the South. The Kansas-Nebraska Bill passed both houses, and Franklin Pierce, apostate New Englander that he was, signed it to the accompaniment of cheers from Southerners. Their jubilance had excuse. They had fought with feverish but calculating realism against the odds of a numerical majority in the North. They had opposed the North's moral pretensions, ethical professions, and humanitarian zeal with a simple formula of political action. Every victory had made their cause appear brighter. They had proved indomitable. With the signing of the Kansas-Nebraska Bill, it must have seemed to them that Professor George Tucker of the University of Virginia said truly when he wrote, "History is the great arbiter of right in national disputes, and the scale of justice on which she happens to light is almost sure to preponderate."

In the breakup of the old parties that followed immediately upon the passage of the Kansas-Nebraska Bill, some anti-slavery leaders saw an opportunity for political cohesion. Many Northerners whose opposition to slavery had been dormant now roused themselves, not necessarily on behalf of anti-slavery, but to stop the extension of the slave power. Northern Democrats, those same "Northern men with Southern principles" who had voted against the Wilmot Proviso and who cared little about the slavery controversy one way or the other, were chagrined by an ever tightening Southern control of the party. "Conscience Whigs" and Free-Soilers were simply adrift. Some of all these came together to form the Republican party.

Meantime the Know-Nothing or American party, which had been jerry-built out of all those elements that hated or feared foreigners and Catholics—and which Henry Wise had called "the most impious and unprincipled affiliation of bad means, for bad ends"—had spent its force. And when its Southern pro-slavery adherents gained control of it in 1855, the Northerners withdrew almost to a man and lined up with the new Republicans. Frederick Douglass, however, thought that the Liberty party, with its seamless devotion to abolition, was due for a revival. He delivered the bloc vote of the Negroes of western New York to that party in 1854, but the Liberty party, as well as its offshoot, the Radical Abolitionist, had used up its ninth life. Douglass went over to the Republicans and carried practically all the enfranchised Negroes with him.

Nor was this all he did. Though at first reluctant to solicit among his own poverty-stricken people, Douglass was soon telling them that "no sacrifice, even to life itself, [is] too much to ask for freedom." Funds were needed for a variety of purposes—to support the Republican candidate, John C. Frémont; to keep the Underground Railroad running; to promote the work of the Emigrant Aid Society, hastily organized to help establish anti-slavery men in the Kansas Territory, and for even more desperate expedients. Men and words and ballots alone would not do in Kansas. What were needed, John Brown told Douglass, were "swords and bullets, and you must help me get them."

And Douglass did. "I got up meetings and solicited aid to be used by him for the cause, and I may say without boasting that my efforts in this respect were not entirely fruitless," wrote Douglass years later. "Deeply interested as 'Osawatomie Brown' was in Kansas, he never lost sight of what he called his greater work—the liberation of all the slaves in the United States. But for the then present he saw his way to the great end through Kansas."

But Kansas was not the way. In the inextricable linkage of violence with politics, Brown's actions in the territory were a danger and a thwart to pro-slavery sympathizers, but they were far from enough to secure the liberty of "all the slaves in the United States." They were barely enough to accomplish what had to be done in Kansas—the making of that state "a clean bed," as Lincoln put it, "with no snakes in it." There were plenty of snakes before John Brown got there. In the preceding March (1855) five thousand Missouri ruffians had crossed over into Kansas to make sure of the election of a pro-slavery legislature. Senator David Atchison had ordered them to "shoot, stab or beat any abolitionists seen at the voting places." The pro-slavery men won that election but, in October, John Brown arrived to keep them from winning another. Fanatical beyond mere ruthlessness and cruelty, he had come, he said, "to promote the killing of American slavery" and "to do the work of the Lord." The work was murder. For a year Brown was a presence in Kansas and the terror of all Missouri, his "name alone equal to an army with banners." But even this was not enough for his great purpose, and when he quit Kansas to solicit more funds in the East —to meet Theodore Parker, Salmon P. Chase, Amos Lawrence, Emerson, and Thoreau, and to renew his acquaintance with Gerrit Smith and Frederick Douglass—Brown knew it was not enough.

So also did Douglass, whose optimism had dwindled. The apparent victory of the cause in Kansas had been wholly vitiated by the Supreme Court decision in the case of Dred Scott, a slave who, having been taken into free Illinois and back again to Missouri, sued for his freedom on the ground that he had lived on free soil. The Court's decision held that masters could take their slaves anywhere in the territories. It held that the Missouri Compromise was unconstitutional. It declared, in effect, that "Negroes had no rights which white men were bound to respect." On the strength of this decision the South renewed its demands to reopen the slave trade, and for a time it looked as if those demands would be met.

It is no wonder that Douglass was discouraged. He said so to Daniel Payne, who seven years before had cried, "We are beaten!" But now, already dreaming of founding the first Negro college, where "the peace of God and the light of learning would shine," Payne demurred. "Oh, Frederick, Frederick! Take comfort. The stars are not altered in their courses." But Payne could not pull Douglass through the depression that enveloped him to the very eve of the Civil War, when at a public meeting a woman, gaunt and fleshless as a ghost, rose to ask the speaker, "Frederick, is God dead?"

John Brown, the self-appointed man of God, had answered that the year before. "God," he had said then, "cries out for blood!" Douglass could not ignore that cry altogether. He was Brown's friend and of his council. He had given comfort to Brown and aid to his plans to free the slaves. When Brown called, Douglass felt duty-bound to answer. Brown called in August of 1859.

The two men met in an abandoned stone quarry near Chambersburg, Pennsylvania. The "terrible saint" had a new and bolder plan. He would do more than run off slaves. He would seize the government arsenal at Harper's Ferry. He would kidnap prominent citizens and hold them hostage. He would make rebellion flame in all the Southern states. Douglass was appalled. For a day and a night he argued. Brown would have the whole country arrayed against him. He was "going into a steel trap" and he would never get out alive. Virginia "would blow him sky-high, rather than that he should hold Harper's Ferry an hour." But Brown was not to be stopped; he craved his martyrdom. He was beyond both reason and fear. "Come with me, Douglass," he said. "I will defend you with my life. I want you for a special purpose. When I strike, the bees will begin to swarm, and I shall want you to help hive them."

A few weeks later he struck. He seized the arsenal and virtually the town of Harper's Ferry, Virginia. He freed fifty slaves. The alarm spread quickly, and all the powers of government mobilized against

him. President Buchanan sent federal troops under the command
of Colonel Robert E. Lee. Virginia, Maryland, and the Carolinas
called out militia. Armed with sticks and stones and squirrel guns,
men and boys from Charleston streamed through the hills toward
Harper's Ferry. It took three days to put down the rebellion, and
only three of Brown's twenty-two men lived to see the end of it.

Meanwhile rumors sped. The seizure of the arsenal was only the
first of a series of raids to be conducted by hundreds of men. The
capture of "Mad-dog Brown" had only scotched the snake. Others
were implicated, among them Thomas Wentworth Higginson,
Theodore Parker, Samuel Howe, and Frederick Douglass. Governor Wise of Virginia charged treason and appealed to the President
for federal warrants. But Parker was in Italy, Howe in England, and
Higginson safe behind the bastion of his family name. Friends urged
Douglass to flee. Did he suppose, innocent or not, that the South
would let slip an opportunity to hang the most prominent Negro
abolitionist?

Eluding by only six hours the federal officers sent to arrest him,
Douglass fled to Canada. But, "Farther, farther, Frederick!" Daniel
Payne urged. So, feeling that he was "going into exile, perhaps for
life," Douglass sailed for England. He did not return until the eve
of the Civil War.

PART TWO

All Glory Gone

CHAPTER FOUR

Faith

1. ISABELLA NO-NAME

SHE WAS called Isabella at first, and the language spoken in her family was Dutch. But to speak of her "family" is an irony, for ten of her brothers and sisters had been sold away, and only her father, Baumfree, her mother, Bett, and her brother, Peter, remained. The parents had no surname. "Baumfree" was a moniker for tall-as-a-tree, and the father refused to have another. Though in later years the name would have fitted Isabella, in her youth it would not stick. She was variously called Bell, Bella, and Lil Bett. She belonged successively to the Hardenberghs, the Nealys, the Scrivers, and the Dumonts, and for more than a year she gave her considerable services to the Van Wageners, but she took the name of none of them.

She held John Dumont, a man of gross appetites, in fervent, idolatrous regard and bore him children, but she did not take his name either for herself or for them. When she married, probably in 1820 and probably at the age of twenty-three, her husband had no name to give her. He was called simply Tom, or Black Tom—not because of the color of his skin but because he "worked roots" or voodoo

and practiced divination. The son Tom begot was called Peter, nothing more. When Peter was a young man in the city of New York
he found the lack of a surname a handicap to such a devil-may-care
free Negro as himself and he adopted the name of Williams—Peter
Williams. He was twice booked into Tombs prison under this name,
and under this name he shipped as a seaman to a foreign port in
1839 and was, save once, heard of no more.

Isabella had not only left him nameless, she had left him motherless. In one way or another she left all of her children—five, or six,
or seven—motherless. There was a frigid winter spot in the blazing
tropics of her soul.

She dismissed Tom, a freedman, while she was still a slave. He
died in a poorhouse in 1830. Peter, the son of Tom, and the children
she had by Dumont were left with Dumont when she ran away. It
is true that she did not run far, or try to lose herself, but this is
scarcely evidence that she missed or wanted her children.

Dumont had promised to set her free in 1826, but when the time
came he was reluctant to make his promise good. In the interval
since her marriage Isabella had got religion and had founded her
faith in God. But she never went to church, and hers was a strange
religion, compounded of Tom's weird conjure lore and Old Testament maledictions. She worshiped in secret, in "a circular arched
alcove" she had constructed "entirely of willows" on an islet in a
stream at the edge of the Dumont estate. Also, according to reports,
hers was a terrible God—a master black magician apotheosized from
every awful attribute of witchcraft, necromancy, and superstition.

She invoked this God for or against Dumont, and then she ran
away. Somehow she knew that Dumont would not try to get her
back. She had been an embarrassment to him, to his wife, and finally,
as they grew up, to his legitimate children. When she left she did
take her second child by Tom, an unnamed infant girl, but within a
month or two she abandoned her to be reared by strangers in the
neighboring town of New Paltz, New York.

Yet there was one curious episode.

Dumont sold the boy Peter. It was 1826. Slavery in New York

State had only fourteen months to go. Peter was five and therefore still useless as a slave, but in some circles it was fashionable to train a Negro child as one would train a monkey or a dog and show off its accomplishments in the parlor. Peter's new master, Dr. James Gedney, apparently tired of this entertainment and transferred title in the boy to his brother, Solomon Gedney. Solomon in turn sold Peter to the husband of a sister, a Deep South planter named Fowler. In defiance of the law forbidding native-born slaves to be taken beyond the borders of the state, Fowler carted Peter off to Alabama.

Isabella exploded, a blazing holocaust—but ignited from what kindling and fed by what fuel it is impossible to tell. She defies analysis. Any of a number of elements in the situation might have sparked a simpler woman to maddened action—the loss of a well-loved child, a blind and twisted jealousy, a passion for fair play, a sense of intolerable humiliation—but Isabella is not explicable in terms of any of these.

She went to Dumont and charged him with perfidy. Then she went to the Gedneys' mother and in broken English screamed, "Oh, I must have my child! I will have my child!" She shrieked out maledictions upon the heads of all concerned, invoked hell and death, and cursed to action the sluggard forces of the law. And she had her child. Under delayed sentence and a bond of six hundred dollars, Solomon Gedney fetched Peter back from Alabama.

But Isabella did not really want the boy. She gave him into the keeping of a family in Wahkendall. Then she herself went to live in New York City.

2. BATHED IN HOLINESS

Perhaps a group of thirty ex-slaves living on Manhattan Island were a little too sanguine when in the early 1830s they addressed a letter to their "Afflicted and Beloved Brothers" in the South: "We get wages for our labor. We have schools for our children. . . . We are happy to say that every year is multiplying the facilities. . . ."

Among these facilities were a theater-hotel called the African Grove, the first Negro newspaper, *Freedom's Journal*, the largest Negro church in the United States, and living space in the Five Points district—where kidnapers prowled in armed gangs and shanghaied any likely Negro, free or not, and sold him south to slavery. But kidnapers could not seriously reduce the Negro population. Negroes kept coming all the time, though a vigorous pro-slavery press thundered against them and against abolition, "this most dangerous species of fanaticism extending itself through our society. . . . Shall we, by promptly and fearlessly crushing this many-headed Hydra in the bud, expose the weakness as well as the folly, madness and mischief of these bold and dangerous men?"

But in New York metaphors were not all that was mixed, often for good but sometimes for ill. Daniel Payne, fleeing Charleston in 1835, would stop there briefly, wander in innocent curiosity into Cow Bay Alley, be "revolted" by the brazen prostitution and open "consortium of white drabs and drunken Negro sailors"; but, finally, through his connection with the Methodist Episcopal Church, meet some white teachers and preachers who would provide him with a scholarship to study at the Gettysburg Seminary and send him on his way. And on a September morning three years later Frederick Douglass would find himself "one more added to the mighty throng which, like the confused waves of the troubled sea, surged to and fro between the lofty walls of Broadway." After a few days "of freedom from slavery, but free from food and shelter as well," he too would meet a mixed group, the Vigilance Committee, find refuge in the home of one of them, and be given steamer fare to New Bedford.

Much of the spirit called humanitarian found focus in New York. Assorted idealists and crackpots, hewing their timbers from the forest of radicalism, were busy building the New Jerusalem. Their hammers rang. The forges of Free Enquirers, Sabbatarians, Emancipationists, Feminists, Owenites, and evangelical sects of all sorts gave off an incandescent glow. Negroes were frequently suffused in it. Many of them attended white churches. They were welcomed in many movements. Situated in what is now Greenwich Village, a

mixed utopian community flourished for a time. The Manumission
Society had founded the first African Free School in 1787, and by
the early 1830s there were seven such schools taught by teachers of
both races and supported by appropriations from the state legislature as well as from the Common Council. "It was due mainly to
[these schools] that there was produced in New York City . . . a
body of intelligent and well-trained colored men and women."

In New York lived John Russwurm, first Negro graduate of an
American college (Bowdoin, 1826). Dr. James McCune Smith,
graduate of the Glasgow University, practiced medicine there "without prejudice to his white patients, who were numerous." Alexander
Crummell and J. W. C. Pennington, one a graduate of Cambridge
University and the other with an honorary degree from Heidelberg,
frequently preached to white congregations.

New York was a haven for Isabella when she arrived in 1829.
Almost the first people she met were the Elijah Piersons, a white
couple of great wealth and inexhaustible mystic faith. Both were
unstable; both had begun a tragic descent into unreality. Their
devotion to the organized Church had been reamed out in the revival of anti-clericalism in the 1820s and rendered them neurotic
prey to a religious eclecticism that was almost as pagan as it was
Christian. They had set out to convert the whole of New York City,
after which, in their grandiose imaginings, they would convert the
world. They had founded an ascetic church called Five Points
House, an esoteric group known as the Retrenchment Society, and
a house for fallen women named the Magdalene Society. Their own
home on Bowery Hill was known as the Kingdom.

Here Isabella went to live with them. Responsive to their religious influence as well as to their kindness, she was quick to substitute their messianic mysticism for the dark and vengeful spirit of
the sorcery she had learned from Black Tom. "Our God is a God of
love," Pierson drummed into her time and again, "and you are one
of His prophets." She had never known a God like theirs. Soon she
was having religious seizures—"I feel so light and so well, I could
skim around like a gull!"—and visions of great intensity—"It is

Jesus!" She was also making prophecies (a practice which must have continued for some time, for Harriet Beecher Stowe, who did not meet her until the 1850s, called her the "Libyan Sybil").

All this seemed to suit Isabella's temperament, and the Piersons seemed her kind of people. They fasted periodically for days at a time, refusing water as well as bread, but Isabella outdid them. When they went preaching in the streets (a "slight, blond" man; a "small, graceful," and dark-haired woman), Isabella preached more fervently. No one could match her prayers. Her voice was timbred like a man's and guttural with the Dutch accent she never quite unlearned. Tall and gaunt, with a strong, dark, homely face jutting angularly below a white headcloth, she attracted attention by her appearance and held it by the power of a personality that no scoffers could shrink.

Under a regimen of prayer, preaching, and fasting, Sarah Pierson's health gave way, and her husband, now mystically renamed "Elijah the Tishbite," refused to have a doctor for her. He himself would effect her recovery according to St. James. "Is any sick among you? Let him call for the elders of the church; and let them pray over him, anointing him with oil in the name of the Lord: And the prayer of faith shall save the sick, and the Lord shall raise him up."

The elders were called, among them Isabella, and they prayed and anointed, but Sarah Pierson died.

But a stranger who had wandered into the Kingdom some time before and announced himself as Matthias explained to a broken Pierson and a faith-faltering Isabella that they had misunderstood the word of God. He *had* raised Sarah up—up into eternal life. Nor was this the only instance in which God's word had been misunderstood, Matthias explained. He would set them right. He, Matthias, was "the Spirit of Truth" that had disappeared from the earth at the death of Matthew in the New Testament. "The spirit of Jesus Christ entered into that Matthias, and I am the same Matthias. . . . I am he that has come to fulfill the word."

And the word was "all things in common." Matthias, who heretofore had been known simply as Robert Matthews, who had deserted his wife and children in Albany, and who had several times been arrested as a public nuisance, very soon had Isabella, Pierson, whose daughter now joined him, and a well-to-do couple, the Benjamin Folgers, completely under his spell. Pooling their considerable resources and turning them over to Matthias, these five moved with him to Sing Sing, New York, to a country place Matthias called Zion Hill. It began as just another experiment in communal living, a material projection of pure idealism such as blistered the American landscape in the 1830s. It ended after two years in a riotous carnival of licentiousness, adultery, and suspected murder.

For Matthias turned the Pierson fasts to feasts, their prayers to pimping. He was not long in convincing Pierson and the Folgers of the divine origin of his "matched souls" doctrine. According to this, Pierson would meet his wife again in the form of another woman: Matthias saw to it. Whatever Pierson's trysts with his own daughter signified under the doctrine, Matthias himself made open love to any woman who struck his sybaritic fancy—and Mrs. Folger did. In a ceremony that Pierson performed, Mrs. Folger became Matthias' soul mate, and Benjamin Folger himself gave her away. A few days later Elijah Pierson suffered what was called an epileptic fit, and in succeeding days a series of them, and then he died.

But the death of this once wealthy, reputable man, known down in the city for his charitable though eccentric works, did not go unnoticed by his relatives. They were suspicious. The body was exhumed and traces of arsenic found in it. Matthias was arrested and charged with murder. Isabella was implicated with him, and was also accused by the Folgers of trying to poison them. But the evidence against her in both these matters was insupportable, and she escaped indictment.

For the truth seems to be that Isabella was not aware of what went on at Zion Hill and Matthias did not corrupt her with this knowledge. He kept her hypnotically transfixed in a religious state beyond all comprehension of reality and worked on her the same spell that, for different reasons and with quite contrary results, he worked on the Piersons, the Folgers, and other members of the cult.

And Isabella remained spellbound longer. She saw Zion Hill as "bathed in holiness" even while the Folgers were testifying to its abominations. Her defense of Matthias in court was so spiritually naïve and sincere that only perfect innocence could have produced it.

3. SOJOURNER

The trial of Matthias was the beginning of a new life for Isabella. Though she was now truly religious, the ecstatic seizures ceased and the visions began to fade. She dropped back into reality like one "once blind but now made to see."

What she saw with mundane clarity was a Negro life sunk to a depth almost beyond recovery. She saw it aswarm in the fetid alleys of Five Points, where Negroes "crawled over each other like flies on a dungpile." It lurked in the shadows of the docks, the stables, and the abattoirs, where, perchance, there might be a day's work free from molestation by immigrant whites who, arriving on every ship, were given first rights in such jobs as offered. She saw Negroes trying to beat back the compacted misery of their days with nights spent in Dickens Place, where assorted whores and their pimps did a brisk trade in flesh and thievery.

For, indeed, this was the life her son became involved in. Peter was now in his teens and his sister had just turned ten, and Isabella, after years of neglecting them, tried to make a home. But Peter was man-size, boisterously genial, already hardened in petty crime. Besides, Isabella had to work.

At first she made her living polishing the brass fixtures that adorned the doors of houses along the east-side avenues. She had regular customers to whom she sometimes talked in an earnest, forthright way about God. The notoriety of the Matthias trial still clung to her, and she was regarded as a strange character. She could be seen any day except Sunday, a can of dampened ashes mixed with sand at her feet, polishing rags hanging from the waist of her kilted skirt, putting a shine on name plates, doorknobs, and hinges.

But this work depended upon the weather, and eventually she took a job in domestic service.

Even so, there was little time for her home. She was a prominent member of the African Zion Church, the church militant. Here gathered all the social forces that Negroes could command. There was plenty of the old-time religion still, and there were many prayer meetings and "love feasts" where Isabella exercised her gifts for prayer and testimony, but here the "most dangerous species of fanaticism" permeated the atmosphere. When anti-slavery ministers like John Marrs and Dempsey Kennedy came to preach, what Isabella heard was less of the word of Christ and more of the battle cry of freedom. At African Zion Church she heard discussions of the questions of colonization, education, and abolition. Once in the early 1840s, William Lloyd Garrison spoke there. Through her association with the church Isabella met Charles B. Ray, the Negro abolitionist, and it was in his home that she first saw Frederick Douglass, the white and wealthy Tappan brothers, and Gerrit Smith. Strange contours shaped and deep new furrows plowed her mind. James Sturges, the English abolitionist, told her, "This [abolition] is God's work too." She did what she could, but her appearance was against the clandestine work of the Underground Railroad, in which many of the Church's members were engaged. She was better suited to public agitation, to haranguing the street-corner rabble. She drew crowds wherever she spoke.

Meantime her son was going to the dogs. All Isabella's prayers could not save him. He professed an interest in the sea, and Isabella gave him the money to pay for a course in navigation, but he spent it on dancing lessons. She got him a job as coachman, but he sold his livery and the stable gear. Three times he went to jail—twice for theft and once for pandering—and when jail threatened for the fourth time Isabella refused to help him, and he sneaked away to sea. She never saw him again.

She had better luck with her daughter. Aged sixteen, the girl married a man named Banks and with him drifted slowly westward.

A son born of their union was to be the only blood kin Isabella was ever known to love.

Once again free of responsibility to a family, Isabella poured her great vigor into "God's work." The steely shards of social reform and anti-slavery magnetized around her faith. Her fanatic tendencies blazed up again, but they were controlled by her developing intelligence and ironic insight. It was almost as if she sported with what Harriet B. Stowe was to call her "strange powers." Gradually her visions returned, but they were not now the apocalyptic visions of heaven's pearl and hell's brimstone. They were hardly visions at all, but sleeping dreams in which voices urged her to "go out into the world, gather in the flock." Sometimes it was the voice of the Reverend Charles Ray, sometimes of the Reverend Henry Garnet, sometimes of Gerrit Smith. Sometimes it seemed the voice of God. She grew impatient with the necessity to earn her living. She felt oppressed by New York, where, she said, "the rich do rob the poor, and the poor rob the poorer," and where the "truth of God is locked away" from sight.

Then one day she felt reborn. "I felt so tall within—I felt as if the power of a nation was with me." It was in the spring of 1843—the year Daniel Payne entered the active ministry of the African Methodist Episcopal Church, the year Frederick Douglass took part in "one hundred conventions." She was working for a Mrs. Whiting, who in answer to a question about her erstwhile maid replied: "She told me that she was going away and that the Lord was going to give her a new name. I thought Bell was crazy. She took a pillowcase and put her things in it, and then she left, saying she must be about her father's business. A new name indeed! And what was her father's business? Poor woman, I thought for a fact she was crazy. She said she was going east."

And she did go east. She renamed herself Sojourner Truth, and hiked slowly through Connecticut and into Massachusetts. She had set out with just enough money for a week's supply of the coarsest food: for the rest of her long life she would allow herself only enough to supply her most stringent needs. Sometimes she earned money by doing a day's work. Often money was given her. In mild weather she slept out of doors. When she needed shelter she asked for it. If she shared a family's meal she paid in coin or labor. She went undaunted everywhere. She was welcomed nearly everywhere. She seemed "sent by God," wrote a Massachusetts man.

"Sister, I send you this living messenger, as I believe her to be one that God loves. Ethiopia is stretching forth her hands unto God. You can see by this sister that God does by his spirit alone teach his own children. . . . Please receive her and she will tell you some things. Let her tell her story without interrupting her, and give close attention, and you will see she has got the love of truth, that God helps her to pray where but few can. She cannot read or write, but the law is in her heart. She is sent by God."

Sojourner Truth had the apostolic manner. In some homes she would announce that she had come to talk about the "angelic elect," but her private conversations differed little from her public preachments. She spoke of the "nation's sins against my people." She carried a white satin banner on which was inscribed, "Proclaim Liberty Throughout All the Land unto All the Inhabitants Thereof." When she had unfurled this on the makeshift rostrum of a camp meeting ground, she would begin: "There is more den one kin' of liberty, an' I come to tell you about all kin' of liberty. . . ."

The first winter caught up with her in Northampton, Massachusetts, where she took up temporary residence. Samuel Hill, Parker Pillsbury, and the brother-in-law of Garrison, George Benson— abolitionists all—received her as one of them. When spring came she was off again, this time journeying west. Her reputation outran her. She was the first Negro woman anti-slavery speaker. Sometimes attempts were made to silence and hinder her. She was beaten with sticks and pelted with stones, and on one occasion received injuries that finally ulcerated her leg. She was beaten many times.

4. GOD'S PILGRIM

Slavery had ceased to be a question of moral debate, though the Garrisonians continued to act as if it were. But Garrison's principle of non-resistance had never been popular outside

New England—and least of all in the West, where slavery was a matter both of politics, as in the South, and of economics, as in the urban East. The question was dangerously surcharged with emotion everywhere. The best interest of Western farmers could not be served by an alliance with slavery, but there were many farmers who hated anti-slavery. Industrial capitalism and slavery were natural enemies, but capitalists joined with slaveholders to fight abolition. The New York Stock Exchange offered five thousand dollars for the head of Arthur Tappan. Midwestern industrialists hired hoodlums to break up abolition meetings. Some "Gentlemen of Property" in Cincinnati posted a notice throughout the city:

Abolitionists. BEWARE!
The citizens of Cincinnati, embracing every class, interested in the prosperity of the city, satisfied that the business of the place is receiving a vital stab from the wicked and misguided operations of the abolitionists, are resolved to arrest to their course.

In Cincinnati, James Birney, converted from Alabama slaveholder to Northern emancipationist, was attacked by a mob under the protection of Nicholas Longworth, the richest man in the Midwest, Jacob Burnet, formerly a judge of the Ohio Supreme Court, and Oliver Spencer, a Methodist minister. The "spirit of lawless violence" that William Jay had deplored in the East was more evident in the West. Pro-slavery sentiment was better organized, more given to deeds than to debate. The president of the new interracial college, Oberlin, Asa Mahan, was stoned in Indiana. Mobbed in Kansas and hounded out of Missouri, Elijah Lovejoy was at last murdered in Illinois.

But violence triggered by any show of radicalism was only half the story. The resolute, refractory, and gentle Quakers were the other half. Their anti-slavery tradition went back more than a hundred years. It went back to Ralph Sandiford, who wrote, and Benjamin Franklin, who published A Brief Exposition of the Practice of the Times—a pamphlet "packed with brimstone." It went back to Benjamin Say, who, "to show his indignation against the practice of slavekeeping, once carried a bladder filled with blood into a meeting;

and, in the presence of the whole congregation, thrust a sword . . .
into the bladder, exclaiming at the same time, 'Thus shall God shed
the blood of those persons who enslave their fellow creatures.' The
terror of this extravagant and unexpected act produced swooning in
several of the women of the congregation."

The Midwestern Quakers no longer carried blood in bladders—
they knew better tricks—and their women were too busy to swoon.
They were busy devising stratagems of elusion, such as the one a
certain Faith Webster pulled. Caching a group of fleeing slaves on
the Kentucky side of the Ohio River one dawn when daylight made
further progress impossible, she returned in the evening to find slave
hunters scouring the area. Faith Webster changed into such clothes
as a slave woman would wear, burnt-corked her pretty face, and
decoyed the posse into chasing her while the slaves escaped across
the river.

Miss Webster had unnumbered colleagues—Quakers and Baptists and those of no denomination—and they were all busy operating
the mysterious railroad that "ran underground from Cincinnati to
Canada." It was not easy to operate. It jeopardized livelihood. It
put life and limb at hazard. But it ran. Whole families ran it—the
Rankins, the Coffins, the Sloanes—and three hundred thousand
slaves escaped.

Sojourner Truth would have joined in this work, but her appearance was just as conspicuous now as it had been ten years before.
So she spoke. She spoke for abolition and for women's rights, which,
thanks to Lucy Stone and Jane Swisshelm, was a subject practically
inseparable from abolition in the Midwest.

"Where dere is so much racket dere mus' be somethin' out o'
kilter," Sojourner told the heckling males at a women's rights convention in Akron. "I think dat 'twixt de niggers of de South and
de womens of de North all a-talkin' 'bout rights, de white mens'll
be in a fix pretty soon. Ef de firs' woman God ever made was strong
enough to turn de worl' upside down all by her lonesome se'f dese
together ought to be able to turn it back an' git it right side up again,
an' now dey is askin' to do it de mens better let 'em. Dey talks 'bout

dis thing in the head—what dey call it? Intellec'. Dat's it, honeys—
intellec'. Now what's dat got to do wid us women's rights or niggers'
rights? Ef my cup won't hol' but a pint an' yourn hol's a quart,
wouldn' you be mean not to let me have my little half measure full?"

Sojourner's ironic wit and her subtle power dominated that meeting. The woman who chaired it, Mrs. Frances D. Gage, later reported that Sojourner Truth "had taken us up in her strong arms
and carried us safely over the slough of difficulty, turning the whole
tide in our favor."

But she was not able always to turn the tide.

There was much hostility in Ohio, where she made Salem and
the office of Marius Robinson's *Anti-Slavery Bugle* her headquarters for two years. (Robinson tried to teach her to read, but
"my brains is too stiff now," Sojourner told him.) It was 1852, when
she judged her age to be "gone sixty," but she went from Ohio
town to town speaking, soliciting subscriptions for the *Anti-Slavery
Bugle*, and occasionally even making sorties into neighboring
states. She could not go into Indiana without facing the threat of
arrest, or into Illinois without the chance of violence. But she went
many times. She said she was "God's pilgrim" and under God's protection, but that protection sometimes wilted in the hot breath
blowing in from Missouri and across the plains of Kansas, where
John Brown, drunk on the wine of his coming crucifixion, would
soon reappear to make good the defiance flung out by Senator William Seward: "Come on, then, gentlemen of the slave states! Since
there is no escaping your challenge, I accept it on behalf of freedom.
We will engage in competition for the virgin soil of Kansas, and God
give the victory to the side that is stronger in numbers as it is in
right."

Sojourner Truth was manhandled in Kansas, and ever afterward
needed the support of a cane, which, she avowed, also came in
"mighty fine for crackin' skulls."

If this was said jocosely, the rumors, the galling jokes, and the
downright lies that followed her everywhere were not. Nor could
the portrait of her drawn by Harriet B. Stowe modify them. The

people who were Sojourner's detractors did not read the *Atlantic Monthly*. If Sojourner was for Mrs. Stowe a "Sybil," she was a "black witch" for many more, and it was said that she worshiped in graveyards. If, as Mrs. Stowe wrote, she had "power and sweetness," there were others more vociferous who said she cast spells.

The unsavory reputation that surrounded her during the exposure and trial of Matthias was revived. Some believed that she was a man masquerading as a woman for reasons that would not bear examination. The St. Louis *Dispatch* reported, "Sojourner Truth is the name of a man now lecturing in Kansas City." Her vigorous, rail-like frame, her scarred, strong face and heavy-timbred voice were deceptive, and there were those who honestly doubted her femininity. But if such doubts persisted (as late as 1877), it was not Sojourner's fault.

In 1858 she had set a Kansas anti-slavery meeting above the usual pitch of turbulence. The meeting had been rigged by the enemies of abolition. As soon as Sojourner began her speech, a man in the audience interrupted her. "Hold on," he said. "Is the speaker man or woman? The majority of persons present believe the speaker to be a man. . . . I demand that if she is a woman, she submit her breast to the inspection of some of the ladies present . . . !"

While the abolitionists gaped in shocked silence, the pro-slavery claque, stamping their feet and clapping their hands, shouted in ribald mockery, "Uncover! Uncover! You are a man!" The dazed abolitionists responded only with cries of, "No, no! For shame!"

The whole auditorium was in confusion, for there were bully boys on both sides, and Sojourner Truth, facing it from the rostrum, whence had fled the chairman and the other platform guests, waited the tumult out. When it had quieted to manageable proportions, she stepped to the edge of the platform and pounded her cane on the floor.

"My breasts," she said, "has suckled many a white baby when dey shoulda been sucklin' my own." Her voice quavered momentarily, and then rose again firmly, tranquilly. "I dar'st show my breasts to de whole cong'agation. It ain't my shame dat I do dis, but yourn.

Here den," she said, ripping her clothes from neckline to waist, "see fer yourself!" Her hard gaze sought and found the face of the man who had first attacked her. She thrust her bared breasts forward and said in angry scorn, "Mought be you'd like to suck?"

5. "FREDERICK, IS GOD DEAD?"

But Sojourner Truth was beginning to feel the wear and tear, the slow erosion of the years. Traveling with Parker Pillsbury on one of his speaking tours through the Midwest, she suffered occasional spells of faintness. Her wounded leg ulcerated. In Battle Creek, Michigan, where she had found her daughter's son, Sammy Banks, with whom she now lived, a physician was able to arrest the infection, but it broke out again periodically and gave her great pain. Nevertheless, she refused to stop for long. She went back into Illinois, Kansas, Ohio, Indiana. She went out into New England, where she was the guest of the Stowes in Andover, Massachusetts. And there was one brief interlude, more pleasant than strenuous. She went to Tawawa Springs, Ohio, to visit Daniel Payne, who, with his wife and her two children, was making his home there.

Payne was as busy as ever. He presided over the work of the African Methodist Episcopal Church in Ohio, Indiana, and Canada. His duties had forced him to live at one time or another in Troy, New York, Philadelphia, Baltimore, Washington, and Cincinnati. In addition to his churchly work, he had organized in each place adult Negroes into study groups and started schools for their children. He himself had done most of the teaching—reading, writing, and "social and civic morality" to the adults; a more formal curriculum to the children.

Now he was engaged in a more ambitious educational venture. He was the only Negro trustee of the new Wilberforce University. It had been founded by the white Methodist Church for "the benefit of the African race." (The exigencies of the war were to close it down in 1862, but Payne was to reopen it the very next year and become the first president of the first Negro-controlled college.)

While Sojourner was his guest in 1858, he took her to visit the college on the outskirts of Xenia. How she reacted to a campus populated exclusively by the illegitimate mulatto offspring of Southern planters is not recorded, but Payne felt moved to remind her that "these also need learning and God as much as any." When he had her speak to the adults of his Moral and Mental Uplift Society, he wished that there had been a thousand "instead of twenty to hear my simple and eloquent friend."

Before the visit ended, Payne read his friend some verses, pieces of his own published in 1850, and from a book of poems by the slave George M. Horton. Sojourner's comment made him laugh wryly. "Dan," she said, "yourn be pretty, but his'n be strong." She regretted that she could not read them for herself, but the bishop made her a gift of his slim volume anyway.

This visit did Sojourner Truth good, and she left Tawawa Springs to go stumping about as usual, attending meetings and speaking.

But all the most eloquent tongues in Christendom could not have modified the momentum or changed the direction of the decade that was now fast drawing to a close. Neither North nor South had been reconciled to the Compromise of 1850. Neither made serious efforts to preserve intersectional peace. If the North's defiance of the Fugitive Slave Law further embittered the South, then the passage of the Kansas-Nebraska Act exacerbated the feelings of the North and brought about a new political alignment of Northern Whigs, Free-Soilers, and Democrats. Professedly anti-slavery, the Republican party pieced out a program attractive to many who cared nothing about the slavery issue. In 1857 the Dred Scott decision did not prove "happily a matter of but little importance," as President Buchanan had said. It was oil thrown on the fire. In 1859, John Brown staged his raid on Harper's Ferry and achieved his martyrdom. In 1860 the Republicans elected the unknown Abraham Lincoln. In that same year Frederick Douglass, deep in despair on his return from England, spoke at an anti-slavery meeting commemorating West Indian emancipation:

"They [Republicans] are men who are brave enough to trip up

a man on crutches, push a blind man off the side-walk, or flog a man when his hands are tied, but too base and cowardly to contend with one who has an equal chance of defense with themselves. The black man, excluded alike from the jury box and the ballot box, is at the mercy of his enemies. . . . All know that the election of Lincoln would destroy all the conciliatory power which this new injustice to the Negro might exert. . . . But what will the colored people and their friends do now . . . ?"

Just at this point Sojourner Truth rose slowly in the back of the hall. "Frederick," she cried, "is God dead?"

God was not dead. Eight months later He was "trampling out the vintage where the grapes of wrath" were stored.

CHAPTER FIVE

Mississippi Delta

1. CRUSADE IN CUBA

THE 24th Infantry of the U. S. Regular Army, colored troops, reached Santiago Bay, Cuba, on June 20, 1898. They were the first to arrive. Their ship, the *City of Washington*, cruised within sight but out of range of Morro Castle until nightfall. The next day, when American gunboats began to arrive, the *City of Washington* was ordered to feint at Morro Castle so as to draw fire from the Spanish guns, and, like a punch-drunk fighter, she lumbered in time and again. The Spanish guns consistently overshot her. It is a good thing they did, for she was no ship for the job. She was a steamer, an excursion boat, and one clean shot would have splintered her wooden decks; but she feinted at the fortress off and on for five days, while the gunboats cannonaded Morro Castle until its guns were silenced. Then the *City of Washington* landed her six hundred soldiers, who marched immediately to Siboney and made camp five miles from the front, where the Spaniards were chewing up elements of Máximo Gómez' ragged army.

The *Comal* reached Cuban waters on June 21. She was a transport. Since she carried, in addition to some Negro regulars of the 10th Cavalry, Batteries B and K of the 2nd Artillery, white troops, baggage, ammunition, rations, horses and mules, she was valuable, and an escort of gun and torpedo boats was sent to pick her up off Dry Tortugas. But in spite of shelling from Admiral Sampson's gunboats, Morro Castle was still hot when the *Comal* arrived, and she steamed sixteen miles down the bay west of Santiago. Here she spent the night making half-mile circles so as to give the horses and mules air. It was very hot, and there was no breeze. In the morning the *Comal* moved within sight of Daiquiri and lay to until the armored cruiser *New York* came in to bombard the villages along the coast above and below the town.

Under the cover of this fire the 10th Cavalry began landing operations. They were at it two days, for they had to land the equipment and swim the livestock through heavy surf to the rocky beach. Two men were lost. Batteries B and K of the 2nd Artillery stayed aboard the *Comal*, which was later joined by the *Anne* and the *Topeka*, also carrying white troops. Then the three ships moved nine miles down to Siboney, where the beach was smoother and where the engineers had built a landing dock.

Meanwhile the dismounted 10th Cavalry had pushed overland to Siboney, which they reached shortly after midnight. Here they rested, and at three-thirty in the morning set out for Las Guásimas, where the enemy occupied a hill commanding the road to Santiago. The 1st Volunteers, popularly called the Rough Riders, had been pinned down at this spot for sixteen hours. When the 10th Cavalry came up, Colonel Leonard Wood, commanding the 1st Volunteers, deployed his troops to flank the hill right and left, and ordered Troops A, B, and I of the 10th to charge the enemy position frontally. Yelling and whooping like crazy men, the Rough Riders stormed up the hill on the right and left without the loss of a single man, but the 10th, charging head on, was met by heavy fire and sustained a loss of twenty-eight men, seven of them killed.

The *Concha* took on the 14th Infantry, a battalion of the 2nd Massachusetts, the brigade headquarters—all white—and the 25th

Infantry, colored, at Tampa on June 7. They totaled thirteen hundred men. Aboard ship, white and colored troops were segregated at once. The latter were assigned to the bottom deck, where bunks were arranged in tiers of four, where it was dark at high noon, and where the only air came down the canvas air shafts when they were turned to the breeze. Topside, white troops lolled on the larboard; Negro troops milled around the gear piled starboard.

The *Concha* stayed tied up at the Tampa dock until June 15, but Negro troops were forbidden ashore except when an officer could take a whole company off to bathe and exercise. This was done twice during the eight days, and by the time the *Concha* sailed she was as ripe as an eighteenth-century pesthouse. It was unbearably hot during the crossing, and Negro troops disobeyed the order against sleeping on deck. Packs of thirty at a time took turns at it, but in seven days no man slept up there twice, and some did not sleep up there at all. They landed at Daiquiri on the twenty-second, where the Cuban troops of General Castillo met them and led them on a two-day march over a jungle trail to Las Guásimas. They arrived just in time to clean up the retreating stragglers from the hill taken by the Rough Riders and the 10th Cavalry. Then they pushed on toward El Caney.

The 9th Cavalry, nicknamed the Black Buffaloes, was short its normal complement when it was ordered from Fort Robinson, Nebraska, to Chickamauga Park, Georgia, on April 20. From Chickamauga the six hundred men marched to Chattanooga, thence went by rail to Port Tampa, arriving on May 2. Here they quartered, and General Joseph Wheeler, in command of the Fifth Army Corps, detailed three officers and six enlisted men to recruitment duty. He wanted six hundred men. The detail found the new recruits in the vicinity of Orangeburg, South Carolina, but before they could return with them the veterans of the 9th Cavalry had sailed, along with some white elements of the Fifth Army.

The 9th disembarked at Daiquiri on June 23, but the sea suddenly became too rough to land the white troops, and the transport carried them to Siboney. That night the 9th bivouacked a few

miles to the rear of the Rough Riders, and the next morning a hatless
and breathless courier thundered in with the news that the Rough
Riders needed help at Las Guásimas. The Black Buffaloes got there
too late, help having been provided by the 10th Cavalry, and returned to camp and spent the next two days building roads. On
June 27 three troops of the 9th were sent to scout and patrol, while
five troops stayed behind roadbuilding until June 30, when they
too moved out.

2. SANTIAGO

Considering that when Congress declared war on
Spain the War Department was only large enough to meet the needs
of a peacetime army of twenty-eight thousand men, and that it had
not for over thirty years transported, even by rail, a larger contingent
than a regiment; and considering the fact that nearly all that was
done between April and August 1898 was done by inexperienced
officers more or less scrambled up in an unwieldy organization of
staff corps, the transportation of seventeen thousand men, all told,
their equipment and accouterments, was commendably done.

The specific objective of these troop movements was Santiago,
Cuba, and the reason the troops converged on that place was also
commendable. It was not because "our rapidly-increasing power,"
or our "commercial needs," or because "more than either, geography
determined it," as Senator Beveridge declared. It is true that all
these played their parts in America's imperialist expansion and the
fulfillment of her "manifest destiny" in other directions; but the
common soldier did not believe that the business in Cuba was of a
piece with annexing the Hawaiian Islands, or building a coaling
station in Pago Pago, or establishing bases on Wake, Midway, and
Howland, or organizing the first Pan-American Congress. These
troops, more than half of them state militia and volunteers, believed
they were in Cuba because America and Americans had been
"shocked in their moral sense" by Spain's "intolerable oppression"
of the Cuban people, by Spain's violation of "all the principles of

justice," and because it was America's "bounden duty to carry freedom to a race of worse than slaves abroad."

The battle at Santiago was to be the first (and last) land battle in pursuit of this noble end.

In defense of the city the Spaniards held two strongly fortified perimeter positions—the village of El Caney and the hills called San Juan. These had to be cleaned out, after which it was thought that the city would fall to the attackers like a ripe mango. Three command divisions were to take part in the initial attack. The first was to be launched from El Pozo, an elevation some three miles from Santiago, from which could be seen the masked entrenchments, the barbed-wire entanglements, and the blockhouses of the San Juan hills. Northeast and to the right, on a hill overlooking all approaches to Santiago, stood the stone fort and the blockhouses of El Caney. Southwest and on the left crawled the shallow San Juan River. Due north stood the city of Santiago on the bay, and on July 1, the day of the attack, the bay grinned and glittered in the bright sun.

General Lawton's command pulled out from El Pozo first. It consisted of three regiments of infantry—the 7th and 12th, white, and the 25th, colored. Their job was to storm and capture El Caney, execute a flanking movement, and then smash against the hills of San Juan from the right. Meanwhile General Kent's division of infantry—the 71st New York and the 13th, white, and the 24th, colored—was to cross the San Juan River, follow an exposed ridge north, and thus flank the hills on the left. Finally General Wheeler's dismounted cavalrymen—the Rough Riders, white, and the 9th and 10th, colored—were to await the reduction of El Caney and then make a frontal attack on the San Juan hills.

Lawton had already gone when the artillery duel began at four-thirty. It was thought that Lawton's infantry could reduce El Caney by midmorning. But this was not the only miscalculation made that day. The American artillery opened up with black powder instead of smokeless, and the Spanish artillery, quickly getting the range, forced the cavalry out of its assembly area before eight o'clock. There was confusion. An American observation balloon floating over the cavalry ranks gave away every movement. Spanish fire converged on them anew. They made for the river, there to seek shelter under its wooded banks, but near the crossing confusion was compounded.

Kent's 71st New York had managed to reach the exposed ridge road running north, but that was all. Spanish fire had completely demoralized them. Now they were milling around in the river crossing like panicked cattle. As the dismounted cavalry approached, the 71st broke through the cavalry ranks, which could not open fast enough to give them passage. Cavalrymen were shoved right and left, and one of them was knocked down and trampled to death. General Kent, "disgusted, with tears running down his cheeks," screamed out entreaties and threats, but he could not stop the 71st's terror-stricken recoil.

The cavalry units finally gained the bed of the river and stood waist-high in the water and waited. The balloon followed them, and Spanish fire followed the balloon. Why it was there none of the men knew. Who ordered it? Who manipulated it? Once it dropped a note saying that the men in the river were being fired upon, but this was quite superfluous information.

Taking the responsibility upon himself, Lieutenant J. J. Pershing, a platoon commander, called the other platoon commanders of the 10th Cavalry together and suggested that they leave the river a platoon at a time and deploy in thin skirmish lines on the shore. His own platoon went first. Three followed. As each platoon scrambled from the river, Pershing's men crawled forward through the light cover to make room. The fire was terrific. Two officers and eleven men were killed in the first five minutes. But the farther the skirmish lines advanced over the six-hundred-yard plain, the thicker the cover grew, and Lieutenant Pershing lost only fourteen men of his platoon before it reached fairly adequate cover near the base of the first hill. Here he waited.

But this was not the attack at all, nor the way it was supposed to be. Back in the bed of the river General Wheeler and some of his staff conferred over the situation, which was not promising. Just behind them in the river a thousand men waited. Another thousand were packed at the ford. Shells burst among them, and they were restless, for it is not easy to stand still and be shot at. It was now after ten o'clock, and Lawton had not reduced El Caney. Lawton was stalled. A part of Kent's command was in retreat. There was no right flank, there was no left flank. Co-ordination of commands had been lost. Retreat or advance? If this was a question in General Wheeler's mind, he did not have to answer it.

For suddenly a horde of men, miraculously moved by the same impulse, plowed out of the river, broke forward toward the ridge road, thronged wildly over it, and started across the plain toward the first hill. They were no one's command. They were a mixed company, white and black, regulars and volunteers, and they went yelling and shouting across the plain and firing over the heads of the skirmish lines as they advanced. Little clouds of dust, thrown up by bullets, bloomed on the hillside. Pausing only momentarily for loading and firing, the line of men—here thick, there thin—swept across the plain through a sheet of Mauser shot and onto the crest of the first hill. The Spaniards retreated to the second line of defense.

At the top of the hill the Americans halted to regroup for the attack on the entrenchments and blockhouses on the second hill. The Rough Riders, with some elements of the 13th Infantry, were put in the center of the line. The 9th Cavalry, which had lost a hundred men, held down the left. Pieced out with some units of the 24th Infantry, the 10th Cavalry held the right, facing the steep southern declivity, which when they poured into it was like spooning sliced potatoes into a pan of sizzling fat. The Spanish fire doubled in intensity when the attack was resumed, and a flood of flame swept over the Americans. But the momentum of the first phase held. Within an hour the blockhouses were taken, the entrenchments overrun, and the Spanish in flight toward Santiago. It was three-thirty in the afternoon.

Meantime the fight that was to have been finished at El Caney by midmorning was still in progress. It was an orderly battle, conducted by the book. At dawn three pieces of artillery had opened up against the stone fort, the blockhouse, and the church tower, but after only one round the dynamite gun jammed, and after only seven the Hotchkiss gun was knocked out. At six-thirty the 2nd Massachusetts was committed. The only visible targets were the fort, the blockhouse, and the tower, and musket fire was ineffective against these. They could not see a single Spanish soldier, but the Spanish saw them. As they moved through the cover of grass and stunted palm, fusillades whined and whimpered from the rifle pits and entrenchments skillfully concealed in the slopes above them. It was like fighting ghosts, but they kept at it for two hours, and then they were withdrawn.

Four companies of the 25th Infantry replaced them. An initial charge carried them within five hundred yards of the fort. Here they were stopped by barbed wire "woven close as cloth" and pinned down by fire from the fort and cross fire from the blockhouse. They had no wire nippers. Working in groups of four, they hacked through the wire entanglements with their bayonets. It took them more than an hour. The operation cost fifty-three men.

But when the work was done the rest of the 25th and all of the 4th Infantry went in. The latter went in on the left and carried to a deep escarpment that blocked further advance but gave them cover from which they poured distractive fire on the blockhouse. The 25th advanced through fire from the fort and the church tower. The charge moved in quick rushes, but it made slow progress.

The 12th Infantry was the last to go in, and it was committed at four o'clock. Compared to the advance of the 25th, its sweep forward over the dead, dark bodies of comrades was triumphant. When Corporal T. H. Jones of I Company, the 25th, saw the 12th advancing, he remarked to Sergeant Butler of H Company, "Here they come to take credit for what our blood and bullets won." In Corporal Jones's company and in H, C, and D companies not an officer was left. The 12th was moving up in battle array, and though the ropy, pitched terrain spoiled their neat order, they nevertheless gave a distinct impression of picture-book soldiers in the final chapter of a storybook war. Impulsively Sergeant Butler ordered Companies I, H, C, and D to a final charge, and in ten minutes of insane fighting they stormed and carried the fort. An officer of the 12th arrived just in time to receive the Spanish flag.

Forty minutes later the blockhouse and the church tower surrendered, and at six-thirty in the evening all resistance at El Caney came to an end.

But the Spanish were not through yet—they simply retired toward Santiago—and there was no sleep for some of the American troops that night. The 25th Infantry was brought forward from El Caney to help the 24th extend and strengthen the lines. The 9th Cavalry gathered the wounded and buried the dead. The 10th Cavalry brought up food and ammunition. These troops worked all night, and in the morning, as General Wheeler had anticipated, the battle was resumed.

It went on for two days longer, but with less and less animation. On July 3, Spanish General Linares asked for a truce, but Cervera, the Spanish naval commander, tried to run his fleet out of Santiago Harbor and had it smashed to bits by the American fleet in Santiago Bay. By July 4 everything was over except the formalities and the shouting, and the war that had been fought "to rebuke a sister nation for her inhumanity," the war that had been fought "for independence, fair play . . . and democracy, against all that was tyrannical" was done.

In the three-day land battle of that war Negro troops of the 9th and 10th Cavalry and of the 24th and 25th Infantry suffered 22 per cent greater casualties than their white comrades in arms.

3. ROPE AND FAGGOT

Before the fight at El Caney one of the Negro soldiers who died in it had written to his wife, "Surely the same strong spirit and quickened conscience which took up the cause of Cuba will secure justice to the American Negro."

And so it seemed that it might. In October 1898 the *Review of*

Reviews commented editorially: "One of the most gratifying incidents of the Spanish War has been the enthusiasm that the colored
regiments of the regular army have aroused throughout the whole
country. . . . Men who can fight for their country as did these
colored troops ought to have their full share of gratitude and honor."
Even the Atlanta (Georgia) *Journal* was "pleased" to note not a
single dissenting voice in the chorus of praise. Perhaps moved more
by this than by political considerations, President McKinley appointed a Negro as register of the Treasury, another as recorder of
deeds, and still another as collector of customs.

All the same, the forces of reaction had only been scattered, not
destroyed, and they were gathering again in no time at all. The ink
was scarcely dry on the pages of the *Review of Reviews* when one
Negro was hanged and ten shot to death by mobs in Mississippi.
That same month, October, a South Carolina rabble attacked members of the "nigger-loving family" of John R. Talbot, collector of the
port at Charleston, and forced them to leave the state. A few days
later in North Carolina, where the election of 1896 had put a handful of Negroes into public office, the Democrats, in solemn conclave
assembled, determined that "Negroes should be made to fear the
lynchers' rope for aspiring to political power."

Red shirts and white shirts, symbols of terror in Reconstruction,
were brought out again. A Presbyterian minister, the Reverend A. T.
Nickelway, later wrote in the *Outlook*: "It is difficult to speak of the
Red Shirts without a smile. They victimized the Negroes with a
huge practical joke. . . . A dozen men would meet at a cross road,
on horseback, clad in red shirts of calico, flannel or silk, according
to the taste of the owner and the enthusiasm of his womenfolk.
They would gallop through the country, and the Negro would
quietly make up his mind that his interest in political affairs was
not a large one, anyhow."

If this was a practical joke, it had the grimmest consequences. On
the day following the election of 1898 a mass meeting of Red Shirts
and other white citizens of Wilmington, North Carolina, passed
resolutions to employ only white labor, to banish the Negro editor

of the *North Carolina Record*, and to destroy the *Record's* printing press. More than a dozen Negroes were killed out of hand that very night, and before the fury had spent itself the following day twenty-three "black men, women and children were shot, stabbed and beaten to death." On receipt of this news in Atlanta a young social historian named W. E. B. Du Bois cried out, "The clock is turned back! The sixties are here again!" Twitching with horror and bitter anguish, he buried his face in his hands.

4. "KEEP POWERFUL FRIENDS"

Quite different was the reaction of Isaiah T. Montgomery when the news reached him down in Mound Bayou, Mississippi. It is reported that he said to no one in particular but to the world at large, "I told you so!" Was there a note of satisfaction in the utterance? Almost certainly. But it was not because he enjoyed blood—he had gone through three years of the Civil War and managed not to draw a drop of it; nor did he like to have Negroes shot down—he was himself a Negro. The thing was that he needed vindication.

The only Negro delegate to the Mississippi constitutional convention in 1890, Montgomery had made a speech there. "Let no one persuade us Negroes to fight a cyclone," he had said then, and the next day cast his vote with those who believed that "every political feud, every factional disturbance, and every race riot can be traced to the ignorant, presuming Negro." He was accused of the basest treachery to his people, and since then it had seemed to him that every instance of terror, every murderous act committed against Negroes in any of the various names of the "public good" somehow justified his stand.

Isaiah Montgomery was a hard man to figure.

He had been a precocious youth, quickly maturing in a precarious age. Born in 1847, the slave of Joseph Davis, elder brother of Jefferson Davis, he grew up on Hurricane Plantation. Joseph Davis taught all the Montgomerys to read, and in addition Isaiah acquired the fundamentals of accounting. At nine he was his master's office boy. At twelve he was doing all the plantation accounts, while his brother helped to supervise the work in the fields, his cousin, Ben Green, served as general mechanic, and his father, old Ben, bossed the whole enterprise.

Joseph Davis was partial to the Montgomerys. It was said that he "never lifted so much as a finger against them." They probably never gave him cause. He trusted them; they trusted him. Many an afternoon in the slack season the master could be found sitting on the back veranda of his house talking "man to man" with the Montgomerys and Ben Green grouped on the steps below him. They talked "plantation business, land speculation and family affairs"— and especially the affairs of young Jefferson Davis, who had been to West Point and to Congress, had come back from the Mexican War a hero, and who, in 1858, a senator from Mississippi, was widely recognized, since Calhoun's death, as the leading spokesman for the South. They talked about the tightening sectional tensions. They talked about the prospects for war.

When the war came Joseph Davis was in his seventies, much too old to fight. Taking a few slaves and some livestock, he went to Montgomery, Alabama, where the capital of the new Confederacy had been established.

> Say, darkeys, hab you seen de massa,
> Wid di muffstash on he face,
> Go long de road some time dis mornin',
> Like he gwine leab de place?
>
> He see de smoke way up de ribber
> Whar de Lincum gunboats lay;
> He took he hat an' leff berry sudden,
> An' I s'pose he's runned away.
>
> De massa run, ha, ha!
> De darkey stay, he, he!
> It mus' be now de kingdom come,
> An' de y'ar of jubilee.

Undoubtedly some of the Davis slaves sang this ditty, but it is highly improbable that the Montgomerys were among them. Old Ben was left in charge of Hurricane Island plantation and of Brierfield, Jefferson Davis' plantation. He took William, his elder son, to Brierfield with him, and put Isaiah and Ben Green in charge at Hurricane. Isaiah was fourteen, Ben three years older.

But in a few weeks the tide of war rolled toward Hurricane. The bluffs on both sides of the river were fortified to protect Vicksburg against the Yankees, who soon made the city a military objective. Shoving out from their base at Memphis, scouts of Grant's army prowled the west shore of the river. Isaiah saw skirmishes between Confederate and Union patrols. He saw the gunboat *Indianola* sunk when Porter's fleet tried to run through the river defenses in 1863. Shortly after that he saw Captain Porter himself. Porter ordered both Hurricane and Brierfield evacuated. He sent old Ben, his wife, their two daughters, and their elder son north to Cincinnati. He kept Isaiah. He was struck by the boy's precocity. He made Isaiah "a prize of war."

Isaiah served Porter as cabin boy on the *Benton* and on other ships that were in the fighting. Isaiah saw the Battle of Grand Gulf. His ship stood by at the Battle of Port Gibson and made a scouting run up the Red River to Fort De Russey. It joined in the bombardment of Vicksburg and was there when that city fell. Though he served for a time as gunner's mate, Isaiah never fired a gun, pulled a lanyard, or breeched a shell, but he was painfully wounded in an accident aboard ship. Captain Porter assigned a nurse to accompany him to Mound City, Illinois. Recovering in a few weeks, Isaiah joined the rest of the Montgomerys in Ohio. He was seventeen.

But life in the North was not for the Montgomerys. Cincinnati was not their environment. Neither the sorcery of their personalities nor the combination of their skills, so effective at Davis Bend, worked to advantage there. They made a living, it is true—the women as seamstresses, the men as laborers—and they pooled their resources; but it was not the living they wanted, or the living they were used to.

Cincinnati was crowded with Negroes, among whom an inflexibly self-conscious class structure had already formed. The Montgomerys were excluded from the status their superior endowments and training argued they deserved. The city and the country around, as far north as Xenia, had been the favorite dumping ground for the mulatto offspring of Southern planters. Many of these mulattoes were doing well. They had urban skills and, often, substantial financial backing. One, a real estate operator named Henry Boyd, was worth fifty thousand dollars. Samuel Wilcox manufactured beds and employed white and Negro labor. A mulatto landscape artist had studied in Rome, and a daguerreotypist was said to be the most skillful in the entire West.

These and others like them were the free Negro aristocracy, and they guarded their status jealously. The Montgomerys were pure black. Fresh up from a slavery that had been for them warm and even rewarding in personal relations with a master class they understood and among Negroes they could command, they were nevertheless peasant. Though slavery was over for them, they looked homeward to Mississippi. The occasional letters they had from Cousin Ben Green brought tears of nostalgia to their eyes.

Ben Green himself was doing all right. He had gone to Vicksburg and set up as a mechanic. There was much to do. "Ruin and army worms is everywhere," he wrote. "About all the plantations is left or made into camps for the colored who work in the woodyards for the soldiers and have not enough to eat. Money comes in driplets but I am better off as most white and colored get no money at all." He reported that Major Compash, who once owned more than a hundred slaves, could be seen in the streets of Vicksburg peddling cakes and bread made by his wife. Farms were going to swamps and weeds because the Negro workers had deserted them. Rumor had it that a railroad was coming through from Memphis to New Orleans, and many freedmen had gone east to help build it. Perhaps things would get better, Ben Green wrote, but, "O, the good land so desolated!"

The Montgomerys went back to Mississippi in 1865, and the next year they leased Hurricane and Brierfield from their old master, Joseph Davis. Ben Green did not have to be begged to join them. In Vicksburg, Natchez, and Jackson they found some of the ex-slaves with whom they had formerly worked and brought them back to the plantations. Each male "hand" was promised rations and fifteen dollars a month. Each head of family—seven in all, making a group of forty-six people that first year—had his own hut and kitchen garden.

Things began to hum. Ben Green restored the forge and made and repaired tools. The first cotton crop was planted in the spring of 1867. In summer the army worm came, but they conquered it. In late summer they rebuilt the levee and the dock at Hurricane. That fall they picked and ginned five hundred and twenty bales of cotton. By settling-up time, just prior to Christmas, the Montgomerys had tripled their original investment, and had done so well that they agreed to buy Hurricane and Brierfield for thirty thousand dollars. Young Isaiah signed the purchase notes. He had not then attained his majority. By 1873 the Montgomerys had become the third largest cotton producers in the state, and their cotton took all the prizes at the Cincinnati Exposition.

But all was not fair weather. Planters in the vicinity of Davis Bend, many of them the "new breed" Ben Green had mentioned in his letters, objected to the Montgomerys on principle. The Montgomerys' tenants were sometimes stopped and questioned about activities on the plantations. Sometimes they were thrown into jail on trumped-up charges, putting the Montgomerys to trouble and expense to get them out again. On at least one occasion a Montgomery well was poisoned and four mules and a horse died of drinking the water. Even the old breed of planters who accepted the Montgomerys and the Montgomerys' help muttered against the new situation that seemed to be developing generally in the life of the state.

It was a situation that the vast majority of Southern whites meant to resist, for it tended to make permanent their forfeiture of political power and to subvert the social principles upon which their at-

titudes, their economy, and their lives had been founded. In Mississippi, as elsewhere in the South, some slaveholders resisted simply
by withholding news of freedom from their slaves. Young men
formed patrols to keep "slaves" confined. In May 1865, Governor
Clark issued a proclamation: "Masters are still responsible as heretofore for the protection and conduct of their slaves, and they should
be kept home as heretofore."

Many professed to believe that slavery still had legal existence.
The only question in their minds was whether the state should adopt
a policy of gradual emancipation. The answer to this was far from
an unqualified and universal yea. Serving as the ears of President
Johnson in 1865, Carl Schurz heard from nineteen of every twenty
Southern men that Negroes would not work except under compul-
sion, that they could not live without a master, and that they
positively "could not be adopted to a system of free labor."

But the legality of freedom was real enough. The presence of
federal troops attested the fact. In November 1865 the new governor
of Mississippi, Benjamin Humphreys, urged the legislature to reckon
with Negro freedom as a reality. "The Negro," he said, "is free,
whether we like it or not; we must realize that fact now and forever.
To be free, however, does not make him a citizen, or entitle him to
political and social equality with the white race. . . ."

Less than three weeks later white Mississippians did reckon with
the reality, but after their own fashion. Following the hasty passage
of legislation that provided, among other things, for binding out
Negro children, without the consent of their parents, to former masters, and the establishment of iron-hard vagrancy regulations applying only to Negroes, the governor signed another piece of legislation
called "An Act to Confer Civil Rights on Freedmen."

It was a new Black Code in twelve sections, and Carl Schurz
summed up its spirit. "It is that the Negro exists for the special
object of raising cotton, rice and sugar for the whites, and that it is
illegitimate for him to indulge, like other people, in the pursuit of
his own happiness in his own way. Although it is admitted that he
has ceased to be the property of a master, it is not admitted that he

has a right to become his own master. . . . There are systems intermediate between slavery as it formerly existed in the south, and free labor as it exists in the north, but more nearly related to the former than to the latter, the introduction of which will be attempted. . . ."

The Mississippi legislation was just such an attempt. All of its provisions were direct threats to the Negroes of the state, but the economic limitations it placed upon them were especially severe. All Negroes must have homes and occupations and written evidence thereof. Negroes employed for a term of service of more than a month must produce a written contract to that effect. If engaged in irregular job work, they must have licenses issued by local authorities. The licenses could be revoked at will. Failure to produce a contract or a license upon demand made Negroes liable to prison or to practical re-enslavement, and though employers could dismiss them with impunity, Negroes could not quit their employment before the time stipulated in their contracts. "Every civil officer shall, and every person may," the law said, "arrest and carry back to his or her legal employer any freedman, free Negro, or mulatto who shall have quit the service of his or her employer."

And, finally, there was a section providing that "no freedman, free Negro, or mulatto can rent or lease any lands or tenements except in incorporated cities or towns. . . ."

It was this provision that immediately jeopardized the Montgomerys. They were still leasing in 1866–68. Even before the law became effective, and even while Negroes were supposed to be under the protection of the federal military, by whom the land had been confiscated from its original owners, Negro leaseholders around Davis Bend had been thrown off the land. And now suppose the law were made to operate retroactively? The Montgomerys would be subject to eviction without compensation. Instead of working for themselves, they would have to work for others.

It was a prospect that Benjamin Montgomery, now growing old, could not face. He summoned his sons and Ben Green for a family conference. William was pessimistic. He had a wife and children and he talked gloomily of going north again to Ohio, where there was good farmland. "I tell you, Pa, the new men won't let us work for ourselves." Ben Green kept silent, as was his habit, but he shook his head disconsolately. They all looked to Isaiah.

"There's Mr. Charles Clark," Isaiah said, "and he's not one of the new men." Clark, indeed, had been a frequent guest of Joseph Davis before the war. "He's not the governor now, but he's still a power. The thing is, if you've got none yourself get somebody with power, and not be stiff-necked. Let's go see Mr. Clark."

Benjamin and Isaiah Montgomery traveled to Jackson to see Charles Clark. He talked with them in his carriage house. He saw to it that they were fed in his kitchen. Father and son returned to Davis Bend in the best of spirits. They had Clark's word for it, law or no law, they would not be molested.

"We got to keep powerful friends," Isaiah said.

There was a pattern of behavior to which slavery had trained them, and within that pattern they could operate effectively.

5. NO NORTH: NO SOUTH

It soon seemed to Republicans in the North that power in the South was being used to subvert the principles of freedom and equality upon which, many Northerners now professed to believe, the war had been fought. Southern state after state passed laws that were meant to bring about the practical re-enslavement of the Negro. In no state did the Negro have freedom of movement or of person. In no state could he vote. In Mississippi, South Carolina, and Louisiana he could not buy or lease farmland, or sell farm products. There was no use for Negroes to protest, as they did, either the laws or the men charged to administer them. All through the summer and fall of 1865 state conventions were busy fixing requirements for suffrage and hammering out constitutions to assure white supremacy. Constitutional conventions simply ignored the resolutions of Negro groups, who were inclined, as Governor Perry of

South Carolina said, "to forget that this is a white man's government, and intended for white men only."

But it was evident that the radical Republicans were not in agreement with this point of view. They had inveighed against Lincoln's veto of the Wade-Davis Bill, which would have penalized the South rather harshly, and they had warned the President "that the authority of Congress is paramount and must be respected." In 1864 they had refused to seat the new senators from Louisiana because the state had denied the franchise to Negroes—and had done this in spite of even Lincoln's expressed hope that "some colored people . . . especially those who have fought gallantly in our ranks," might be let in. If, after the death of Lincoln, Johnson seemed determined to follow a program of conservative reconstruction, the radical Republicans were just as determined that he would not. Their disapproval swelled to militant anger. Thaddeus Stevens, "the first Republican madman," declared that "the very foundations of their [Southern states'] institutions must be broken up and relaid, or all our blood and treasure have been spent in vain."

When Congress convened in December 1865, the radical Republicans were set for a knockdown, drag-out fight. It was not long coming.

Though the open issue and the only issue for some was Negro suffrage and civil rights, there were other issues not strictly political in nature. Knowing politicians could not ignore them. The power of the executive had been enormously increased during the war, and that had to be curtailed, the balance between it, the legislative, and the judicial power restored. The unindemnified loss of billions in slaves and other confiscated property had to be adjusted. The runaway pace of industrialism in the North; the relative economic paralysis of the South; the future of the poor whites, whose man Johnson was; the rise of the money merchants, corporations, trusts, and monopolies—all these were involved in the problem of reconstruction and the task of binding up "the nation's wounds." All these were at issue in the fight between radical and conservative.

But it did not seem so when the radicals made their first move.

Effectively controlling Congress, and led by Thaddeus Stevens and Charles Sumner, they refused to admit to Congress the South's newly elected representatives. They argued that the South had not purged and redeemed itself. They argued that the conditions of redemption had not been properly established. They argued that the readmission of the states was not, as Lincoln had presumed and Johnson was trying to prove, an executive matter: it was legislative. To fix the conditions upon which the South might have congressional representation, Stevens pushed through a proposal to set up a Joint Committee of Fifteen with broad discretionary powers.

Meantime the new Black Codes were attacked as contrary to "elemental justice," as undoubtedly they were, and not only the radicals but the Puritan idealists contended that the federal government must step in to protect the Negro against his former master. But how? In February 1866, Congress passed a bill giving sweeping adjudicative and economic powers to the Freedmen's Bureau, a wartime emergency agency. President Johnson vetoed it. Three days later he publicly defended his veto in language so personal and intemperate that some Northern newspapers accused him of being drunk. Yet "drunk either with wine or power," a few weeks later still he also vetoed a bill designed to "protect all persons of the United States in their civil rights, and to furnish the means of their vindication."

Stung by the President's stubbornness, by his rejection of the Joint Committee of Fifteen's preliminary report (which said, in part, that "the South deliberately proposed to oppress white Unionists and freedmen"), and by his vituperative censure of the Republican party, Congress overrode the veto of the Civil Rights Bill. In June it passed the Fourteenth Amendment to the Constitution and sent it to the states for ratification.

Having shown their power, the radicals were now determined to consolidate it in the elections of 1866. The squabbles between the President and the Congress had made clear the issues, and the Republicans propagandized them. The national debt must be saved from "the inevitable repudiation" that awaited it if rebels were returned to power. Freedom must be maintained, "not for a limited time but for all time." The "Constitution must know no North, no South."

Charles Sumner was the most brilliant and persuasive speaker in the Republican party. His altruism was as incorruptible as Stevens' vindictiveness was adamant. One was fire, the other rock. One attracted the misty-eyed idealists, the other the tough-minded pragmatists. Stevens acted; Sumner spoke—and when Sumner spoke people listened. "Thus is Equality the Alpha and the Omega, in which all other rights are embraced. Equality is the first of rights. . . . Strike at the Black Code, as you have already struck at the Slave Code. There is nothing to choose between them. Strike at once, strike hard! You have already proclaimed Emancipation; proclaim Enfranchisement also. . . ."

President Johnson had only pieces of parties behind him, and no machinery through which the pieces could operate. Moderate Republicans and Copperhead Democrats met in Philadelphia and, for what it was worth, pledged their support to him. It was not worth much, and the "Tennessee tailor" did nothing to increase its value. His choleric temper got the better of him as he stumped the Midwest. He slung personal abuse at his public enemies. Northerners heckled him, and he replied with rancor and without the dignity both his position and his policy required. Preaching tolerance for the South, he himself grew increasingly intolerable. He was again accused of drunkenness. He injured his own cause.

On the other hand, the Republicans got help not only from Northern industrialists and financiers, who envisioned the free South as a vast reservoir of cheap labor and a fertile field for investments; they got it also from certain events that supported the well-propagandized opinion that the South "menaced hate" and that no one, "white or black, who was friendly to the Union was safe" there. In the spring a Memphis riot brought death to forty-six Negroes and destruction to four of their churches and twelve of their makeshift schools. On their way to a political meeting—marching, as was the almost universal custom in those rallying days—a band of

New Orleans Negroes were attacked by whites. A fusillade of shots peppered the Negroes' ranks; they were set upon by the police as well as by the spectators. When the frightened Negroes barricaded themselves in the Mechanics' Institute Hall they were shot like fish in a barrel. Fifty-eight were killed and a hundred wounded, and others were killed as they tried to flee. "It was an absolute massacre," reported General Sheridan after an investigation, ". . . murder which the mayor and police of the city perpetrated without the shadow of a necessity."

Following such incidents as these, all bloodily embellished by the Northern press and pulpit, the Republican victory came easily. The Republican Congress would have a two-thirds majority—143 to 49 in the House; 42 to 11 in the Senate. Let Johnson veto all he had a mind to!

And he had a mind to veto much, but that handy power was soon shriveled by a Congress that believed the elections to be a prescription to carry through with Reconstruction on the basis of the report of the Joint Committee of Fifteen. Even before the preceding Congress adjourned, it had tied Johnson's hands—as President, with the Tenure of Office Act; as Commander in Chief, with a decree that military orders must be channeled through the General of the Army, a new rank, to which U. S. Grant, the North's Civil War hero, was appointed.

This done, the first Reconstruction Act was passed. By its terms each of the ten states still technically in rebellion was designated as belonging to one of five military districts over each of which an officer of general rank would exercise vast civil powers. His immediate function was to prepare the states in his district for readmission to the Union by registering all citizens, black and white, and by ordering elections for conventions to adopt state constitutions providing for Negro suffrage. Once the new constitutions had received congressional approval and the states had ratified the Fourteenth Amendment, readmission to the Union would follow.

By 1868 the process had been completed in all but Virginia, Texas, and Mississippi, and these, forced to capitulate if they would avoid being ruled as conquered territories, came around in 1870, by which time the Fifteenth Amendment to the Constitution had been ratified. By which time, too, the Union League and the politicians who infested the Freedmen's Bureau were keeping the strength of the Republican party solid through a thorough control and manipulation of the Negro vote. Negroes sat in the highest councils of the reconstructed states. Sixteen, representing seven of these states, sat in the United States Congress. Two from Mississippi were elected to the Senate. Hiram Revels, one of the latter, went to Washington in 1870 to take the seat once held by Jefferson Davis.

6. BLACK MAN'S PLACE

If there was a kind of poetic justice in this, the Montgomerys did not appreciate it. Isaiah was to refer to the Negro Mississippi congressman John R. Lynch and to the Negro senators, Revels and Blanche K. Bruce, as "outlanders." He was to pass remarks about "all these new people in here," and to profess himself "mighty dissatisfied with the way things are running."

That he inquired closely into the way things were running is doubtful, else he would have known and been pleased by the fact that Hiram Revels fought in the Senate for the removal of the restrictions placed on ex-Confederates. He would have known that John R. Lynch, a member of the Mississippi legislature and Speaker of its House before he was elected to Congress in 1873, not only petitioned Congress on behalf of the old master class but opposed with all his unavailing strength the bill that increased taxes fourteenfold and resulted in the tax sale of six million acres of Mississippi farmland. (In 1873 the Montgomerys paid taxes of $2447.09.)

But Isaiah Montgomery was a jangle of contrarieties, though still in some almost organic way a pure product of his times. By training and experience he was one thing, by instinct and temperament another. He had tremendous self-esteem but in the face of his own material success, which he seemed truly to believe the doing of God, abject humility. Reared in the paternalistic pattern of slavery and in the ways of thinking that slavery encouraged, all his life his public acts and utterances marked him a believer in the innate inferiority of his race, yet as a free man he was sensitive and proud to the extent of vowing that he would starve rather than work as a menial for any white man.

He was generous and "charitable," but he did not hesitate to demand interest as high as 50 per cent on loans, and he was known to take advantage of his workers at Davis Bend by markups of 20, 30, and even 40 per cent on supplies from the commissary.

He founded a Negro colony that eventually spread over thirty thousand acres of rich Delta land, and this undoubtedly stimulated race pride and ambition and contributed to race progress. But when John R. Lynch, described as "the ablest man of his race in the South," importuned him to "work with us for the uplift of our people," Montgomery expressed such aversion to joining forces with reputable Negro leaders of Mississippi as to appear psychopathic. Nevertheless, he considered himself an ardent "race man"—though his ardor would be difficult to prove by the fact that, in the year Lynch was elected to Congress, Montgomery voted for J. L. Alcorn in the gubernatorial election, who was pledged to re-establish the "Bourbon system," and who had, consequently, been repudiated by the Negroes of the state. As the only Negro in the Mississippi constitutional convention in 1890, Isaiah Montgomery spoke and voted for Negro disfranchisement.

Were these the acts and attitudes of a self-seeker or of an uncommonly wise man? Perhaps Montgomery saw that Negro political and civil equality, forced upon the South by a vindictive and perhaps venal Congress, could not last. To see this in those times of extreme disorganization required, certainly, uncommon insight. And especially in Mississippi, where there was the greatest confusion of attitudes, trends, and forces: humanitarian zeal and inhuman hate, both personal and racial—and neither with a clear advantage; flux and counterflux; movement from the land to industry in the cities; from the cities back to the land; from the South, North; from Southeast, West. There was a ruined Southern oligarchy, and there were powerful segments of Northern capital organized to keep it ruined and to forestall the resurgence of Southern political power. If many conservative white men insisted on the necessity of satisfying the requirements of Congress, at least an equal number were opposed. Although most Democrats went along in principle with the editor who wrote that "nigger voting, holding office and sitting in the jury box are all wrong," many did not at first act on the principle they espoused. Accepting what seemed to be the inevitable instead, they spared no effort to enlist the Negro vote.

And the efforts themselves were confused. On the one hand there were unsegregated barbecues and picnics "at which Negro bands and glee clubs entertained," and on the other there were economic pressures, threats, and violence. Though the radical Republicans enjoyed the overwhelming advantage of Negro support, they regarded it as a necessary evil, and they would not countenance Negro control of the party, or allow "social equality," or encourage widespread economic opportunity for Negroes. After the withdrawal of the Freedmen's Bureau in 1870, while native Delta planters were enticing Negro workers with small social and economic advantages and declaring that "every step taken in the development of the section has been dependent upon an increased Negro population," other elements, including, naturally, the poor whites, were convinced that "every Negro that leaves the state is a blessing" and that "the South cannot hold up her head until the last Negro is gone."

While the Klan and Klan-like organizations rode through the countryside murdering Negroes and burning their schools and churches, Blanche K. Bruce, the Negro senator from Mississippi, and his wife "entertained a distinguished group which included the wives of Supreme Court justices and other officials."

Whether or not Isaiah Montgomery saw through the confusion of the 1870s and '80s, one thing he saw clearly: the Montgomerys' present security lay in their plantations on Davis Bend. Here they were removed from the political confusion of Vicksburg, Jackson, and Natchez, and they would not need, God willing, the authority their white friends no longer possessed. And if they minded carefully their own business they would not provoke the authority now in the hands of strangers. None of the Montgomerys attended the political meetings called by the enthusiastic Negroes of Vicksburg and Jackson in 1867 and '68. They did send Ben Green as an observer. Green reported trouble ahead. The positions of mob and nabob had been reversed. In December 1868 there were rumors that "Negroes throughout the South had a thorough understanding, and planned to repeat all the atrocities of Santo Domingo." Considering that the "atrocities" in Santo Domingo had come to an end fully a half century before, and considering the much-bruited "abysmal ignorance" of Negroes, the rumor was fantastic, but Mississippi gave it credence. Governor Ames appealed to the military commander of the district to keep an armed force ready.

But armed forces of sorts were even then ready and going about their business of murder. General Nathan B. Forrest, the implacable racist who had refused to recognize the Union's colored troops as soldiers and had ordered the wholesale killing of those captured at Fort Pillow, had already organized the Ku Klux Klan. There were, besides, the Knights of the Black Cross, Heggie's Scouts, and the Washington Brothers. A member of Heggie's Scouts boasted that on one occasion the Scouts killed "a hundred and sixteen niggers and threw their bodies in the Tallahatchie." Catching a group of Negroes in baptismal rites in Yockana Creek, the Klan of Lafayette County drowned thirty of them. All through the late sixties and the seventies ubiquitous bands of terrorists murdered Negro preachers and land renters, "black Republicans and some Jewish merchants."

As Isaiah Montgomery saw it, undoubtedly the best thing was isolation. He did not want to be thought involved or to be caught unprotected in the white man's world. But the isolation of Davis Bend was not quite enough. When the military commander of the district, General Ord, named old Ben Montgomery a justice of the peace, the wave of reaction of native whites to this first appointment of a Negro official washed over the Montgomerys on their plantations. Said the Jackson *Clarion*: "General Ord has heretofore exhibited a wisdom in his administration, but we doubt not lovers of peace . . . will condemn this action as insulting to that race whom God has created the superior of the black man, and whom no monarch can make his equal." While old Ben held his breath, Isaiah assured the white neighbors on Davis Bend that his father would not hear cases involving whites; that, in fact, he did not want to be a justice of the peace anyway—but what could he do?

Back into play came that ceremonial submissiveness to whatever will was ascendant and to whatever climate of opinion prevailed.

There was of course much for the Montgomerys to do simply to mind their own business, and they minded it with unremitting care. It was Isaiah's ambition to make the plantations self-sufficient, as in the days of slavery. A commissary was built. Once a year Isaiah journeyed to Cincinnati to buy "furnishings"—the shirting, shoes, and jeans, the gaudy calicoes, the cheap candies, and the shoddy toys the workers would buy for their children at Christmas. From the plantation smokehouse came the fat back, from the cane mill the sorghum. A sawmill was built. With the help of the Freedmen's Bureau the Montgomerys salvaged some old machinery and built a cotton gin. They loaded their cotton directly onto the steamer from their own dock. In 1869 a disastrous flood swept away their dock, breached the levee, and ruined part of the crop. They had recovered by next planting time, but in harvest season the dock, which was already stacked with the first bales of cotton, was mysteriously destroyed by fire at night. Old Ben thought some careless worker had dropped ashes from his pipe. Ben Green suspected vandalism. Isaiah kept his own counsel, but when the dock was rebuilt he went to the white planters on Davis Bend and offered them its facilities free of charge. You had to "stay right" with the white folks.

In common with other planters, the Montgomerys had trouble keeping workers, for if freedom meant anything to great numbers of ex-slaves it meant freedom to move about. "Every little accident would make them get up and leave," Isaiah recalled years later, "and when there were no accidents, they'd find excuses." Not all of the excuses were simple. ("I'se jes' movin' ter town perminint so's ter save de trip dere ev'y Sa'dee.") In town and city were schools for their children, domestic work for their wives, and wage work for themselves. Competition for farm labor was keen and ruthless among river-county planters. Many of them lured workers from neighboring plantations and even from neighboring states. They painted rosy pictures and made big promises, but such deception did not pay off in the long run, for there were the railroads providing free transportation to distant places and offering the princely wage of a dollar and seventy-five cents a day. Though this was less than the two to three dollars paid blacksmiths, carpenters, and brick-masons, it was far more than the wage of farm hands.

But the city was Babylon, and slavery had taught no defense against Babylonian temptations. Idleness was the test of freedom, but idleness had to be supported. "In catfish season they [Negroes] fattened and did well," and in winter they got rations from the government, until General Gillem, commissioner of the Freedmen's Bureau, cut them off in 1867. The practice, he said, abetted "indolence and independence," as no doubt it did. But in that year and the following hard times struck, and even the most industrious were forced into idleness. So many Negroes died of yellow fever, cholera, and smallpox that confident forecasts were made of the Negro's complete extinction. In 1867 the Natchez *Democrat* was certain that "the child is already born who will behold the last Negro in the State of Mississippi," and the eminent clergyman, Dr. C. K. Marshall, who seems to have got direct word from heaven, foresaw with satisfaction that "On the morning of the 1st of January, 1920, the colored population will scarcely be counted . . . a few . . . here and there who may still earn precarious bread as they pass away."

The graveyards filled up in bad times, the jails in good. Fear of the law could not restrain the petty pilfering that had been so easily learned in slavery. And drunkenness was another thing, for during slavery "not to be drunk during the holidays was disgraceful" and aroused the suspicions of the masters, who freely supplied the whisky. Now any chosen day was a holiday, and there were drunkenness and quarrels and profanity, and these led straight to the lockup. Of the 1416 people who "served time" in the Vicksburg

workhouse from March 1868 to the next February, 992 were Negroes, "and Negroes idling in jail are a problem."

But General Gillem had a solution. He would lease the convicts.
It was a strange kind of lease that gave a planter-capitalist named
Edmund Richardson control of state prisoners in 1868. Under the
terms of it the state paid Richardson eighteen thousand dollars a
year for the maintenance of prisoners and he could employ them as
he saw fit. He saw fit to employ them not only on his own plantations but to hire them out to other planters at fifteen dollars a month
a man. Richardson's contract lapsed in 1871, but five years later the
almost incredible Jones Hamilton, who played with plantations, race
tracks, railroads, and steamboats as a reckless boy plays with mar-
bles, fainaigued a similar agreement. Through Hamilton the Montgomerys got some convict laborers for the plantations on Davis
Bend.

Skilled and tactful campaigners though they were, the Montgomerys could not ward off all the strokes of chance or impregnably
defend against all the common afflictions. The production of cotton
rose, but the price went down, and the cost of agricultural credit
soared from 15 to 30 per cent. In 1877 a hundred bales of cotton
brought only as much as fifty had brought ten years before. The
land, too, was petering out. In 1878 old Ben Montgomery died, and
some of the sentiment went out of the Davis Bend plantations. William again talked of leaving. But where would he go? What would
he do? He was not one of those "burr-head ignoramuses" cluttering
the roads in search of excitement. Good timber covered nearly a
thousand acres of Brierfield, and Isaiah had plans for it. He sent
William and Ben Green to Vicksburg to set up a sawmill. They
turned out barrel staves, puncheons, and railroad ties. They sold
scrap lumber to the steamboats. The end of the Montgomery place
on Davis Bend was near at hand.

It came when Joseph Davis' heirs disputed the Montgomerys' title
to Hurricane and Brierfield. It was an easy suit to settle. When the
Davis lawyers came from Jackson to see Isaiah, he did not argue.
They did not bother to take their hats off in Isaiah's parlor and in

the presence of his wife and three young daughters. They referred to him as a "nigger man," and reminded him that he was just a "nigger boy" when he signed the purchase notes in 1867. He was only twenty then, and even had he been white that was too young to sign a legal instrument and make it stick.

Isaiah did not even engage a lawyer. What lawyer would take a Negro's case against a white man? He did write to "Miss Varina," Jefferson Davis' wife, and he got an answer, too. Miss Varina expressed her sympathetic concern that he avoid all trouble, but the matter was out of her hands: neither she nor her husband was a party to the suit.

So Isaiah yielded without a struggle. If he yielded on a quid-for-quo basis that involved, explicitly, relinquishing the property and a fourteen-thousand-dollar equity in order to retain the good will of men who could and probably would ruin him otherwise, and, implicitly, the acceptance of white supremacy and the fact that the end of slavery brought an end to his immunity, he was responding to the reality he saw everywhere about him. He knew what was required of him in the face of it. He had no illusions. The old masters were back and accounting for every move in terms of their social responsibility, *the* social good. Wedding the rage and passion of the poor whites to the purpose of restoring the South as it was (though in that South the poor whites lived degraded and denied), they, the old planters, new capitalists, and poor whites, marched under slogans as under a cloud of banners. "Mississippi Is a White Man's Country, and by the Eternal God We'll Rule It!" "God Almighty, in farming out His privileges to mankind, drew a line as to qualifications." And the masthead of the *Mississippi Register* proclaimed, "A White Man in a White Man's Place. A Black Man in a Black Man's Place. Each According to the Eternal Fitness of Things."

Isaiah Montgomery was an artless evocation of the real present and of the predictable immediate future. He could see the superiority of white men growing ever more preponderant over colored until at last black men were squeezed into some sterile, half-forgotten corner, there to live on sufferance or to die. Isaiah did not want to die.

Accepting the thirty-five hundred dollars that was offered him "partly as a gift, partly as a reasonable share" for the crop left standing in the fields, and gathering his household goods and his wife and children, he joined his brother William and Ben Green in Vicksburg. The year was 1883. Isaiah had something over six thousand dollars in cash and part ownership of a thriving sawmill. He had acumen, energy, and a considerable deposit of good will in the patronizing thoughts of some influential white men, including those who had done him out of Davis Bend.

If he also had a will to personal power and dignity, born, paradoxically, out of his own slavery, he knew the precincts wherein it could be exercised. It took only a small gift of insight to realize that whatever power and dignity he acquired must ultimately derive from the vexed temper, the indifference, and the scorn of white men for black. This was the lesson he had learned too well ever to forget. This was the knowledge that gave meaning to his "I told you so."

7. THE BOSS

For a year and a half Isaiah devoted himself to the enterprises of the Montgomery clan. Besides the sawmill, there were now a store and a few parcels of real estate which he had taken care to buy in the neighborhood of Negro expansion. He reasoned it unlikely that either the greed or the envy of white entrepreneurs would disturb him in the possession of them there. He seems to have given little thought to anything outside the little world of family. Ridiculous, grim, and tragic things were happening on his very doorstep, as it were, but he did not bother to lift the shade and look out of the window. In 1884 he could have been a member of the Mississippi House or even of the Senate. The fusion system, which aligned Negro Republicans with white Democrats, operated in all the predominantly Negro river counties, but when the Republicans, led by the redoubtable Jim Hill, approached him, he turned them down.

When the white Democrats themselves came later, Isaiah, deferential and polite, said no to them too.

He wanted no part of politics. It was a white man's country; let white men run it. John R. Lynch, once a United States congressman, and Blanche K. Bruce, once a United States senator, pleaded with him to work with them for "the uplift of our people," but Isaiah would have no part of that either. He considered Lynch and Bruce "both foreigners, both Fred Douglass men," and he execrated Frederick Douglass. Had not Douglass agents come into Mississippi in the seventies and urged Negroes to migrate to a fool's paradise in Kansas? What did Douglass know about the uplift of the colored people in the South? And had not his second wife been white? "The farther you stay away from white people's politics, the better," Isaiah said. Thus when the Colored Farmers' Alliance and Cooperative Union began to make sounds like a political organization and to co-operate with the white National Farmers' Alliance in 1886, Isaiah resigned.

But white folks' politics of the most corrupt kind was tied up with the vast land grants to railroads, and Jones Hamilton had something to do with the land grant to the Yazoo-Mississippi Railroad, and Isaiah Montgomery had something to do with Hamilton. Through Hamilton he had once hired convict labor. Now through Hamilton he met Colonel Harold Dermott, a land agent.

In 1886, Isaiah made several mysterious trips north toward Memphis, but exactly where and why no one seemed to know. Whenever he went, he left detailed instructions for his brother at the store and Ben Green at the sawmill. On the fifth trip he took Ben Green, and upon their return Isaiah called the family together to announce that he and Cousin Ben had bought from the Yazoo-Mississippi Railroad eight hundred and forty acres of land in Bolivar County. The price? A song, Ben Green said laconically.

Though at first it seemed scarcely worth a song, in a few years it was rich in myth and legend. Legend says that, standing knee-deep in water, Isaiah flung wide his arms, exulting, "This is for my people, a place where God dwells, and liberty." Legend says that he prayed against the water that covered the land farther than the eye could see through cypress, gum, and blackjack trees, and "in the morning the water was gone." Legend has it that when the first colonists stepped off the train and faced the uncleared wilderness Isaiah addressed them in these words: "Have you not for centuries braved the miasma and hewn down forests like these at the behest of a master? Can you not do it for yourselves and your children unto successive generations, that they may worship and develop under their own vine and fig tree? Why stagger at the difficulties that confront you?"

Whatever legend says, the fact is that the swamp forest of Bolivar County was enough to stagger any man. It was completely uninhabited and, some thought, uninhabitable. Having been induced to buy tracts sight unseen at eight dollars an acre, the fainthearted fled without a second look, but others who had put all they had into the venture stayed. With saw, ax, and dynamite, all purchased from Isaiah, they cleared eighty scattered acres that first summer. Montgomery and Green brought in a sawmill and cut logs for cabins and lumber for railroad ties. When a settler's funds were exhausted, Isaiah either extended credit at 15 per cent or set the settler to work clearing more land.

The following spring the first log cabins went up, the first families moved in, and the first crop was sown. There were fifty-nine people now, including a half dozen infants and several infirm old women. The men cleared land, the women and children worked in the fields. There was trouble from depredators. Bears and coons got into the corn, "deer in herds like cattle" fed upon the sugar cane. Sometimes panthers slunk out of the forest, and "the howling of wolves was common music at nightfall." Until drainage ditches were dug and a levee erected, every rain brought flood. There was swamp fever. There was death.

Nevertheless, a townsite gradually emerged. It was bisected by the railroad. Well east of the depot and facing the tracks, Isaiah's trellised, gabled cottage went up, and in the fall of 1888 he brought his family on from Vicksburg. Also he acquired on a commission basis two thousand acres more. He built a "general mercantile emporium," a funeral parlor, and an assembly hall. In the winter he held the first series of "citizenship meetings." But the name he called them stretched a point.

The colony's government was paternalistic, its society approbational. When things did not please Isaiah he spoke about them in meeting. If Dillon Henry left his plow to spend an hour at the depot at morning train time, Isaiah gave Dillon a public dressing down. If Millie Poe ventured to shop in the white stores of Shelby, where lower prices made the five-mile trip worth while, Isaiah brought her to public shame for her disloyalty. Nothing seemed to escape Montgomery's eyes; everything came at last to his ears. He was the colony's conscience, its guide and guard. Strangers were not tolerated unless they came to take up land. Couples had to produce certificates of marriage. Illegitimacy was punished by immediate expulsion of erring mother and child. If there was no really rational moral design in all this, it was at least highly practical. "Here in this place," Isaiah told the colonists, "we are building a place of safety, a refuge."

And a refuge it seemed to be to a score of Negro families who fled there from other parts of the state in 1889. The political campaign of the year before had brought a return of intimidation, terror, and violence. The Republican grip on municipal governments was beaten loose. In Jackson, where a biracial Republican organization had held power since 1866, terrorist tactics were so successful that only one Negro even attempted to vote. ("He was an old negro and looked silly and he was not hurt, but told to hustle out in double-quick time, and he hustled.") Negroes were killed in numbers estimated as high as three hundred. But the Republicans swept the national elections of that year, and with both houses of Congress controlled by Republicans, the conviction grew in Mississippi, as elsewhere in the South, that federal control of elections would be again imposed and the Negro vote restored.

The conviction did not seem groundless in view of the introduction of Henry Cabot Lodge's Force Bill. Negro Republicans from forty Mississippi counties gathered in Jackson and boldly demanded that the Democrats adopt a fusion ticket. Failing this, they held a convention and proposed their own ticket with a slate of Negro candidates. This was too much. A bloody wave of violence swept over the river counties. Hundreds of Negroes fled. Some of those who fled to the colony in Bolivar County were allowed to remain. Isaiah lectured the new colonists on the evils of political participation.

But in his own eyes he was neither deceitful nor traitorous when, in 1890, he made his deal with the Democrats. He was silent about it, but he was as clear and simple as a mountain stream. He operated without enchantment under the only social and doctrinal imperative he knew. Mississippi, the South, the United States was the white man's country. If the Negro was to be free from molestation, from pressure and, above all, from fear in a little corner of this white man's country, then thanks to the tolerant grace of the white man.

So in 1890, when the sentiment for calling a constitutional convention swelled irresistibly in Mississippi, Isaiah Montgomery entered politics for the first and last time. His purpose was to keep his people out of politics forever. He went straight to the heart of the matter. He got in touch with the white Democratic leader. What he said to J. Z. George is quite unknown, but the sentiments that the Jackson *Clarion-Ledger* attributed to George were known to everyone. "If every Negro in Mississippi was a graduate of Harvard, and had been elected as class orator . . . he would not be as well fitted to exercise the right of suffrage as the Anglo-Saxon farm-laborer, *adscriptitius glebae*, of the South and West. Whose cross 'X,' like the broad arrow of Locksley, means force and intellect, and manhood—*virtus*."

In the nature of things Mississippian, the constitutional convention would have been all white, but there were the Republicans sitting tight in Washington, and the "bloody shirts" among them were supporting the Lodge Force Bill, and if the Negroes were to be disfranchised without "calling forth an iniquitous Federal inquisition," they must be made at least to seem to disfranchise themselves.

When John R. Lynch called a gathering of Negro Republicans to form a slate of colored convention delegates, Isaiah was there. He said he wanted to be on that slate, and the logical inference was that he wanted to be on it to "protect the rights of Negroes." He was named as the Republican candidate to the convention from Bolivar County. In the county contest that followed, he was elected easily, although he did not campaign actively. He did not have to, for he had an understanding with George that in Bolivar County the practice of fusion would be temporarily restored. George swept Isaiah in, and he was seated in the convention without protest—the only Negro delegate and the lone Republican.

The one hundred and thirty Democrats who assembled in the constitutional convention on August 12, 1890, were tired of needing the Negro vote, in sacrifice to which, the best among them knew, honor, integrity, and truth had melted like snow. "Sir, it is no secret that there has not been a full vote and a fair count in Mississippi since 1875," a delegate told the convention. "In other words we have been stuffing ballot boxes, committing perjury, and here and there in the state carrying elections by violence and fraud. . . . No man can be in favor of perpetuating the election methods which have prevailed in Mississippi since 1875 who is not a moral idiot."

But did this mean that the Negro vote was to be allowed? Certainly not. For the plain truth was that even the best men—those who did not want to "die and leave their children with shotguns in their hands, a lie in their mouths and perjury on their souls"—even these had this in common with the worst: they wanted to restore and preserve white supremacy. They wanted this so badly and with such a passionate singleness of purpose that it can only be called madness. And as for violence and fraud, they would no more be done away with than the Negro himself, for as a matter of simple fact, to the end of bringing about the legal and official repudiation of the black man as a political equal, as a citizen, and as a human being, they employed the very ends best calculated to insure that this same Negro would be fair game for the systematic depredations of planter, cotton-gin operator, and merchant, and the acceptable object of the unrestrained violence of any white man who bore a grudge.

And Isaiah Montgomery? He knew as well as any man what the purpose of both the best and the worst white men was. And he served that purpose not only because he saw the logical consequence of not serving it—the white man's intrusion upon his private domain—but also because he believed that the elimination of the Negro vote was in the best interest of the Negroes in the state and the nation; because he believed that Negro disfranchisement would bring an end to terror, violence, and race hatred, and would eventually create that salubrious emotional climate in which "the best white people will protect the colored" even against the latter's own profligacy and lawlessness. Called upon to speak as a member of the committee on franchise, Isaiah said this in effect. Then, in clear conscience, he proceeded to endorse the registration requirement, the tax requirement, and Section 244 of the constitution, which imposed a literacy requirement that not one in ten thousand Negroes could meet, and which was to serve as the model for other Southern states, all of which had completed the process of Negro disfranchisement before the battleship *Maine* was sunk in Havana Harbor. In a speech applauded by the whole white South and ex-President Cleveland, Isaiah endorsed the section the expressed intent of which was "to eliminate Negroes with or without education, and to remove no white voters from the rolls." He helped to postpone the day of the South's commitment to respect the citizenship of the Negro, and he helped to fix the traditional ways of thinking about what the Negro's place in American life is and how best to prepare for it.

And this was by no means all. For Isaiah Montgomery secured at the same time that exemption from interference in which he meant to remain undisturbed in the control of his colony of Mound Bayou and the lives lived there.

For though he was reverently called "The Honorable," a harsher, truer title would have been Boss of Mound Bayou. For years he was the mayor, and he hand-picked the three aldermen. Though the white sheriff of Bolivar County appointed the Negro deputy for Mound Bayou, Isaiah named him. Isaiah chose the town constable. He hired the first schoolteacher and guaranteed the salary of the first preacher. By 1893 there were four thousand Negroes in Mound Bayou and the colony spread over twenty thousand alluvial acres and was still growing. Isaiah owned either in whole or in part with his cousin Ben Green the cotton gin and the warehouse, the feed and fertilizer store, the lumberyard, the general merchandise emporium, the burial business. He owned uncounted first mortgages. He was turning a profit of eight thousand dollars a year on rough lumber alone, and he was reputed to be—and probably was—the only Negro in the United States who could put his hands on fifty thousand dollars "cash money" in an hour's notice.

Insulated by such power, he did not turn a hair when Ben Green was murdered. First Cousin Green, the taciturn, plodding mechanic who kept the cotton gin and the sawmill going, and who had done Isaiah's bidding for thirty years, seems to have grown dissatisfied in 1892.

Perhaps his wife had something to do with it. He had married her almost surreptitiously while Isaiah was crowning the eminence of his disfranchisement speech with a call on President Harrison and House Speaker Reed. By all accounts, Mrs. Green was a woman of exceptional strength of character, bred from three generations of freemen. At any rate, Cousin Ben grew recalcitrant. Isaiah was "head of everything." Ben Green was heard to complain that Isaiah "consistently drew off the larger share of profits" from their joint enterprises. Suddenly, in 1892, Green dissolved the partnership, and between him and Isaiah mistrust and enmity bred. One day in 1896 Ben Green was shot to death.

In a town fiercely suspicious of strangers, no one had seen a stranger. The town constable and the deputy sheriff had the assistance of the county sheriff, but no clue was ever found, and the final official word was that Ben Green had "met his death at the hands of parties unknown." He left a widow and a young son. He also left among his kindred a precedent for dying violently. Long after Isaiah himself was in his grave, the precedent would overtake a Montgomery daughter and a daughter's spouse.

Isaiah made no visible show of loss at Ben Green's death. Indeed, he was not bereft. He acquired more property, including Cousin Ben's half interest in the cotton gin, the operation of which proved too much even for the sagacious widow. He invested a piddling sum in a prosperous tri-state fraternal-benefit association and persuaded its officers to build the headquarters in Mound Bayou. What better site for a Negro institution than an all-Negro town? Isaiah practically guaranteed that if it did not bother white folks, white folks would not bother it. A popular jingle had it:

> A nigger's a nigger,
> You can tell by his face;
> And he's got no business
> In a white man's place.

It was comforting to know that a white man had no business in a black man's place either.

8. PATIENCE IS THE PAY-OFF

If, on the local level of Mound Bayou, Isaiah Montgomery was creating not only an environment for Negroes but a generalized Negro mentality more or less tractable to a single will, another was attempting a very similar thing on a much grander scale.

The patience to wait for the main chance, an unerring instinct for compromise, and a sure knowledge of the subtler uses of adversity had brought Booker T. Washington a long way since his slave birth in Virginia in 1856, '57, or '58. These qualities, directed by a cunning cast of mind, had carried him through Hampton Institute, brought him the especial favor of the white teachers there and of General Samuel Chapman Armstrong, the president, and had been his chief recommendations to a group of Alabama white men who, in 1881, were looking for someone to head a school they proposed to found for Negroes. Now as principal of that school, Tuskegee Institute, Washington was the best-known Negro in the South. He meant eventually to be the best-known and most influential Negro in the United States. In 1893 he was well on his way.

Booker Washington had already won the gratitude of certain whites. He had done this in the early post-Reconstruction period by assuring the white South that black men would not again aspire to, much less usurp, the place of white men. It never occurred to him or to the South that there might be a real and complex question as to what and where was the Negro's place.

On the land, traditionally held to be his tether and his domicile? Except for the fortunate handful of Negroes (only 120,000 of more than 4,000,000) who had managed to bull their way to ownership of a few paltry acres, a place on the land in the South meant a return to slavery or peonage. The Southern aristocratic ideal, the storied sense of noblesse, which had certainly moved some planters to render slavery tolerable, was now decayed. Many of the aristocrats themselves were gone, leaving the land in the care of those who took satisfaction in using the methods of slavery to control the Negro's freedom. And even for a place on the land there was increasing competition. There were poor whites and growing numbers of small dirt farmers made landless by the strangulation of the cotton market and the operation of debt and mortgage laws. They too must eat, and to eat must work—and on whatever terms they could get. And the terms, inevitably disadvantaged by the clamoring crowd of the dispossessed, were in substance and sometimes in degree the same for these whites as for the blacks: sunrise-to-sunset, tumble-down-shack, fat-back-and-molasses, pellagra-rickets-and-consumption terms. Tenant terms. Cropper terms. And as for those few landowning Negroes, their prospects were the same as for the small landowning whites—an endless accumulation of debt to the supply merchant, who demanded mortgages on the crop, the chattels, the land, and even the tools with which to cultivate it.

Many Negroes fled these terms and these prospects. Most fled northward, cityward. And did they find a place there? Scarcely. They were "an industrial superfluity." Competition with European immigrants, tough since the raw 1840s, grew subtly vicious in the closing decades of the century, and Negroes lost. Fannie B. Williams, a feature writer for the New York Age, reported:

"It is quite safe to say that in the last fifteen years, the colored people have lost almost every occupation that was regarded as peculiarly their own. . . . White men wanted these places and were strong enough to displace the unorganized, thoughtless and easygoing occupants. When the hordes of Greeks, Italians, Swedes, and other foreign folk began to pour into Chicago, the demand for the Negro's place began. One occupation after another that the colored people thought was theirs forever, by a sort of divine right, fell into the hands of these foreign invaders. . . . The Swedes have captured the janitor business by organizing and training the men for this work in such a way as to increase the efficiency and reliability of the service. White men have made more of the barber business than did the colored men. . . . The 'shoe polisher' has supplanted the Negro bootblack, and does business in finely appointed parlors, with mahogany finish and electric lights. Thus a menial occupation has become a well-organized and genteel business with capital and system behind it."

Negro efforts to organize and get capital and systems behind them came to nothing. Though scattered groups of Negro workmen's protectives had achieved sectional cohesion in the National Bureau of Labor, they had little strength, and some of this was drained off in the political campaign of 1884, the rest thoroughly dissipated in the campaign of 1892. President Cleveland said in his first inaugural that "there should be no pretext for anxiety touching the protection of the freedmen in their rights," and he repeated the sentiment in his second inaugural; but he kept silent while Southern states disfranchised the Negro and the Supreme Court rendered its "separate but equal" decisions, and while evidence of the drastic curtailment of the Negro's citizenship rights grew more incontestable every day.

No attention-commanding voice was raised in behalf of the Negro, but many were raised against him. None was louder than South Carolina's Ben Tillman's when it thundered, "If you want to rise, keep the nigger down!"

This injunction was heard and heeded even in the North. White craft unions refused Negroes admission. Industrialists, who did not like unions anyway, were smart enough to encourage this prejudice. What industrialists wanted was a large, uncommitted surplus of labor, and Negroes were that surplus, and so long as the industrialists had it they could scorn to negotiate with white organized labor. Used as strikebreakers, Negroes called down upon themselves a triple measure of the enmity of the white laboring man, thus closing up the evil cycle. Neither white nor black worker had any clear notion of the forces affecting his life. Each approached whatever situation confronted him from within a pattern of thought generally held to be valid: the immutable superiority of white men to black.

The voice that might have shouted an effective denial to this was stilled in 1895.

Frederick Douglass' death, one of his admirers said, presaged an even more troubled future for the Negroes, and that future was soon upon them. Within seven months of Douglass' funeral, Booker T. Washington stood before a packed throng at the Atlanta Cotton States Exposition and delivered his people over to the whims of the prejudiced, the exploitation of the venal, and the machinations of the crafty. Washington's exposition speech exploded in the national press like a pyrotechnic display in salute to the "New South." "You can be sure in the future, as in the past," he told an audience swelling with gratitude, "that you and your families will be surrounded by the most patient, faithful, law-abiding, and unresentful people that the world has ever seen." The speech was firmly based upon the premise that "the Negro enjoyed the friendship of the Southern whites." But the irony of this was evident even while Washington spoke.

At that very moment the South Carolina state convention was vigorously pushing the disfranchisement of Negroes. On that very day a North Carolina court found guiltless a white farmer who had killed a "lazy" and "abusive" colored tenant. On that day "Florida officials promised a mob at the outset of the trial of a Negro that he would be hanged." Under the headline "An Eye for an Eye," the Memphis *Commercial Appeal* described the mutilation-slaying of a Negro prisoner by a white mob. Two days after Washington's speech Wilcox County, in Washington's own state of Alabama, published its education budget for 1896. It provided salaries of $28,108 for the teachers of 2285 white children, and $3940 for the teachers of 10,745 colored children. Within the week Washington spoke the management of the Tennessee Coal, Iron and Railroad Company announced the replacement of "eighty-seven negro laborers by others, mostly Chinese."

Within a month President Cleveland wrote Booker T. Washington: "Your words cannot fail to delight and encourage all who wish well for your race; and if our colored citizens do not from your utterances gather new hope and form new determination to gain every valuable advantage offered them by their citizenship, it will be strange indeed."

Certainly valuable advantage might be gained, but it was not of the sort President Cleveland had in mind, and it had little to do with citizenship. Indeed, it had more to do with citizenship's opposite and its denial: the exclusion of Negroes from the body politic, the ultimate civic isolation that was the Negro "place," and that made possible—and even, it seemed, desirable—an Isaiah Montgomery and a Mound Bayou. And what was strange indeed and quite apparent before Isaiah Montgomery died, and his daughter was killed like a common criminal by a white sheriff, and before Eugene Booze, the husband of another Montgomery daughter, was murdered by parties unknown, and long, long before Mound Bayou had become, ironically, a focal point for Negro insurgency in Mississippi —what was strange was that whatever hope and determination Negroes gathered came from circumstances quite different from any Washington had foreseen or Cleveland desired: came, first, from the final resurgence of Negro political power in the fusion campaign that sent a North Carolina Negro to Congress in 1897 and returned roughly a hundred Negroes to public office "throughout the Southern land . . . where other black men were gratefully hearing the news and surging up in emulation."

And before this had quite expired a second circumstance was already in being—the quarrel with Spain over Cuba. It does not matter that it was a quarrel sought for and one that could easily have been avoided. It does not matter that the real cause was that "the taste of empire" was in the mouths of some American leaders and that, though they "envisaged now the kingdom, the power, and the glory," it had nothing to do with the Lord's Prayer. Most Negroes had not heard of Albert J. Beveridge or of Cushman K. Davis, and Negroes thought, as the common man everywhere in America thought, that the war with Spain was a crusade of righteousness, for liberty from oppression, and for "the law supreme . . . the law of God." And to Negroes—and of even more consequence to them—it was a war to complete the revolutionary struggle of a "colored people" led by the "Black Thunderbolt," Quintín Bandera, and the mulatto, General Antonio Maceo. And if the American people, including especially the white people of the South, could give such booming enthusiasm to a war for the freedom from oppression of a foreign colored people, was not this a matter from which to gather new hope?

"Surely," wrote a Negro who died at El Caney, "the same strong spirit and quickened conscience which took up the cause of Cuba will secure justice to the American Negro."

CHAPTER SIX

A Doctor's Dilemma

1. MY PEOPLE

ONE DAY in January 1890 a neat little man hastened
along Dearborn Street in Chicago. He was dressed
in a black bowler hat and a black chesterfield overcoat, below the
flopping tails of which his scurrying legs, oddly encased in white
duck, seemed to twinkle as he walked. A small black satchel swung
in his hand. His naturally pale face was flushed pink with cold and
his breath frosted on the light brown, almost blond mustache that
covered his upper lip.

Except that he might be driven by the cold, there was no need
for so great a hurry, and he realized it and tried to slow his pace.
But quickness of movement was a habit with him, and, anyway,
he thought, perhaps the nurse he had engaged was not as thorough
as she was recommended to be. Perhaps he should not trust her with
all the last-minute preparations. He thought about the medical profession. He thought about physicians and nurses in general, and
about Negro nurses in particular. Negro nurses? Where could you
find one? The subject was his special demon, and lately it had been
riding him without pause.

Just a month before, he had made a decision and a promise. The Reverend Louis Reynolds, pastor of the African Methodist Church, had asked him to use his influence to have Reynolds' sister admitted to a nurses' training course in one of the Chicago hospitals. Dr. Williams smiled ruefully now as he thought of it. Because he was on the surgical staff of the South Side Dispensary, where he gave clinical instruction to Chicago Medical College students, and because he was a member of the Illinois State Board of Health, people thought he had influence. But did he? He had never thought about it. Now all at once he suspected that those colleagues of his who knew his history considered him an exception, and the thought made him blush. None of them had ever mentioned race—so why should he? The students to whom he lectured had no idea that he was a Negro.

He was, it seemed, caught in a dilemma, one horn of which was his personal career in medicine, and the other a tradition of racial ties that knit itself through three generations of his family. Mixed blood had mixed and confused and lost to him some of his nearest kinsmen. Was it to confuse and lose him too? With a sudden ache he thought of his father as he had thought of him when he talked to the Reverend Mr. Reynolds. "No," he remembered having said then, pausing while the minister's eyes glinted bitterly. "I don't think I'll try to get your sister into one of those training courses. We'll do something better. We'll start a hospital of our own, and we'll train dozens and dozens of nurses."

Dr. Williams meant to make good that promise.

2. MIXED HERITAGE

Daniel Hale Williams was born in Hollidaysburg, Pennsylvania, in 1858, of a class so mixed in nationality and blood that some of his cousins used to say that they were of the "scrambled race." In the line that stretched immediately backward from him were a Scotch-Irish grandmother, a German-Negro grandfather, and a pure German great-grandfather. Though his own mother could prove only Negro and white blood, a heavy Indian strain showed plainly in her straight black hair, high cheekbones, and luminous eyes.

His father, also called Daniel, was a strong-minded, substantial man, proud, independent, and—for all his Caucasian ancestry, and, indeed, perhaps because of it—ambitious for the progress of Negroes, to whom he habitually referred as "my people." Before the Civil War he missed few of the national conventions by means of which Negroes sought to make their voices heard. After the war he moved his family to Annapolis, Maryland, and became a zealous member of the Equal Rights League, "arduously traveling and speaking" in its name. He wore himself out in this service and died at forty-seven, leaving his wife, Sarah Ann, with seven children and enough to live on if only she were careful.

Sarah Ann was not careful. She had difficulty handling responsibility or even recognizing that there was a responsibility to handle. Her first independent move after the death of her husband was to put the two middle girls in an expensive convent school, leave the youngest with their grandmother, and take the two older girls to Illinois. Price Williams, the older son, was twenty and already on his own in the North, teaching and reading law. Daniel, the youngest child of all, she apprenticed to a shoemaker in Baltimore. Daniel's enemies were to say later that his mother had deserted him, but this may not have been the instance they referred to, for there was another. After a year Dan gave up his apprenticeship and bummed his way to his mother in Illinois. A few months later, however, Sarah Ann, reckless, restless, and homesick, returned east without him. He was twelve. He was on his own.

But he was on his own in a section of the country particularly attractive to those Negroes who were anxious and ambitious to make good use of freedom. The South was beginning again to set rigid in its opposition to Negro social and cultural mobility. As we have seen, and as even Booker Washington was later to say, the postwar South meant for Negroes "poor dwelling houses, loss of earnings each year because of unscrupulous employers, high-priced provisions, poor school houses, short school terms . . . bad treatment generally, lynching and white-capping, fear of the practice of peonage, a general lack of police protection, and want of encouragement." In spite of black Republicans, Reconstruction and the Fourteenth Amendment, the Freedmen's Bureau and Yankee missionaries, Negroes were virtually re-enslaved in many places in the South.

The West was relatively new and absorptive and flexible. No cultural mold had been unalterably fashioned, no social pattern set. It was a cultural frontier where even sons of the South—inheritors of an ancient dream of aristocracy—learned "a democracy native to the frontier." In the Ohio Valley and farther up in the Rock River Valley, and farther still along the upper reaches of the Mississippi, gathered, as Parrington points out, "a multitude of rough libertarians [who] took seriously the doctrine of equality and proposed to put it into practice." In the 1870s the expanding West was a heady land and a hearty land. Here a man could blaze his own trail; here a man could make his way.

Or, so far as that went, a boy. Twelve-year-old Daniel Hale Williams made his way. He worked on lake steamers and saw something of the Northwest. He worked in barbershops and learned a barber's skills. He worked on river boats, and once or twice found himself in Cincinnati, where he may have seen and heard a Negro youth of about his own age—one Gussie L. Davis, who had yet to write "The Baggage Coach Ahead," "Send Back the Picture and the Wedding Ring," and other popular tunes, but who was already "stealing a knowledge of music" as he swept the classrooms of the Cincinnati Conservatory. The city in the early seventies was not much different from what the Montgomerys had known in the early sixties. It was still a mulatto mecca. Years later Dan was to reminisce about the beauty of its "high-toned" ladies.

But the life of the wanderer was no life for Dan Williams. He wanted to settle down, to get an education, to follow the admonition he had more than once heard fall from the lips of his father: "We colored people must cultivate the mind." His ambitions were vague but they tugged at him persistently nonetheless. He was often lonely. When his oldest sister, Sally, wrote asking him to join her in Edgerton, Wisconsin, where she was in the hair goods business, he went gladly. He opened his own barbershop. For a time his restlessness was eased.

Edgerton was a frontier village. There was no school, for there were as yet not enough children to justify one. Traveling lecturers avoided it, and the occasion was rare when even one of the ubiquitous clan of book canvassers set up shop for half a day in the vestibule of the Grange Hall. Janesville, however, was only a few miles away, and Dan was impressed with it on shopping trips there with his sister. It had a population of ten thousand and was still growing. It had schools, an opera house, and a Young Men's Association. Henry Ward Beecher and Robert Ingersoll frequently lectured there. There were flourishing industries—woolen mills, shoe factories, farm-implement manufactories. There was also, Dan noted on one trip, a large barbershop run by a Negro named Anderson.

Sally too was no longer happy in Edgerton. Attractive, fairskinned, and aged twenty-six, she was tired of spinsterhood. She had admirers in Edgerton, two of whom had quite substantial means, but she refused to have any of them. She would not "marry white, even if a white man was the last man on earth." But there were at least a few colored men in Janesville, and shortly after Dan and his sister moved there in 1876, Sally married one of them—a man named Turner—and went to live in Portage. Dan, now twenty, was again alone. In a special way, he was alone all his life.

He used to say later that in Janesville he "came to himself." This was a Janesville colloquialism that meant he became acquainted with himself and found his direction. It was not easy to come by either self-knowledge or the direction he would take. He sometimes wished he could recompose the basic ingredients of his personality, and all he knew about his direction was that it must challenge him and lead, as tradition devised, to some center in the Negro world. Finding such a road was trial and error and finally happenstance.

Harry Anderson wanted him to stick to the barber's trade with music as a side line. Anderson had not only the best and busiest shop in town, serving the town's best people, but his string orchestra played for the best people's dances, and it accompanied touring stars, among them Helena Modjeska, who came to entertain in Mayer's Opera House. Anderson had plenty of time to influence Dan. He and his Irish wife (for "in these parts colored women are in short supply"—to which Dan's response was an echo of his sister's: "But I would not marry white") took the young man into their home and treated him as if he were one of their own children, of which they had five. Beneath Dan's shy reserve lay a hunger for affection and a need to deserve it. Under the influence of the Andersons, Dan took up the guitar and learned to play the bass fiddle; he joined Anderson's orchestra and traveled with it all over Wisconsin and into the bordering states.

But a barber-musician's career was not for Dan either. Other influences poured in upon him—from Professor Haire's Academy, where he enrolled to study Latin, mathematics, and zoology; from lectures in Apollo Hall, where he heard Robert Ingersoll thunder, "Every library is an arsenal, filled with the weapons and ammunition of progress, and every fact is a *Monitor* with sides of iron and a turret of steel. . . . Nothing but truth is immortal." And from Jenkin Lloyd Jones, Welsh pastor of the Unitarian church; and from his older brother, now a successful lawyer back East, whose name kept appearing in the Negro papers. For a year after getting his high school diploma, Dan clerked and read Blackstone in a lawyer's office. But the law was not for him.

He realized this one day when he read in the Janesville *Gazette* an account of a local medical case. He knew Dr. Henry Palmer, the physician on the case, in the way a barber would know an important patron, the town's leading medical light and a civic worker who had once been mayor. Dr. Palmer was probably Janesville's most influential citizen. His opinions frequently appeared as editorials in the local paper; his every activity was news. Now he had a case of gunshot wound, and he was giving "it all his skill and knowledge," which, the paper said, "were considerable." He was "striving desperately to save a life."

From the moment he read the account Dan knew with overwhelming certainty that he had found the road he wanted to take. The only problem was to get on it. Putting aside self-doubt, beating back his natural shyness, he spoke to Dr. Palmer the next time he cut the physician's hair. Dr. Palmer may have been curiously stirred, or—though there was no question but that he took his profession with passionate seriousness—he may have been amused. But after all, the first surgeons were barbers. And why not? At any rate, within three months Dan Williams joined two white apprentices in Dr. Palmer's office, and two years later, under the lax medical standards that generally prevailed, he was qualified to enter into the practice of his profession.

Dr. Palmer had impressed upon his apprentices the fact that scientific theories were changing and medical knowledge expanding, and that the only way one could keep up with advances was by attending medical school, "taking one's lumps in hospital," and learning both theory and practice. Dr. Palmer made them feel that anyone who set up in the practice of medicine without a certified M.D. was little better than a quack.

Medical studies cost money, and Dan had none. He could not count on his mother, who had recently come into her own father's considerable property. Though he felt a warm love for his mother, as neglected children often do, he knew her for what she was—thoughtless, extravagant, selfish, and completely involved in her own life. Borrowing a hundred dollars, for which Harry Anderson stood security at the Janesville bank, and which was barely enough for books and fees, Daniel Williams went down to Chicago.

3. DOCTOR IN CHICAGO

If Negroes thought of Cincinnati as the mulatto mecca in the 1870s, in the 1880s they were beginning to think of Chicago as the new Canaan. Lured primarily by prospects of employment, but also by the city's reputation for racial liberalism, black migrants were trickling in from the South, principally by way of the coal fields of Illinois, whence the competition of foreign labor was driving them, and the cornfields of Kansas, where in the late seventies so many had gone that conditions comparable to the "contraband camps" of the Civil War resulted. As President Hayes's policy of letting the Southern states alone came more and more to mean the consolidation of white supremacy and the unhindered imposition upon Negroes of those social terms already described—political repression, cultural isolation, and peonage—the trickle into Chicago became a stream. From about three thousand in 1870, Chicago's colored population topped ten thousand by 1880. And, indeed, the "foolish hegira," which even the influence of Frederick Douglass could not bring to a stop, was taking on serious proportions for other Northern cities, where the characteristics of the latter-day Negro ghetto began to evolve.

There was no ghetto, however, in 1883, when Daniel Hale Williams, brand-new M.D. from Chicago Medical College, opened an office at Thirty-first Street and Michigan Avenue. It was a substantial neighborhood, racially mixed, and Dan's office adjoined those of white physicians. He soon discovered that good hospital staff appointments were hard to get because "Chicago hospitals were as tightly organized as personal clubs" and they "did not welcome strangers." Toward the end of his third year in private practice one valuable appointment came his way: he was taken on to do minor surgery at the dispensary connected with Chicago Medical College and to serve as a demonstrator in anatomy to medical students there.

Meantime, such private cases in surgery as he undertook were performed in the dining rooms and kitchens of his patients' homes. He had rather more of these than his white colleagues, partly because his predominantly Negro patients had difficulty getting private rooms in hospitals, and partly because the distrust of hospitals, still commonly referred to as "butcher shops," was stronger among Negroes than among whites.

But gradually a question was projected into the mind and heart of

Dan Williams. It was of such varied and complex aspects that he resisted it and refused for a time to face it. But somehow it seemed to get involved in all he did.

It was a question both of identity and of identification. He had learned from his father who and what he was, but the years of his childhood had been relatively simple. Alignments had been ordained, commitments inevitable. One was committed to Negroes because one was himself a Negro, and this was his complete and unassailable identity.

True, there were those mixed bloods, a few of Dan's relatives among them, who blurred or lost this identity, but Dan's father was not one of them. Blue-veined and blue-eyed, and with only the barest crinkle in his hair, Dan, Sr., would have no truck with that society of Negroes who, in so far as they could, withdrew from all things Negro and racial, created their own twilit and traumatic half-world, and subscribed to the proposition that whiteskin was best, and brightskin far better than black, and blackskin was very bad indeed. They were a cabal as secret, designing, and exclusive as the Medici. The elder Dan Williams would have nothing to do with them. He talked constantly about his "people," by which he meant the Negro people. When he moved his family to Maryland after the war his first act was to pay his respects to George Forten, an ex-slave, a worker for the Equal Rights League, and as black a man as ever put on clothes.

An identification of such pristine simplicity was not easy for Dan, Jr., in Chicago in the eighties and nineties. His professional life was a complication. He wanted to go as far in his profession as intelligence and skill could take him, but also he had inherited a compelling sense of duty to his people. The two seemed irreconcilable.

So long as Negroes remained too poor to afford the private facilities of hospitals—or prejudice kept them out of hospitals—and so long as he devoted himself principally to their care, he could have only limited access to those avenues of new medical learning and surgical skills that hospitals provided. It seemed that he must sacrifice career to race or race to career. The idea of passing into the white race occurred to him but he rejected it. He could not deny his people the service he could give them; nor could he deprive them of whatever pride they might take in whatever success he achieved. Were they not already boasting that he was "the first Negro ever appointed to the Illinois Board of Health" and that his latest appointment "on merit as surgeon to the City Railway Company" had broken a precedent?

Unless he were to accept standards of behavior and attainments of mind lower than those he was used to, Dr. Dan Williams had no choice on the social level but to live in the world of the mixed bloods. It was a privileged world. Inhabited largely by the bastard sons and daughters of former slaveowners, but also by those who, like Dan himself, had come by their white blood legitimately, it boasted of its ancestry, its tradition of freedom, its culture. By virtue of education and the manners sedulously imitated in the "big house" and carefully passed on, like priceless gems, from parents to children, the mixed bloods could attain the better jobs on the scale running from the personal service of valet, butler, barber, and tailor to petty but secure clerkships in civil service. A few acquired independent businesses, and a very few acquired professions. There were bookkeepers, brewmasters, and undertakers, schoolteachers and journalists. They had a security undreamed of in the Negro world of common labor. They were zealous to educate their children, often at great sacrifice. They were equally zealous to guard against misalliances that might introduce a too dark strain into their white blood. They were conspicuous and self-conscious consumers not only of goods but of culture; and they were very, very careful to make ineradicably clear the difference between themselves and the common run of Negroes.

And yet this world of mixed bloods—a new world, it might be said, dropped unordained and maculate, foreboding and perverse, from the womb of genetic chance—soon developed a necessary and important dual function.

More consciously than it admitted, and not altogether insusceptible to the flattery it implied, it served as model and preceptor to the lately freed. It was, too, liaison, intercessor, and spokesman between the white world above and the black world beneath. In a sense, for all its differences from each, it complemented both.

It was no easy thing to do. The people of the mixed-blood world were often troubled and driven to despair by a sense of race duty that operated irresistibly somehow against their will and, as many of them thought bitterly, against their world's best interest. Fierce tides of hatred and self-hatred, pride and fear and love dragged many an anchor from the harbor of sanity. It is little wonder that later historians have been forced to note the high incidence of psychotic behavior: the suicides; the mad sacrificial joy with which families encouraged scions to pass over—knowing that in passing they were lost to them forever—not inevitably to a fuller, better life, but to a kind of painless limbo; the crazed pride with which mothers, for all their rigid insistence on morality and sexual virtue, gave up daughters into the arms of men because, simply, the men were white. Dan Williams himself was to be sacrificed to this pride when the mother of the mixed-blood girl he loved would not let her "marry a man identified with colored people," though the man was Dr. Dan, honorable and eminent and in appearance white almost as snow. It was a traumatic world, surely, where, as Pauli Murray reports in *Proud Shoes*, a woman was still counted sane who ranted at her neighbors thus:

"I'll tell anybody I'm a white man's child. A fine white man at that. A Southern aristocrat. If you want to know *what* I am, I'm an octoroon, that's what I am . . . and I don't have to mix with good-for-nothing niggers if I don't want to. . . . And I'll tell you another thing. My father was one of the best criminal lawyers in the South. He was in the North Carolina legislature. Before the Civil War he saved fourteen poor Negroes from the gallows free of charge. He got many colored folks out of trouble and kept 'em from rotting in jail. . . ."

However mad some of the individuals in the mixed-blood world might be, the function of that world was sane enough, and Daniel Hale Williams was soon pushing that function to the limits of consistency—and there were some who said beyond. But the fact was that Chicago was changing rapidly, and Dr. Dan saw needs where others did not. Every day brought a new quota of Negroes into the city. They were crowding into the south side, in the area of Dan's office, faster than the white people could sell and move out. By 1890 there were twenty-five thousand of them, and Chicago was beginning to lose its reputation for equality of opportunity and lack of prejudice. The south side was becoming a ghetto, where vice and prostitution flourished. Dr. Dan's venereal cases doubled, then tripled. He did not like it. He did not like what it signified in ignorance and social degradation. The crime rate jumped. Saturdays Dr. Dan spent long after midnight bandaging battered heads, sewing up knife wounds, and probing for bullets. It was not the work he wanted to do. He felt that it was not the work that should need doing.

Among his friends he began to talk about conditions in the ghetto. Basically shy and retiring, he was no crusader in the ordinary sense. His earliest conversations on these matters were contemplative and tentative rather than persuasive. He talked about the young men who loafed all day in front of the poolrooms and the honky-tonks and the "dirty little pork and greens shops" that were squeezing up on both sides of State Street north of Forty-third. It gave him a particular wrench to see Negro girls frequenting these places and seeking distraction on street corners. These young people, for want of something better to do, Dr. Dan told his friends, were candidates for careers in crime and vice. The young men could find occasional employment only as strikebreakers—and this subjected them to violence; the young women, even when they had finished high school, could get no employment at all.

Dan soon realized that to talk to his friends was not enough. Some of them laughed at him. What had he to do with the problems of ignorant Negroes coming up from the South? He was a medical man, not a social worker, and his friends refused to take him seriously except as a physician. What they did not understand was that social problems were inextricably mixed up with a Negro physician's practice. He tried to make this clear.

There was, for instance, the case of a Negro patient who needed a hysterectomy, but no hospital would take a Negro as a private patient, and no hospital would let him operate. Could he perform a hysterectomy on a kitchen table? Should he send his patient to a charity ward? As a member of the state Board of Health, he knew what charity wards were. They were crowded, they were often filthy, they were always inadequately staffed. Even a white woman could not hope to get the care she needed in a charity ward, and if this was true for a white woman, then—— "To attack the medical problems of Negroes," Dr. Dan wrote later, "[is] necessarily to attack the problem of race."

This was a construction so realistic and so simple that Dan Williams was surprised that it had not occurred to him before.

His medical career was a matter of friendly interest to some of his white associates in the profession. He often met with them informally to discuss new medical theories and surgical techniques. Also in the Hamilton Club, a political organization behind which stood the portly power of ex-Postmaster General Walter Gresham, there was some talk of hospital staff appointments, clinic lectureships, and the like—though always as if his being a Negro were completely irrelevant. Naturally this was flattering, since the assumption seemed to be that professional competence was the sine qua non, and he was not averse to dreaming that perhaps his skill and intelligence had been enough to secure his appointment to the South Side Dispensary.

But were they enough really? Would he have got the position with the City Railway Company if the question of his race had come up and he had had to answer it? He did not think so. And could he say honestly that his appointment to the Illinois State Board of Health had nothing to do with political expediency, a matter of the Republicans hoping to make Negro voters happy?

To pretend that only his personal qualifications, without any regard for his racial background, made for success in his career was to leave out of consideration the fact that he practiced medicine principally among Negroes, and was to pretend that certain problems of medical care were not peculiar to Negroes, and was, in the final analysis, to desert Negroes altogether. Would the competence that might open doors for him under the condition of being thought an exceptional Negro also open doors for other Negroes? He did not think so. Assuming his entrance at those guarded doors of the white medical world, and assuming further his climb to eminence there, could he then bring subtle pressure to bear to fling the doors wide for all? Again he did not think so.

These were the conclusions Dr. Dan had reached when he told the Reverend Mr. Reynolds, "We'll do something better. . . . We'll get down to brass tacks."

Getting down to brass tacks meant hounding his friends, colored and white. "There must be a hospital for Negroes," he told them, "but not a Negro hospital." There was a great and decisive difference. "It must be an institution expressive of interracial good will, one where colored and white can work together, but it must be dedicated to medical service and the training of Negroes—internes, technicians, nurses, all the nurses we can train."

No one could remember seeing Dr. Williams so excited as he was during the closing months of 1890. Once his retiring personality had polarized around the idea of the hospital, he "radiated an almost sparkling magnetic force," and his appeals, though quiet, were irresistible. He formed committees of white and colored people and put them to work. He skipped from meeting to meeting and from rally to rally. He personally solicited funds. He sustained enthusiasms. He won from staff members of Mercy Hospital and the faculty of Chicago Medical College pledges of services to the embryonic institution, already named the Provident Hospital and Training School. He wanted the highest standards and the best men to maintain them, so, excepting himself in surgery and Dr. Charles Bentley in odontology, the staff he began to organize was white. Drs. W. W. Jaggard and H. T. Byford of the Medical College faculty were to be obstetrician and gynecologist, Frank Billings chief consulting physician, and the renowned Christian Fenger consulting surgeon. Within a few months a three-story building at the corner of Twenty-ninth and Dearborn had been selected and a first payment on it made. It had room for a dozen beds, and this seemed enough for a start.

But the start was still several months away. A great deal of money was needed, and money came slowly. Times were not good in the ghetto. The first ominous clouds of the depression that would spread over the whole land in 1893 already darkened the lives of Negroes. Besides, Dr. Dan was a busy practitioner. He could not attend all the meetings or chair all the committees. The faithful friends of the idea worked hard, but these faithful friends were practically all of the mixed-blood world, for only they had the time to give, and only they had important connections in the white world. Under-privileged Negroes, though they stood to benefit, were resentful and suspicious. Provident Hospital and Training School looked like a "half-white dickty" to-do to them.

The mistrust of Negroes wounded Dr. Dan more deeply than the prejudice and indifference of whites, but he redoubled his efforts. The founding of Provident was a challenge to the integrity of his sense of race. He would help his people whether or no. He passed over an opportunity to study with Dr. F. B. Robinson, a renowned abdominal surgeon. He talked in Negro churches; he talked at meetings in poor Negro homes; he talked to Negroes on the streets. "It will be our hospital," he told them. Grudgingly, gradually, they came to believe him.

Finally he approached Millionaire Row and got contributions ranging from two hundred to five hundred dollars from the Kohl-saats, the Armours, Marshall Field, and the Pullmans. Eighteen months after the start of the campaign the moment came to draw up the papers of incorporation. The line where Daniel Hale Williams' signature should have appeared was never filled in. At the time of the signing he was performing a hysterectomy on a Negro patient. His sterilizer was a wash boiler, his operating table a dining-room table, and his operating room a cleared space off the steaming kitchen of a home on the west side of Chicago.

4. OUR PEOPLE

The "grand opening" of the country's first interracial hospital in May 1891 was a huge success. "Everybody who was anybody," the papers said, and many who were nobodies in the ghetto community, were there. They came bringing gifts of "sheets, beds, old linen, sugar, soap, black currant jelly and loaves of bread," and some of these gifts "were kept up month by month." Wealthy white people made financial gifts too, but Provident remained just this side of extreme destitution. Though desperately needed and gratefully received, eggs, butter, and vegetables were not medicines, and books, "a Japanese screen worth $6.50," and a clothes wringer, whatever therapeutic values they might be imagined to have, were not forceps and Reverdin needles and cystoscopes. Dances, benefit dinners, and church bazaars staged by the Ladies' Auxiliary and the Provident Hospital Association did not keep the petty cash box supplied. At the end of the first year, having admitted one hundred and eighty-five patients, nearly a third of them white, Provident had a deficit of close to a thousand dollars.

But finances were not the only cause for worry. Dr. Dan wanted to add Negroes to the staff, but he did not wish to compromise the severe standards he had established. To do so would be to destroy his own concept of Provident, to play fast and loose with the reputations of the men who had consented to give their services to it, and to reduce good will to condescension and sincere sympathy to scornful patronage. He could not risk losing a competent white staff. He did not want it said that Provident was "just another nigger institution," with all the phrase implied of carelessness and irresponsibility. As a Negro physician, he was on the defensive for his people: they had yet to prove themselves.

So even applicants to the nurses' training school had to meet standards that were more than ordinarily high. The level of training

Dr. Dan imposed on the school and the caliber of the men and women who gave instruction required that nursing students have "a broad intelligence already fairly trained," and those personal attributes—"punctuality, neatness, moral fitness and a gentle manner" —that might prove insurance against mediocrity and failure. Of the one hundred and seventy-five applicants the first year, Dr. Dan accepted seven. His cousin's daughter and the sister of the Reverend Mr. Reynolds were among them. They were all high school graduates. They were all light-skinned and of the mixed-blood world. What seemed to give this inexorable circumstance an unfortunate blush of policy and planning was the fact, equally inexorable, that the two Negroes on the medical staff and the one interne were also of the mixed-blood world. The only other Negro physician who had applied did not meet the standards, and he had been rejected. His name was George Hall.

In Negro life in Chicago, as elsewhere, ambitions were stirring. A harsh, aggressive species was beginning to press up, claw up through the multitude. As a class it had not yet put either a great social or a great emotional distance between itself and the throng. A protective tribal instinct operated. It operated now in the mass as it had operated during slavery to condition the relations of the great number of field slaves to the few, more privileged house servants and free people of color, most of whom were mulattoes, and most of whom the field slaves thought were in league against them. They were suspicious and resentful. George Hall was of this breed.

A dark-skinned man of genial bearing, Hall was well known and well liked in the ghetto. Here his opinions were respected, and one of his opinions was that he was just too dark for Dr. Dan Williams' taste.

It sounded plausible enough to the people in the ghetto. That the course of study at Chicago Medical College was then the stiffest in the country meant less to them than that George Hall, their friend, was a doctor the same as Dr. Dan. Medical training was medical training, without discrimination as to the level of it, and in Hall's dingy office hung a medical diploma. It was from one of the

more than twenty Eclectic schools in Chicago. As a member of the
Illinois State Board of Health, Williams knew what those schools
were. They were still back in the pre-bacteriology, pre-antiseptic
age. Their graduates could not meet the standards the head of
Provident insisted upon.

But Hall had a following, and he had the powerful shibboleth of
"color-struck dickties" around which to rally it. This gave him a
kind of authority Dr. Dan was never to have and was never to learn
to cope with. Apparently approached by some of Hall's crowd, the
hospital's board, totally comprised of Negroes, grew concerned for
the welfare of the Provident and the solidarity of the race. They
persuaded Dr. Dan to appoint Hall to the children's clinic—"to look
after measles and chicken pox, and such," Hall said bitterly. Indeed,
it was no flattering appointment; another type of man would have
refused it. Hall was required to call in a consultant on even the
simplest cases. He was never to forget or forgive.

Hall's inclusion on the staff was eventually to wreck the medical
standards and play hob with the administration of Provident's affairs, but for the time being things went on much as before. It was
a struggle to keep the hospital going. Most of the patients were
poor, three fourths of them required expensive surgery, and many
of the accident and physical-violence cases brought in from the
streets, the stockyards, and the railroads could not pay anything.
Though Dr. Dan and some of the white physicians on the staff
brought in their private patients and sometimes turned their fees
into the hospital's general funds, as the record shows, there was
never enough money. The record also shows that the finance committee regularly sent out appeals for "arnica, Pond's Extract,
Brown's Ginger, plasters, camphor from your medicine chests." As
the depression of 1893 deepened there were many weeks when the
board and the staff met emergency expenses from their personal resources, and "more than once Dr. Dan reached into his own pocket
and gave the superintendent money for the day's food."

The Chicago World's Fair brought some relief. The Chicago Negro weekly newspaper, the *Crusader*—and, indeed, Negro weeklies

throughout the country—gave passionate publicity to Provident as an "interracial venture of great significance, where white and colored work together for the benefit of mankind." This appealed to Bishop Daniel Payne, who believed that "to help mankind is to love God." As gentle as always, but tottering now, and now more than ever like a graveyard thing (for he was to die in November), he came bringing a gift of five hundred dollars from his diocese in Ohio.

The aging, gray-maned Frederick Douglass, himself only two years from death, also played a part in lifting the "siege of Provident's debts." He was in Chicago as Haitian commissioner to the fair. Once recorder of deeds for the District of Columbia, once grand marshal of the United States, and lately minister to Haiti, he was still the race's spokesman and still the most famous Negro in the country. Negroes flocked to see him and to do him honor, and he urged them to contribute to Provident. An interracial hospital was his kind of thing. He did not "approve of organizations distinctively racial. . . . There are societies where color is not regarded as a test of membership, and such places I deem more appropriate for colored persons." So Negroes went to Provident and left their pennies, dimes, and dollars.

Of course Douglass himself went—and not merely because he and Dan Williams had discovered the faint possibility of a blood relationship and called each other "cousin." He went with those twin furies, Ida B. Wells and Fannie B. Williams, "whose tongues were never still on the question of equality," and he left the fifty dollars that he had solicited after a lecture in a Negro church. His visit was well advertised in advance, and "Dearborn Street was packed with every Negro in Chicago." Visibly tired, Douglass declined to make a speech, but he waved a greeting to the crowd, and the crowd shouted with one voice.

Things were easier after the summer of the fair, and Dr. Dan could give more of his attention to the practice of medicine. Chicago Medical College, which had expanded into postgraduate work and was about to be absorbed by Northwestern University, had moved to within five minutes' walking distance of Provident. Dr.

Dan enrolled in a course in bacteriology. He had another opportunity to study abdominal surgery with Dr. Byron Robinson, and
now he could take it. Sometimes he was the assistant, but more
often he simply watched and listened as the great scowling gynecologist and "stomach man" operated and lectured. Williams absorbed medical knowledge as if his mind were a sponge. Even the
cantankerous Robinson, known to be stingy of praise, spoke of him
as a "skilled surgeon . . . one of the best . . . of wide experience
and good judgment."

Dr. Dan had earned such mentions for his work at Provident, and
as they were repeated by men of the highest professional repute it
became common for physicians to crowd into the hospital's small
surgery to watch him work. His manual dexterity was amazing. He
was bold and ingenious, but generally he knew the full medical
history in every case, and his daring and resourcefulness were
grounded in a thorough knowledge of anatomy and exercised on
carefully calculated risks. He was never reckless. When he made an
incision he knew what he expected his knife to find.

The operation that brought him national fame and international
recognition was an emergency. One day in July 1893 a tough young
street fighter named Cornish was brought to Provident. He had a
one-inch knife wound in the chest just left of the breastbone. It
seemed superficial, but within a half hour the man was seized with
a paroxysm of coughing, and within the hour he had collapsed from
shock. Dr. Dan diagnosed the injury as a damaged blood vessel,
perhaps the heart itself. Unless something was done, obviously the
man would die.

There was no precedent to follow. In those days, even opening
the thoracic cavity was considered an invitation to death. The latest
authoritative work treating the subject of wounds to the heart—
Surgery, by C. W. M. Mollin, a Fellow of the Royal Society of
Surgeons—had been published but two years before, and it stated
that the only treatment was "absolute rest, cold, and opium," after
which the patient invariably died.

To follow this treatment now would do no harm to Dr. Dan's

reputation. But if he did not follow it? If, venturing into the unknown, he challenged death with the weapons at his command? They were not today's weapons. There was no X ray. There were no sulphur drugs to fight infection. There was not even a choice of anesthesia, and blood transfusions were unknown. As he watched the patient grow steadily weaker, Dr. Dan alerted the hospital's one interne. He had decided to operate.

Besides the interne, only five professionals (four of them white) were there when medical history was made. Not one of them "but must have shuddered when Dr. Dan put the point of his knife to Cornish's inert body." It was over in a matter of time no one remembered to record, so tense was the atmosphere. The man was still alive when the last suture was made, and this was success from the medical point of view. But was it a *real* success? The answer came fifty-one days later, when, following a second operation to remove five pints of bloody serum from the chest cavity, Cornish was discharged. He lived for more than twenty years afterward. He was the first human being to survive an operation on the heart.

When the news got around Dr. Dan was besieged by medical men and reporters, but he gave only one interview. This was to the *Inter Ocean*, a newspaper controlled by Herman Kohlsaat, who was one of the first white men to contribute financially to Provident, and who, together with Marshall Field and Otto Young, would one day make possible a new, modern Provident. And even that interview said more about the interracial policy of the hospital, its mixed staff, and its nurses' training school than about Dr. Dan himself and the precedent-breaking operation he had performed.

Though Daniel Hale Williams did not know it, he was about to begin an undertaking that would have as its final result an estrangement from his people so nearly complete that a once favorite cousin would exclaim bitterly, "He wanted to be white. He wanted to be white, so let him be it!"; and that would make the furious curse of George Hall seem fulfilled at last: "I'll punish him worse than God ever will. I'll see he's forgotten before he's dead!"

And for Dan Williams, the estrangement from the lives and the struggles of his people was indeed a worse punishment than any he could have imagined coming from God.

5. SONG OF LOVE

The state of Negro affairs in the last decade of the nineteenth century left something to be desired. The Democratic party's victory over Reconstruction was complete. The Negro remained a source of fear and hatred in the South on the one hand, and the victim of evasion and neglect in the North on the other. Any effort to improve his condition seemed only to worsen it. By 1894 all but a tardy handful of Southern states had disfranchised him. By 1896 the Supreme Court had pronounced its "separate but equal" doctrine, thus assuring the continuance of the tradition of racial difference and those discriminatory practices by means of which many Southern whites could satisfy their "consuming monomania"—the perpetuation in law of an incontestable superiority to blacks. By the middle years of the last decade of the century Negroes were being lynched at the rate of one every fifty-six hours.

For Southern attitudes Southern spokesmen of course were not slow to find justification in a kind of pseudo reality. It was a false reality created in part by the systematic exclusion of Negroes from the general cultural life and in part by an ineradicable tendency to romanticize what had been dearly loved and tragically lost—namely, a way of life, as imagination reproduced it, so aristocratic, gracious, and precious in particulars, and so beneficent, generous, and fruitful in principles that it might well have served and even should have served as a model for all mankind. It was a pseudo reality that was sustained for long years after the North's outcries ("The South of popular story is a figment of the imagination, I tell you!") against the actuality were stilled, and long after the entire machinery of attitudes, custom, and law had been adjusted to the Southern point of view.

Since the American world accepted as unquestioned fact the "inherent and irredeemable inferiority" of the Negro, it was not necessary to keep padding the fact, except as the padding was poultice for a raw conscience. And it was poultice.

"You could ship-wreck 10,000 illiterate white Americans on a desert island, and in three weeks they would have a fairly good government, conceived and administered upon fairly democratic lines. You could ship-wreck 10,000 Negroes, every one of whom was a graduate of Harvard University, and in less than three years, they would have retrograded governmentally; half of the men would have been killed, and the other half have two wives apiece." Thus Mississippi Senator John Sharp Williams spoke the common Southern opinion in the 1890s.

This, of course, was the pained conscience at work. It was at work in all those Southern spokesmen—from John P. Kennedy (*Swallow Barn*), through Thomas Nelson Page (*Red Rock*), to Thomas Dixon (*The Leopard's Spots*)—who helped to create and tried to breathe life into the stereotypes of the Negro character, the Negro mind, and the Negro soul. That character was at once depraved, comic, and benign; that mind was at once dull and crafty; that soul was either inexplicably angelic or primally debased beyond redemption.

By reason of his exclusion from the cultural life and his inability to gain traction in the intellectual life, the Negro had no effective defense against these attributions. Sutton Griggs might publish novel after novel from a corrective point of view, and Pauline Hopkins might write books crying out in agony, "We are not like that! Dear God knows we're not like that!" but they had to peddle their books from door to door. Even Charles Chesnutt, a close friend of Dan Williams, who had won distinction as a racially unidentified writer of stories for the *Atlantic Monthly*, might write "uncompromisingly and impartially, sparing neither whites nor Negroes, Southerners nor Northerners," those soberly documented novels of Southern life, but *The House behind the Cedars*, *The Colonel's Dream*, and *The Marrow of Tradition* tended to modify the common opinion and correct the false concepts, and the white reading public paid scant attention—and a fine literary talent fizzed out like a drenched fire.

Certainly one result of the implacable resistance to the assertion of the Negro will and the Negro concept of himself was this: perhaps realizing that sometimes the battles you do not fight are the ones you win, Negroes began or seemed to begin to live up to the baleful attributions, both in their literature and in their lives. It was extremely unhealthy, as first a few and then a growing number realized. But slowly their vaunted talent for compromise, for compliance and conformity took over. In his famous "Atlanta Speech" in 1895, Booker Washington urged these as the characteristics that should henceforth define Negro life. Temporarily bewitched by the country's almost frenzied reception of Washington's ideas, men who were later to proclaim their dignity as Negroes and their rights as American citizens fell into line as if moved by the hand of God.

How unhealthy all this was showed up in the life of Paul L. Dunbar, who for a brief time was the most widely read poet in America. Dr. Dan first met Dunbar when the poet served as Douglass' assistant at the Chicago World's Fair. Later he was to know him better as a friend and as a patient brought hopelessly drunk to the alcoholic ward of Freedmen's Hospital in Washington. But in 1893 the poet—then twenty-one and the author of one volume—was just beginning his short, brilliant, tragic career.

White friends in his home town of Dayton, Ohio, had brought his poetry to the attention of William Dean Howells, then America's most influential man of letters. Charmed by the dialect pieces written frankly in imitation of Stephen Foster and Irwin Russell, Howells encouraged Dunbar to develop this vein. This was the vein, the critic said, that "in the charming accents of the Negro's own version of our English" most clearly defined "the range between appetite and emotion, which is the limited range of the race."

But it was not really Dunbar's vein. He was not at home in it; he could not do what he wished to do in it—sing of the aspirations and depict the depths of Negro life. Yet here was the arbiter of American letters advising him to develop it. For Dunbar's second volume, *Majors and Minors,* Howells wrote for *Harper's Weekly* a full-page review devoted solely to praise of the dialect pieces. For the third volume, *Lyrics of Lowly Life,* Howells wrote the introduction. "Paul Dunbar is the only man of pure African blood and of American civilization to feel the Negro life esthetically and express it lyrically."

But it was not Negro life. It was what the white South had seduced America into believing was Negro life, and no one knew this better than Dunbar. But he had an aging mother to provide for and a young and beautiful wife to support, and writing was all he knew to do for a livelihood. Dialect poems and stories, or the pallid romantic novels he fashioned around idealized white characters, were all the public would accept from him. He poured them out, and his publishers handsomely bound and illustrated them, at the rate of nearly one volume a year.

Fame sickened him even as he pursued it. He took to drink. It assuaged his bitterness and frustration and what a recent critic has called his "self-hatred." He drank more heavily. He disgraced himself at his public lectures, notably at Yale and at Northwestern. His wife left him. She loved him no less than he loved her, but she could no longer protect their love from shame and abasement and him from himself. No one could, not even his cherished mother, to whom he fled in 1905. In the last months of his life he somehow managed to gather his energies and turn out some of the most poignant of his lyrics in pure English, among them this:

> He sang of love when life was young,
> And Love itself was in his lays,
> But, Ah, the world, it turned to praise
> A jingle in a broken tongue.

He died in 1906 at the age of thirty-four.

6. THE NADIR

In some areas appearances did not entirely betray those who, like Booker Washington, pretended to believe that everything was fine in the Negro situation and in race relations. Negro secondary schools and colleges were crowded. Most of them were substandard, it is true, but the white denominations that supported them and the white men and women who taught in them were sincere in their efforts on the Negro's behalf. Negro churches, such as the African Methodist Episcopal, the African Zion, and the Colored Methodist, enjoyed an unprecedented growth in membership just before the turn of the century. They could claim "23,000 churches, with unusually wide activities, and spending annually at least $10,000,000."

Some of this money went to Negro businesses, of which there were a sufficient number to make for the presence of four hundred delegates at the first convention of the National Negro Business League in 1899. The delegates represented restaurant and hotel chains, bakery companies, co-operative grocers and catering firms, and some of these were substantial, but they were hardly in a class with the Negro insurance companies, mutual aid societies, and burial associations that were organized in the same period.

Fraternal orders, such as the Masons and Odd Fellows, had long been established among Negroes in the 1890s, but new groups came into being. Negro banks, too, sprang up. Some, like the State Street Bank of Chicago, flourish still, but most collapsed after a year or two. Negroes supported orphanages, homes for the aged, and asylums for fallen women. The National Association of Colored Women, founded in 1895, set up kindergartens for the children of poor working mothers and social clubs for young girls.

Individual Negroes, too, gained recognition, and this was sometimes inflated beyond all deserving by a people who were culturally starved and hungering for heroes. Sports figures, theatrical personalities, and just "characters" were made to shine like gods. Negroes of really fine accomplishment had a way of getting absorbed by the white world, usually abroad. Henry Tanner, the painter, whose works hang in the Luxembourg, the Franklin Institute, the Chicago Art Institute, and the Metropolitan, went to Europe in 1891 and lived in France until his death in the 1930s. Sissieretta Jones and

Marie Selika (whose voice and artistry were "above criticism") were so much in demand on the concert stages of Europe that one found time to visit her homeland only a few times in a half dozen years and the other never returned at all. Negro papers in the nineties tried to follow such careers, but it was rather like firing a cannon at the stars.

While the front pages of Negro papers were often roseate with success stories, the editorial pages were gray with gloom—and for reason. The lynching rate climbed steadily. The anti-Negro activities of organized labor, which refused to see the unity of interest between white and black workers, were most severe. Negroes were pitilessly lampooned in the national press.

Negro editors gloomed especially over political prospects. They remembered Reconstruction, when Negroes sat in legislative bodies in the South, and there were black sheriffs, postmasters, magistrates, superintendents of education, and officials of all kinds. "Politics," wrote John Langston, a Negro leader, "is the key to unlock all doors." But with Reconstruction finished, the doors were as tight-locked as they had ever been in slavery, and the key hung out of reach.

When Grover Cleveland, who had already served a presidential term, was again the Democratic nominee in 1892, few Negro editors saw any reason to change the opinion most of them had expressed in 1884: "If Cleveland is elected . . . it will be a cold afternoon for this country and especially for the Negro and the laboring classes." For, meantime, Cleveland had denounced the Federal Election Bill and had praised Isaiah Montgomery for helping to engineer the disfranchisement of Negroes in Mississippi. But Cleveland was elected. "Equality follows the badge of citizenship wherever found, and, unimpaired by race or color . . ." he said, hitting the proper note of exhortation in his inaugural speech. But it seemed unlikely that he himself would do anything to lift the Negro from his plight.

Only one monument to the liberalizing, fluid period of Reconstruction remained—the Freedmen's Hospital, in Washington, D.C. And even that was threatened by indifference and neglect.

7. FREEDMEN'S OWN

An old friend of Dr. Dan's and an early benefactor of Provident Hospital was soon to prove that the indifference and neglect were not total.

Ex-Postmaster General Walter Q. Gresham had left the Republican party to campaign for Cleveland and the Democrats, and Cleveland rewarded him by appointing him Secretary of State in the new cabinet. It was not a post in which a man would ordinarily concern himself with Negro affairs, but Judge Gresham was one of those interfering Yankees who stuck his long nose into all sorts of matters that were but disingenuously his concern. He stuck his nose into Freedmen's Hospital and Refugee Camp, and what he sniffed was foul. He pressed the Secretary of the Interior, Hoke Smith, so hard that that Southern gentleman's resistance was completely smashed and he promised to start reforms.

Then on a visit home to Chicago, Secretary Gresham sent for Dr. Dan. He told Dr. Dan that Freedmen's was going to be completely reorganized and he wanted him to apply for the executive position there. He brushed aside the physician's solicitude for Provident. That hospital was in fine condition, as Gresham well knew, with a staff as strong as any in the city, and with a small surplus of funds. "If it's service to your race you're thinking of," Gresham said, "Freedmen's needs you more than Provident."

This was a line of argument Dr. Dan could not ignore, and it had the greater strength from the fact that his mother and two younger sisters had moved to Washington just a few months before. He promised to apply.

There were other applicants, among them one who wrote, ". . . no colored physician can fill the place properly because they have less respect for their own race than a good Christian white man feels." Dr. Dan's application was supported not only by Gresham's political influence but by enthusiastic letters from the most eminent medical men in the Midwest and by his own professional distinction. He got the job.

It was the end of December 1893 and he was to assume his new duties the first day of February. He wanted to leave Provident's affairs in order. He had a large private practice to dispose of and other personal matters to attend. But friends who knew he had worked unceasingly for seven years urged him to take a vacation, and he went off reluctantly to southern Illinois. There on a hunting trip he had an accident that sent a load of buckshot through his foot. By the time he could return to Chicago and Provident, inflammation of the veins of his leg had developed. Time dragged. Three days before he was to leave for Washington he left the hospital. It was too soon. Lymph vessels and glands became involved, and the celebrated endocrinologist, Dr. Christian Fenger, had all he could do to save his colleague's life.

This unfortunate accident and Dr. Dan's delayed recovery gave George Hall an opportunity he had awaited with well-concealed impatience. The gladhand, the backslap, the bluster had won him a reputation for affability even at Provident, but his manner hid a satanic vindictiveness and a designing ambition. Though now at last, having attended evening classes at a second-rate medical school, he had a degree in allopathic medicine, he cut no figure in the professional world. His colleagues at Provident rated him a mediocre physician, and he had not been promoted.

He felt unfairly treated. He felt that his unfair treatment had the most inexcusable of reasons—his dark skin. Stored up in him were explosive quantities of professional and personal jealousy, for neither his own attainments nor the blatant attractions of a red-haired octoroon wife had won him entree to that mixed-blood world with which most of his Negro colleagues were associated by birth. Hall wanted this at least as much as he wanted professional preferment. He believed that one signalized the other. All the emotional tensions of the struggle for status, complicated by the severe intorsions of color caste within the race, worked in Dr. Hall to an intolerable degree.

The last thing he wanted was for Dr. Dan to stay at Provident, where he might continue to block his promotion. Yet at the same time he did not want his rival (for so Hall conceived him to be) to have the Negro world-wide recognition of the appointment to Freedmen's. Dan Williams was not what Hall would describe as a "race man." He did not put race above all other considerations. He did not give Negroes the "breaks" just because they were Negroes. If he could not block Dr. Dan's appointment, Hall thought he might at least besmirch Dr. Dan's name.

Thus, while the latter lay critically ill, Hall, radiating great waves of race consciousness, addressed the Negro public through the Washington paper, the *Colored American*. He implied that Dr. Dan was stalling, that he was satisfied with the deluge of publicity. "Freedmen's new chief," Hall wrote, "will never assume his post there." Hall persuaded James Blackever, a Negro politician of questionable ethics and little power, to write the Secretary of the Interior. Blackever enclosed a copy of Hall's newspaper diatribe, which was, he told Hoke Smith, "written by an associate of Dr. Williams." As for himself, he continued, he had been in Chicago, "where I left Dr. Williams following his everyday profession. . . . Everyone knows that he is only baffling with the Department . . . at the expense of those he was sent to serve."

It was easy to induce Robert S. Abbott to take up the attack. His mind was as dark and twisted as Hall's—and for the same tragic reasons. "Freedmen's Hospital is in charge of an invalid who has drawn eight months salary without performing a single week of service. . . . He is a fitter subject for a hospital than for the management of one." But Abbott, whose first paper came out as irregularly as a groundhog in a variable winter, was not then the powerful editor of what was to be the most influential Negro weekly in the world.

Dr. Dan was hurt by these attacks, not in his standing with the federal officials, who had been kept informed, but in that deeply personal way he was always to be hurt when his own people accused him of disloyalty. He had no defense against such attacks. He was too modest to point out the sacrifices he had made to establish and keep Provident going. He told no one how drastically his income would be reduced by taking the position at Freedmen's. Weakened by the long illness that nearly took his life, and upheld only by the hope of turning Freedmen's into "an institution in which Negroes could take pride," Daniel Hale Williams packed his instruments and his medical library and in the fall of 1894 set out for the nation's capital.

8. CONFLICT IN COW TOWN

Washington was a great change from Chicago. The capital city for a century and a half, it was just beginning to look like it—and this only to the eyes of the uninitiated. Reeking marshes sprawled inward from the Potomac River and infested Georgetown, Anacostia, and LeDroit Park with seasonal plagues of mosquitoes and frogs. In spring the river sometimes flooded and inundated the Negro quarter at the very foot of the Capitol. Radiating from this, the principal avenues, Pennsylvania, Massachusetts, and Connecticut, had long since claimed the embassies, the clubs of the influential and wealthy, and the ornate homes of the nouveau riche. The intersecting streets, too, had established their character. Solid rows of red brick fronts, broken here and there by architectural oddities in stoops, steps, and porches, frowned down like fortresses on tiny patches of front yards graced with fences of iron, stone, or hedge. But behind the stone and marble of the avenues and the brick of the middle-class streets, behind and between and in every crack and corner squeezed the noisome alleys and courts of the poor—some black, some white, and some few red Indians.

A little to the northwest but outside the boundaries of the city proper, the federal government had established two institutions for Negroes. Founded in the irritable frenzy of the Civil War and Reconstruction, they stood side by side. One was Freedmen's Hospital, Asylum and Refugee Camp—the very name of which signified emergency—and the other Howard University. Over the years they had come to be the twin symbols of what President Grant had called "the Government's undiminished regard" for the welfare of colored people. Over the years, without either losing or quite fulfilling their separate functions, they had mingled their identities and grown so close together in physical fact that one could not tell whether the slums of Cow Town, to which the hospital was attached on one side, made progress toward the respectability of the university or the university declined to the slums.

Actually, though, there was no mobility in Cow Town. Poverty and repression had vitiated all but the rawest instincts of survival. The sign of the slums, as the poet Dunbar pointed out, was the hospital and asylum. The inhabitants of Cow Town, ignorant and untrained, could get no handhold in a city where there were no factories, no mills, no industry of any kind, and where the jobs in domestic and personal service were traditionally pre-empted, as they had been in slavery, by an altogether different caste and class of Negroes.

This other class made the university the symbol of their lives. They had ambition. One who drove a senator's horse today aspired to carry his official messages tomorrow, and to be perhaps his clerk (for there were already a few Negro clerks in government) a year from now. In short, there was competition, struggle, and it was all the more unremitting and ruthless because positions of prestige were so few and because the competitors for them had started from the same place, with similar advantages and handicaps, and were, in a way of speaking, sprung from the same loins.

So Dr. Charles B. Purvis did not see why Dr. Daniel H. Williams had any more claim to head Freedmen's than he. A member of the university's faculty of medicine, Purvis had run the hospital for a dozen years. That he had run it badly, as a sinecure, no one seemed to detect until Judge Gresham interfered. But the two positions had given Purvis tremendous prestige in the Negro community, and he did not care to lose it. He made trouble of a nagging sort. He injected politics into the situation. He tried to rally the university trustees and faculty by declaring that the advantages the university medical students enjoyed would be lost if a non-faculty man, and a stranger to boot, ran the hospital.

But the truth is that Freedmen's was more asylum and refugee camp than hospital when Dr. Dan took over. Housed in six buildings, five of them wooden, barracks-like structures, on three acres of ground, it had been built for an emergency and the emergency had lasted thirty years. The patients were wards of the government—the indigent, the homeless, the useless, the habitually drunk, the insane, and the blind—dumped there by the authorities of distant cities where, though native to them, they were not tolerated. Those who were able were required to render such services as cleaning the yards and buildings, and making "bedsacks, sheets, chemises, aprons, handkerchiefs," and the like.

The medical care they got was not only negligible but negligent and dangerous. Surgery was sometimes performed "by students who needed the experience." The mortality rate was more than an excessive 10 per cent. There were no trained nurses. On his first morning Dr. Dan was shocked to see a "ward mammy" take up a position between the rows of beds in the female ward, clap her hands, and shout, "All you 'leven o'clockers, take yo' medicine!" Freedmen's, a monument to the government's "undiminished regard" for the welfare of Negroes, resembled nothing so much as a medieval pesthouse. Yet to be its surgeon in chief was to attain the highest administrative post the federal government accorded Negroes. The head of Freedmen's was an important man in the Negro world, and in that world his position commanded great esteem.

The prestige value of the job meant practically nothing to Dr. Dan. He did not know how to employ it to surround himself with influential friends who might prove useful. He cared little for society. His friends were people to whom he was attracted by intrinsic qualities and professional interests. He did sometimes go to visit his "cousin," Frederick Douglass, who, in semi-retirement, quietly waited for death in nearby Anacostia, and once a week he dined with his mother and two sisters in Kingman Place, but for the most part he was so deeply involved in Freedmen's that he had no time for anything else.

His first job was to reorganize the hospital, and within a month this work was begun. He established seven departments. His reputation in the medical world, coupled with a local scarcity of professionally broadening opportunities, made it possible for him to enlist an unpaid, biracial staff of twenty of Washington's "most competent and successful" specialists. This was the kind of organization he had started with at Provident, and he extended it here. He saw an interneship program as necessary, since, excepting Provident, there was not a hospital in the United States that welcomed colored medical graduates. He refined the hospital's ties to the university medical school, which was still an evening school for students who had to work days to support themselves. He wanted to substitute a nurses' training school for the two-nights-a-week instruction in practical nursing that Purvis had installed and offered to women of pitifully inadequate background. If Dr. Dan conceived of Freedmen's as both a hospital and a center of medical training for Negroes, he also felt it was a challenge to the belief that Negroes could not "do" and learn and apply as well as whites.

There were difficulties. The annual budget of fifty-two thousand dollars was inadequate for a two-hundred-bed hospital and training center. Purvis sniped from nearby and used his still considerable influence to undermine the work. He encroached on the authority of Sarah Ebersole, whom Dr. Dan had brought on from Chicago to run the training school and nursing staff. There was, finally, the indifference of the Secretary of the Interior, a Georgian who preached white supremacy and "cared not a fig" about Freedmen's.

Nevertheless, things were accomplished. Dr. Dan's abilities won over the university administration and all of the medical faculty save Purvis. A biracial staff worked as smoothly at Freedmen's as it had at Provident. After less than a year young white medical graduates were applying for interneships, and Dr. Dan admitted the best qualified of them along with Negroes. He demonstrated and lectured in surgery. Steadily the caliber of the medical service rose to match the reputation the deprived masses of Negroes were all too prone to give anything that was theirs and racially identified with them. While surgical cases increased almost 200 per cent, the mortality rate dropped lower than 3 per cent. By 1896, Freedman's was admitting five hundred surgical cases a year, and Dr. Dan was proving in the East his right to the reputation he had earned in the Midwest as one of the "country's greatest surgeons." Not only local medical men pressed for opportunities to watch him operate, but soon men were coming from Johns Hopkins in Baltimore and the University of Pennsylvania in Philadelphia.

In spite of the success of the biracial program, prejudice was far from dead. Some Negroes thought that Dr. Dan's knowledge and skill should be kept within the race, and that Freedmen's should admit no white patients and have neither white internes nor white members on the medical staff. Freedmen's was theirs: Dr. Dan was theirs—one of them. The whites had hospitals to which Negroes were not admitted even as patients, much less as staff physicians and surgeons. They had, too, their professional groups, like the District Medical Society to whose meetings Negroes were never invited (though it was known through the proud testimony of an eaves-dropping Negro waiter that Dr. Dan's operations had been subjects of discussion there twice in three months). White medical men were simply using Freedmen's as a good thing, and Dan Williams was rather a fool to permit them to do it. Or—perhaps there was some-thing else. Could it be that Williams was more desirous of having the approbation and acknowledgment of white people than of giving service to his own?

Whether or not such insidiously inspired talk reached the ears of Dr. Dan, he was soon to give it the lie. He had been instrumental in establishing a local group for the professional benefit of colored physicians, and though certain men like Purvis had boycotted and maligned it, the Medico-Chirurgical Society had flourished. It was a mixed group, for Dr. Dan knew that the exchange of ideas and expe-rience with advantaged white men would be good for Negroes in the profession. But he also knew and respected that powerful defensive impulse in Negroes to have something that belonged exclusively to them. Born of the race's experience of indignity and kept strong by the galling indifference of whites, the impulse did sometimes lead to a development of initiative and racial self-respect. The Negro church systems, the militant Negro press were products of it. And perhaps, Dr. Dan wrote his friend Dr. Charles Bentley, the impulse "could be made to work to the advancement of Negro medicine."

Acting on this thought, Daniel Williams invited a representative group of Negro physicians to a meeting in Atlanta, Georgia. There they organized the National Medical Association. It was their own, and for more than half a century it was to remain the only national medical body to which Negroes could belong. Refusing the presidency, Dr. Dan consented to be the association's first vice-president. It was in this capacity that he met Booker Washington, some two or three months before the Alabama educator was hurled onto the national stage by the storm of applause that greeted his "Atlanta Speech."

The three men—George Hall, Charles Purvis, and Booker Washington—who were each in his own way to contribute to the inevitability of Daniel Hale Williams' withdrawal from Negro affairs and the race milieu had now entered his life.

9. WASHINGTON, FAREWELL

In the next two years circumstances seemed to shape right for Purvis and events to fall wrong for Dr. Dan. Frederick Douglass died in February 1895, and Judge Gresham the following May. With the passing of these two men, Dr. Dan lost the only politically powerful friends he had.

But more unhappy in its immediate consequences was the death of his only brother that same year. Price Williams, errant, jovial, braggart, had always been his mother's favorite child. At his burial her reason snapped. Dan was head of the family now, the last male in his line, and in the days that followed he contemplated resigning to devote himself to Sarah Ann's care. His two younger sisters, with whom the mother lived, were virtually helpless. It was a time of great strain and personal anxiety for the physician. Even after his mother's reason returned, the strain did not lessen.

For, meantime, Dr. Charles Purvis had managed to create and win attention for the politics involved in Freedmen's. The time was ripe. Both major political parties had been thrown off balance by the Populist revolt of 1892, and neither had recovered fully. Populists, Democrats, and Republicans had "sought to win the Negro vote . . . and resorted to desperate means." Party lines were still blurred West and South. The Populists increased their total vote by 40 per cent in the congressional elections of 1894, while the Democrats, seriously split and unable to close ranks in the South, lost 25 per cent. The panic of 1893, which sent more than a hundred railroads into receivership, and the depression that spread through '94 and '95 put the country in a sullen mood. Politicians of both major parties knew that something must be done, or the power of doing anything might be taken out of their hands. The Democrats had no great strategist: they had only William Jennings Bryan. The Republicans had Marcus Alonzo Hanna. And Hanna had many people, including Negroes. The Democrats were routed in 1896. The Republicans swept back to power.

Purvis was a Republican who knew his way around the hustings (he had campaigned vigorously for McKinley) and the halls of Congress. There was an old congressional committee, set up to investigate "all charitable and reformatory institutions in the District," but it had grown moribund. Purvis thought the committee's work should be revived. The patronage that went to Negroes was in short supply, and one way to replenish it was to find cause to get rid of Negro Democrats in office. An investigation of Freedmen's might help to accomplish the trick. Purvis began knocking on congressional doors. He was, he said, not only a campaigning Republican, as everyone knew, but a deserving Republican, as all Negroes knew. It took him six months to get this subtlety across.

Meanwhile, however, he was not idle in other directions. In February 1897 the Washington *Bee* revealed that Dr. Purvis had been persuading Howard University medical students "to sign a paper against Dr. Williams"—perhaps, the *Bee* hinted, on pain of not being awarded their degrees. But Purvis had also put his persuasive powers to another use. Sporting as a figure of influence in the Republican party, he had convinced Dr. Dan's assistant and the director of nurses' training at Freedmen's that he, Purvis, could do for them what no one else could. Dr. William Warfield, the assistant, was incompetent; Miss Ebersole, chief of nurses, was aging and tired. Both had comfortable berths at Freedmen's, and both wished to stay on. In instance after instance during the subsequent investigation, Dr. Warfield and Miss Ebersole perjured themselves.

As the investigation dragged on and Purvis' trickery came to light, it seemed to Dr. Dan that politics of this kind soiled him personally and put his professional reputation at stake. Aided by white associates, who knew his worth to Freedmen's, he defended himself with all his force. Jeremiah Rankin, the president of Howard University, was the final key witness. He testified that Dr. Williams was "a choice man in the job, a first class surgeon," and that "everything he has done has been fully justified."

In spite of his complete exoneration by the congressional committee, Dr. Dan was tired and discouraged. Alice Johnson, the daughter of an ex-slave and the famous Jewish sculptor, Moses Jacob Ezekiel, had had her troubles too. Until the illness of her mother brought Dr. Williams into her home, she had isolated herself from society. She was proud of her father but ashamed of her illegitimacy which, since it had been no secret from her student days at Howard, was the subject of whispers and cruel taunts. Her uncommon beauty brought her insults, especially when, boarding the horsecars, she advertised her Negro blood by sitting where Negroes were forced to sit. White men followed her, molested her. She began to go heavily veiled. Finally she stayed home altogether.

The illness of her mother was the turning point in her life. She and Dr. Dan became friends. He brought her quietly among his own few social acquaintances, mostly temporary residents of Washington—the poet Dunbar, ex-Congressman John Langston and his family—and gave her a measure of protection she had never known. They had a quiet courtship. Alice hated Washington, and Dr. Dan could not be unmindful of this. Six weeks after he was exonerated he resigned from Freedmen's, and a few days later he and Alice Johnson were married. Dunbar wrote a "ditty" for the occasion.

> Step me now a bridal measure,
> Work give way to love and leisure,
> Hearts be free and hearts be gay—
> Dr. Dan doth wed today.
>
> . . . .
>
> 'Tis no time for things unsightly,
> Life's the day and life goes lightly;
> Science lays aside her sway—
> Love rules Dr. Dan today.
>
> . . . .
>
> So with blithe and happy hymning
> And with goblets harmless brimming,
> Dance a step— Musicians, play—
> Dr. Dan doth wed today.

The bridal couple read it as their train sped toward Chicago.

10. DIRTY WORK

Chicago was glad to have Daniel Hale Williams back. He had scarcely resettled there when professional demands upon him grew so heavy that he found himself with patients in five hospitals at once. Most of his patients were white, but they had to seek him out in his ghetto office, for he had not considered breaking off his identity with his race.

As a matter of fact he was even then engaged in a correspondence with Booker Washington, who, having visited Freedmen's the year before, had written, "I was not in your hospital two minutes before I saw, as I had never seen before, what you are." He had asked Dr. Dan to "come to Tuskegee for two or three days" to help set up "medical and nurse training departments." Exactly what the school principal had in mind the physician did not know, but his own ideas were solemn and grand. He wrote Washington about the building of a great medical center "to serve not only Tuskegee but thousands of those poor people who die for want of . . . attention."

This was too much for Washington, whose ambitions were completely organized around himself and who cared nothing for a medical center that might overshadow him and Tuskegee. Dr. Dan tried various approaches, all of them self-effacing, but Booker Washington knew that Daniel Hale Williams was a name of some luster and that it might shine more brightly than he cared to have shine the names of those associated with him. The "sage of Tuskegee" apparently had decided to drop the whole matter when Dr. Dan, still pursuing it, wrote, "When you come to Chicago, come to see us."

Booker Washington did come to Chicago in the fall of '98, but he did not see Dr. Dan. He penned a note saying that his "time was more than taken." He did not say that some of it was taken by the unctuous Dr. Hall.

The ghetto was beginning to sense itself as a cultural and ethnic unity. Striving for independence and self-respect, it nevertheless tested the flexibility of the surrounding white community by constant encroachments upon it, invading and absorbing when it could, resenting bitterly when it could not. The ghetto wanted to be two things at once: an imperium in imperio and an interrelated community of the city. It hated the repressive prejudice that threw it back upon itself, while at the same time it reveled in its self-sufficiency. A clangorous race chauvinism marked its every move, every event.

The ghetto was where Dr. Dan made his home, and where he believed in all conscience he belonged. If as a professional man he honored the obligation to offer his services to all alike, as a social being he felt a compulsive loyalty to the struggle for the community's advancement. "We need not be dependent on white people," he told his friend Charles Bentley. He resumed his place on the finance committee of Provident and his old post as chief surgeon. He gave his services free to the new Negro Old Folks' Home. The

Reverend Reverdy Ransom was making the first attempt at social settlement work among Negroes, and Dr. Dan gave his support to this, contributing money to the Institutional Church and Social Settlement, and free medical care to those members who could not pay for it. With a small group of Negroes, he helped to organize the United Brotherhood Fraternal Insurance Company.

But at the same time he wanted and needed the stimulation of new ideas and new professional knowledge, and this stimulation could come only from outside the race. There were not enough forward-looking Negro doctors in Chicago to provide it. Their only opportunities to keep abreast were through an alliance with Provident and through postgraduate courses at Northwestern University. But few could afford, in either time or money, postgraduate work. Their associations with advantaged white men in the profession were one-sided and tenuous. They were admitted to the Chicago Medical Society and could attend its discussions, but listening to papers was an entirely different thing from studying problems in the morgue and the laboratory, and from watching men at work on them in surgery. And this was what Dr. Dan wanted. He resumed the associations with white men that had been cut off by four years of absence.

That he was welcomed as a contributing member of the small vanguard of medicine soon became evident. His monographs began to appear in the *Chicago Medical Journal* and in the *Journal of Obstetrics* and to be reprinted in professional publications all over the country. He performed operations before growing numbers of surgeons at Provident, at St. Luke's, and at Mercy, and the colored papers were quick to point out that he was the first and (then) the only Negro to do so. He lectured to the Chicago Medical Society and to similar groups in distant cities, always insisting, however, that Negro physicians, too, be invited to hear him. In Dallas and other Southern cities he refused "to operate in lily-white hospitals." The *North Carolina Medical Journal* wrote soliciting a paper, but this Southern publication had been printing articles purporting to offer scientific proof that the shape of the Negro skull marked the race's inferiority. Dr. Williams took pleasure in replying that he was a Negro and "too busy just now to send an article."

He considered it an outrage to be looked upon as a Negro who had become exceptional by virtue of a skin color that indicated his white blood. "The color of the skin," he pointed out more than once, "furnishes no correct index" to anything. He believed that what colored men needed was opportunity. When opportunity came and they muffed it, he was dispirited.

Through acquaintances in Washington and through the Negro press he kept in touch with Freedmen's. Things had steadily deteriorated. The institution had been thrown to the political lions and had attracted the ambitions of men who were at once unscrupulous and mediocre. William Warfield, who had been Dr. Dan's assistant, was one of these. Though his own testimony before the congressional committee had proved him perfidious, he was perhaps less perfidious than Purvis and his political connections were just as strong; he had been chosen to run the hospital. But now the Negro press gave currency to an exciting rumor that there was to be a new national hospital for Negroes, the "modern Freedmen's." Architects' drawings were published; estimates were discussed. Dr. Dan was emboldened to write Booker Washington.

For by the early 1900s the principal of Tuskegee had become the virtual dictator of Negro affairs. He had been hoisted to this eminence by a group of powerful men—Baldwin, Carnegie, Frick, Huntington, Peabody, and Rockefeller—whose "psychology of materialism and reaction," as one historian points out, "dimmed the fervor of real American idealism" with a pretense that the alternative to the industrial control of wealth was chaos, and with the belief that private philanthropy was an adequate substitute for social justice and equality. In so far (and it was very far indeed) as Washington decried the Negro's participation in organized labor and politics, and in so far as he advocated extreme compromise in every situation that might upset the status quo, he was their man. He would help maintain the South's quiescence by keeping Negroes—the truly revolutionary force, the catalytic power—out of politics.

He would hold Negroes to the "Negro's place." He would assure industry's power over a recalcitrant white labor force by delivering a cheap, docile, and plentiful supply of Negro labor. He was the man for the great industrial barons, and they did right by him. They raised him to the nth degree of power over Negro affairs. From 1895 almost until his death in 1915, Booker Washington was "the umpire in all important appointments of Negroes; the channel through which philanthropy flowed, or did not flow, to Negro institutions; the creator and destroyer of careers; the maker and breaker of [Negro] men." "He was appealed to," wrote Mary White Ovington, "on any and every subject: how many bathrooms to put in a [colored] YMCA, whether or not to start a day nursery in some town, and so on." The so-called Tuskegee machine, which Washington built with great precision out of the talents of self-seeking men, ran with devilish efficiency on the fuel of his egomania.

Daniel Williams was quite naïve in some respects, but he was not alone in his ignorance of the fact that even when the deepest interests of the race were at stake Booker Washington was strictly committed to the quid pro quo. The worldly wise and somewhat cynical Mrs. S. Laing Williams told Dr. Dan this. She was amused by his shocked reaction. "You're so *nice*," she remarked lightly, and went on to tell him how her husband, a lawyer, wanted a position with the Chicago office of the Department of Justice, and Booker Washington wanted a stop to the critical attention he was getting in the Chicago Negro paper, the *Broad Ax*. Mrs. Williams was a journalist, and she knew the *Broad Ax* editor well: indeed, most of the unsigned pieces critical of Washington were her own. Soon the paper was printing her name over pieces "glowing with praise for the Wizard of Tuskegee." Mrs. Williams' husband got the job.

But all Dr. Dan had to offer Washington was a dedication to the welfare of their "common race," and he offered it.

"It would be a calemity," he wrote (he never learned to spell with consistent accuracy any but scientific terms), "to the whole aspiring race for the new Freedmen's to be put in charge of a mediocre man." He wished it to be unmistakably clear that he did not want the job himself, but he begged Washington to use his influence to see that only the best men were considered. "Now is the time when we can do much for our young men and women who are groping in the dark for leadership. They can do little for themselves without opportunity and guidance. . . . I am appealing to you for the interest of deserving men who will never know anything of this unselfish move on your part."

There were two things wrong with this. The "*we* can do much" was a phrase likely to jar on the sensitive ear of Booker Washington; and Washington did not want people whom he helped to be ignorant of the fact. His answer to Dr. Dan was noncommittal, and the matter might have stopped there but for a stroke of chance.

The most important cog in the Tuskegee machine was Washington's private secretary. Washington admitted that Emmett J. Scott was the only Negro in the country indispensable to him. Scott knew Washington better than his chief knew himself, and he had that nice combination of cynicism and personal loyalty that his job demanded and that Washington had an expert's eye for. Now Scott fell ill with appendicitis, and Washington wired Dr. Dan to come at once. Dr. Dan went, operated, and saved Scott to his chief. Dr. Dan had a quo for Washington's quid.

"It [Freedmen's] is too important for our men of science to be dealt out through favoritism," he wrote. "I want you to understand me. My interest is sincere, it is not for preferment. . . . I so much want your interest and help in this important matter, this one grand opportunity of our time, to finally develop an exceptional institution. If it is lost or carelessly handled, it will put our doctors and nurses back 25 years."

After a whole summer of silence came Washington's reply. He had been awaiting, he said, an opportunity to see the Secretary of the Interior. Now he had seen him, and the Secretary wished from him, Washington, "recommendations for the reorganization of Freedmen's." Would Dr. Dan send him by "return mail the names of six or eight colored doctors . . . the very highest and best. . . . Of course we want to include your name."

Dr. Dan did not include his own name, understandably, since not only was his pride involved but he had told the simple truth when he said he did not want to be considered for the position. But there was another name he left off the list, and Washington's response undoubtedly upset him: "Do you not think it a good idea to put Dr. Hall's name down? . . . Of course I understand the conditions surrounding him, but sometimes I find it pays to overcome littleness with bigness and to do our whole duty regardless of how people may feel toward us."

Dr. Dan assumed that he had been called upon to submit names because, as an officer of the National Medical Association, he was in a position to know the work of Negro physicians and who were best qualified among them. His sharply worded answer was in the nature of a rebuke to one who would accept standards lower than they should be.

"In selecting the names sent you, I drew upon my knowledge of what each individual had actually done to merit recognition, and not upon newspaper notoriety. I believe the names seldom appear in the Negro press, though they are powerful factors in race progress. They are doing something. . . . 'The man who is doing something,' quietly adding to the sum total. That is the man who can get my endorsement.

"I cannot say that I consider the party you named in that class. There is so much that you do not know and have no way of knowing.

"All the Gentlemen I named are not friends of mine . . . but I do know of their ability and honor, and assure you that they are men of such standing that I would be perfectly willing to serve with them. . . . And again, I want to impress most sincerely, Mr. Washington, that I am in this for the advancement of my people, to make conditions better for them, to prepare them for serious life work. I am serious in everything I undertake. If I go into this, it is not for social prestige or outside show. . . ."

But if there was much that Booker Washington did not know, there was considerably more that Dr. Dan himself had no way of knowing. He had no way of knowing that even during the yearlong course of this correspondence Booker Washington was in constant and intimate touch with George Hall. Slipping into Chicago, Washington would see Hall and his wife, Theodocia, without letting Dr. Dan know he was in the city. He became an intimate in the Hall household. Mrs. Hall did "little things" for him, and he called her "Teddie," though "only in private." He sent little gifts, sometimes to her alone, sometimes to both. She wrote Washington: "When the Dr. [Hall, her husband] returns he will find your delightful gift awaiting him. To say he will be pleased is putting it very mildly. The Dr. indulges in a sort of hero worship for the 'Wizard of Tuskegee,' you know, a condition to which the rest of the family must also plead guilty."

"Teddie" was as skillful in the arts of ingratiation as her husband, and her husband had proved very skillful indeed.

He had used his skill at Provident during Dr. Dan's absence. He had attained only slight professional advancement there, it is true, but he was crafty and devious in a way that only his Negro colleagues understood and, in the delicate nature of co-operative relations between Negro and white, dared not expose. He got on well with the white people who counted on the supervisory council and the staff. He was more careful not to be wrong than to be right on principle. He did not press his ambitions openly, but seemed desirous only to be helpful. He smiled and flattered and went along. When a vacancy occurred on the board, he was named to it, and he greased his way onto the powerful executive committee of that body. Finally promoted to the department of gynecology, where "he was permitted to do uncomplicated surgery on hernia," he presented himself to the public as the medical rival of Dr. Dan.

Not many Negroes knew better. Booker Washington invited him to Tuskegee to lecture. He went to Georgia and South Carolina to set up clinics and to operate in them. (Not one of the clinics lasted a year.) Once at a demonstration in Birmingham, Alabama, "a country doctor had to take over Hall's operation to save the patient's life."

But when the *Tuskegee Student*, Booker Washington's nationally distributed paper, edited by Emmett Scott, carried a laudatory article on Daniel Hale Williams, Hall wrote the principal:

"My grievance is the use the *Student* is put to, exploiting a man whose professional rivalry with me is known to you and to everyone around Tuskegee. . . . When my friends, on whom he has taken special pains to impress how important he is to you at Tuskegee, asked me about it, I said it was not true. So you can well imagine I was embarrassed beyond all measure when there appeared in the *Student* a column and a half of Appreciation of this great man!"

Of course, Dr. Dan did not know about this either. Involved as he was in many professional commitments, he was not especially aware of how "Hall was pushing himself into the [administrative] routine of Provident." Nor did he have any way of knowing that, while Hall was nourishing his own reputation for loyalty to the ghetto and to the race, he was destroying Dr. Dan's bit by bit. He did it mainly by hint and innuendo, but he was also known to remark that "That fair-complexioned fellow doesn't seem to know what race he wants to belong to," and to ask, as if in disinterested curiosity, "Do dark colored people ever go to the Williamses'?"

It was easy to make such insinuations stick. The Williamses' social acquaintances were of the mixed-blood world. Besides, Dr. Dan's professional life took him daily into the white world, and it would have been strange indeed if the white world did not sometimes figure in his social life. His white colleagues liked him as a person. Some of them did not know he was a Negro. So wide was the gap between white and black that they could not conceive of a "colored" man of such great professional skill and reputation. "I was well acquainted with him for two years before I knew he was colored," wrote Dr. J. Wyllys Andrews.

Dr. Dan was vulnerable, and Hall made the most of it. Again he wrote Booker Washington: "When I think of my unquestioned well-known stand for Tuskegee and all concerned, in Chicago and everywhere, as compared with one who has never opened his mouth in public to advocate the school or the policy of its principal, I think I have every right to seriously object . . ."

But the principal was playing some game of his own. He answered Hall, ". . . When I am in Chicago I shall hope to have the privilege of talking to you and of telling you more in detail just how I feel toward you." But in that same week he also, at long last, answered Dr. Dan: "For the present, let the whole matter concerning the party [Hall] about whom I wrote you pass out of your mind. Nothing has been said or done to obligate me to anyone else in the matter, and there is no special reason why he should be taken up just now at least."

When the special reason came, it was political.

11. RESIGNATION

Having served more than three years of the term of the assassinated McKinley, Theodore Roosevelt wanted to be elected President in his own right in 1904. He had been a hero to Negroes during and just after the Spanish-American War. In a speech during his campaign for the governorship of New York, Roosevelt had quoted one of the officers who had served with him in the war, " 'Well, the 9th and 10th [Cavalry] men are all right. They can drink out of our canteens,' " and he had added on his own, "I don't think that any Rough Rider will ever forget the tie that binds us to the 9th and 10th Cavalry." Such remarks earned him a majestic reputation among Negroes: his voice drew all ears.

Once safely in the governor's mansion, however, he changed his tune. He wrote in an article for *Scribner's* magazine, "They [Negro soldiers] are, of course, peculiarly dependent on their white officers. . . . None of the white regulars or Rough Riders showed the slightest sign of weakening; but under the strain the colored infantrymen began to get a little uneasy and to drift to the rear."

Negro newspapers crackled with outrage. Teddy was a hero no longer. He was instead "a turncoat," "a treacherous friend," who, as one Negro paper put it, "grins and grins and stabs you in the back."

Roosevelt tried to regain his status with the race. Within a month after succeeding McKinley he entertained Booker Washington at lunch in the White House. Negroes were "delighted at this signal recognition," and delighted the more because it "shocked, boiled . . . and exasperated the South." Two years later Roosevelt exasperated the South again by appointing a Negro as collector of the port at Charleston and declaring that "color was no sufficient reason to keep a good man from office." He would not, he said, "close the door of hope" to any American citizen. It helped.

But, in the election of 1904, Roosevelt's Democratic opponent, Alton B. Parker, presented a claim to the Negro's allegiance. Descended from an old anti-slavery family, the New York jurist had stood up for "Negro rights," and his endorsement by a scattering of the Negro press indicated at least that Northern Negro voters were no longer "blind Republicans." In order to line up the Negro vote, Roosevelt needed the active support of Booker Washington; and Washington, of course, wanted the added power and prestige he could derive from the President.

Washington himself called on the help of George Hall, who had organized and now bossed the Chicago ghetto's Hyde Park Republican Club. Aided by Hall, Washington managed to swing the Chicago *Bee* to Roosevelt. He bought out the Chicago *Conservator*, another Negro opposition paper, and put his own men in control. Washington complained to Hall about a certain Negro reporter, and Hall replied: "If you will just leave that newspaper reporter to me, I think when I get through he will be good. He is hugging me now to save himself and I am sawing off his limb close to the tree." Hall sawed off many limbs, and Booker Washington showed proper gratitude.

For, once Roosevelt was elected, the principal of Tuskegee set about to promote Hall's name far beyond the limits of Chicago's Negro community. "Send me," he urged, "your best photograph, put in the most prominent and successful operations you have performed. I can use these in a way to be of great service." The piece his public relations staff subsequently put out appeared in thirty-five Negro newspapers, a dozen of which had national distribution.

Then, skillfully timed to ride this wave of publicity, a rumor floated up from Washington, D.C. The principal of Tuskegee was strongly endorsing a Chicago physician for surgeon in chief at the new Freedmen's. Though everyone seemed to surmise that the Chicago physician was Hall, professional men who were acquainted with him and knew his mediocrity as a surgeon and physician could scarcely credit it. Dr. Dan knew no more than the rumors and the surmises. No letters concerning Freedmen's, or anything else, had passed between him and Booker Washington for months. Long since discouraged over the misuse of "the one great opportunity of our time to be of service," Dr. Dan shut the matter from his mind.

Moreover, he was very busy. His reputation was such that he was called as far west as North Dakota to perform surgery on a mining millionaire, and east to New York to attend a bishop of the Episcopal Church. Once a year he went to lecture and hold clinics, without fee, at the Negro Meharry Medical College (in Nashville, Tennessee) and other places in the South. He was still surgeon in chief at Provident, where his operations drew crowds of other surgeons. But he was finding it increasingly difficult to work at Provident. Hall had gained administrative power there. Dr. Dan's private patients were given short shrift and treated with little discourtesies. "The operating room would not be ready [for him]. Nurses would not be detailed to him."

But the professional esteem in which Dan Williams was held increased rather than lessened. In 1908, Negro doctors from all over the country gathered at a banquet in Chicago to celebrate Dr. Dan's twenty-fifth year in medicine. There were gifts from individuals and from groups. There was a silver bowl engraved with the names of thirty-seven Chicago physicians, white and colored, but George Hall's name was not among them. He had responded to Dr. Carl Robert's invitation to join in honoring Dr. Dan, "Curse him! I'll punish him worse than God ever will. I'll see he's forgotten before he's dead!"

And the circumstance that Hall seized as the opportunity to start, he thought, his "rival's" name toward oblivion was the very circumstance that signalized at the time the highest recognition of Dr. Dan's skill.

Dr. Dan was appointed associate attending surgeon at St. Luke's, an honor no other member of his race would attain for a quarter of a century after his death. He entered upon his duties at once. Though these duties required a reorganization of his private schedule, they in no way interfered with his other work; but Hall persuaded the Provident board that Dr. Dan's acceptance of the St. Luke's appointment was "an act of disloyalty to the Negro race." The board ordered Dr. Dan to bring all of his patients, "rich and poor, black and white," to Provident. The order was absurd. In the light of Dr. Dan's career, it was an outrage.

Daniel Hale Williams resigned from Provident. He did more—he resigned from the Negro race.

12. RESIGNATION RESCINDED

The old man had not stirred for a long time. His nerveless hands lay helpless on the blanket that swathed his legs. His eyes were closed, but should he open them he would see across a tiny bit of lake to the woods that half encircled this retreat in northern Michigan. In the later afternoon a woman came out onto the screened porch, tipped across it, and gently snugged in a corner of the old man's blanket. It was a kind of ritual, and when she heard the usual "I'm not 'sleep," the woman smiled. She was a German woman, and she had been the old man's housekeeper since his wife died in 1921. Now it was 1926.

"I'm bringing the post," the woman said, holding up a packet of letters.

"Margaret, you're not bringing," the old man said. "You're already here. Won't you ever learn English?"

But Margaret knew English very well, for now, as she had done for several months, she opened the letters and began to read. "Dear Dr. Dan . . ." or "Dear Dan . . ." There were some twenty letters, all from fellow members of the American College of Surgeons—

Coleman Buford, Cary Culbertson, William Fuller, Willie Mayo—
of which the old man was a charter member. The housekeeper's
voice went on and on, and suddenly Dan Williams interrupted her.

"Margaret, tomorrow," he said, "we must have that lawyer out
from town. It's time I made my will."

When the will was opened five years later it was seen to contain
the following bequests: medical books to the Mercy (Negro) Hospital of Philadelphia; two thousand dollars for the operating room of
a new interracial hospital on Chicago's south side; five thousand
dollars each to Meharry (Negro) and Howard (Negro) Medical
Schools, "to be used for impoverished students"; eight thousand
dollars to the National Association for the Advancement of Colored
People.

PART THREE

Men in Motion

CHAPTER SEVEN

Paths to the Future

1. "NIGGER DEMUS"

WHILE IT WAS quite possible to set up limits, material and ideological, to the Negro's physical penetration of the white environment, it was something else again to curb a cultural tide. And that tide was rising. Though it had its unnoted beginnings in the preconscious days of slavery, the rise was marked by a convenient date—1879. Then it was that the Fisk Jubilee Singers set out to bring to the attention of the world those Negro songs called "spirituals." Then it was, too, that an aging Negro opened the floodgates through which poured and pounded northward, eastward, westward thousands of his people, bringing with them their sorrows and their songs, their laughter and laments, and their incomparable quality as agents of social change.

Being unlearned, Benjamin Singleton understood only a part of what he did, but the Senate committee that called him to testify in 1880 probably understood even less. Indeed, the committee saw only the political issues involved in the migration, which they thought, and tried to prove, was a Republican plot to discredit Southern Democrats and lessen Southern representation in Congress. The committee thought that "Pap" Singleton, perhaps unwittingly, was a tool in devilish hands. But, "No," the old man told them, "I was the whole cause of the migration. Nobody but me."

This of course was not the whole truth, for the whole truth involved—as Southern Democrats well knew—fraud, violence, and murder. "If I votes the Republican ticket," one Southern Negro swore in evidence, "I wakes up nex' mornin' in the graveyard." Seventeen hundred pages of testimony affirmed the likelihood of this and, without knowing it, so did Pap Singleton. "I am the Moses of the colored exodus," he declared. And he was—a leader who embodied the longings and the restless strivings of his people and who, before his work was done, led eighty thousand of them westward from "the land of night" toward the Kansas sun.

They went singing:

> We have Mr. Singleton for our president. He will go on
>   before us and lead us through. . . .
> Marching along, yes, we are marching along.

Mistaking the biblical Nicodemus for Nigger Demus, they sang:

> Nigger Demus was a slave of African birth,
> And was bought for a bag full of gold.
> He was reckoned a part of the salt of the earth,
> But he died years ago, very old.
>
> Good time coming, good time coming,
> Long, long time on the way. . . .

They sang for themselves, as folk do everywhere, and no more than they themselves did others guess that the songs they sang— their rhythms and their moods—would be originative of forms and modes far above the level of "folk" and would, in time, fix the cultural identity of America for the rest of the world.

At the moment, since these were "nigger songs," they were of no account. They did not meet the sacred standards of taste fawned on by men who had come back from Europe with costly copies of the graphic masters, who had read the songs of Scott and Byron with streaming eyes, and who (for all their claim to wide learning and broad aesthetic judgment) did not sense in these songs of wandering, of labor, of sorrow, and of joy the epitome of what they themselves had made and the essence of the culture they had produced. Nor did they hear in them the sounds of the life they had begot or—since this surely was the hardest thing of all—recognize them as specifics against the very thing they most feared—the revolutionary intransigence of five million blacks. For the truth was, of course, that these songs had their provenance in the heart of time and place, and this "nigger music" laid a grip upon realities that were constantly denied. And to be appreciated, the songs and music had finally to go from the world that made them into a world that they would shape.

But since realities cannot be denied forever, it is no wonder that a young Negro who heard these songs for the first time when he was seventeen should recognize them instantly "as of me and mine," and should, when he came to write the first book of his private revolution, head each chapter with a bar of this dark music. Nor should it surpass credit that a young printer with a face like night, hearing this music in all the many-timbred sonances of a massive Negro choir, did "weep and also feel exalted as by the might of angels."

2. LESS THAN ENOUGH

Though they were born in the same year, 1868, William Burghardt Du Bois and Robert Sengstacke Abbott were as different as parentage, background and training could make them. Their only point of resemblance was negative: neither looked like the "men of war" in the Negro song both loved.

Small though strong of frame and feature, Du Bois bore clear traces of his French Huguenot lineage. His forehead was broad, his nose fine-chiseled, and his lips thin in a sharply tapering amber-colored face. Abbott was so black of skin that it was once remarked that if he were cut he would "bleed ink." His ancestry was pure Ibo. His face was a flat plane over which his nose spread like thick molasses to the heaped mound of his lips. Heavy-fleshed and squat, he had the hammered-down look of primitive African statuary. Du Bois was flame blown on by jets of air. Abbott was flesh oppressed by brooding midnight. One was excitation and intellect. The other was solemnity, intuition, and lumbering brain. If neither man looked like men of war, both were to prove themselves such men.

Du Bois was the first. Descendant on his mother's side of those brown-skinned, Dutch-speaking Burghardts who had come through the western passes from the Hudson to the valley of the Housatonic, who had in time fought in the Revolution and the War of 1812, meanwhile establishing farms and families, Du Bois was reared to a sense of independence, and revolt was in his blood. His paternal grandfather, Alexander Du Bois, lived many years, and from this old man, who still gave certain words the sound of French, William heard snatches of Alexander's life.

He had been born in the Bahamas of a rich bachelor and a mulatto slave and brought to America and enrolled in the Cheshire School, but upon the death of his father, who left no will, the white Du Boises had dropped him to fend for himself. They told him he was "colored," and so he sought a colored country, Haiti, to "learn in pride the meaning of the word." He learned it. Returning to the United States, he revolted against the white Episcopal parish in New Haven and shaped more to his liking a new "colored" parish named St. Luke's.

The grandson, William, learned early that he himself was "different from other children." The difference did not matter much in Great Barrington, Massachusetts, at first. He played with white companions (there were no other Negro children) on the hills and in the river. He had a lively imagination, he could think of things to do, and he was, it seems, the leader of the town's gang of schoolboys, and perfectly at home in the town's best houses.

But when he entered high school he discovered that the parents of some of his schoolmates considered his brown skin a misfortune. He grimly determined to show them it was not. His temper quickened, hardened. The irascibility that later marked the man and was called "airs" and "insolence" must have entered him then. He excelled in his studies. He was "spurred to tireless effort." Though he did not have the physique for sports, he did well in them. Winning the first of many scholarships, he declared his wish to go to Harvard and was told that his place was in the South among "his people." He rebelled, and brooded for six months, but by a sudden "miracle of emotion" he felt "part of a mightier mission." He enrolled at Fisk.

Fisk University in Nashville, Tennessee, was his first experience of the Negro world. The whole "gorgeous color gamut" of it excited him nearly to delirium. Girls and boys of a species he had never known left him tongue-tied and dreaming "boastful dreams" of great remedies for the sickness of the world. For already he knew the world was sick. He heard the Negro folk songs and was "thrilled and moved to tears." Studying under white teachers too wise, honest, and noble to flaunt the role of missionaries, and living, learning, and larking with "darkly delicious" young men and women, if Du Bois felt that he was experiencing the best of two worlds, he did not shun the worst of either.

In two summer vacations he went deep into rural Tennessee and taught a Negro school. He saw the galling, unrewarding drudgery of Negro country life, the wrenched and wretched existence of Negro peasants. He sensed the "senseless cruelty" of a social system controlled—often exclusively controlled—by ignorant white men. He saw, he said, the race problem at nearly its lowest terms. Nothing had prepared him. In his senior year at Fisk he crammed in history, politics, and economics. Harvard offered scholarships in the South that year, and Du Bois applied for one. He was astonished when he got it.

He was twenty when he entered Harvard in the junior class. He knew what he wanted and where he could get it, and he went straight to Albert Bushnell Hart in history, William James in psychology, Santayana in philosophy, Barrett Wendell in English, and George Herbert Palmer in social problems—this last being as close, in 1888, as Harvard got to sociology. If some of his classmates also had something to offer, Du Bois did not share it. Herbert Croly, Augustus Hand, Norman Hapgood, and Robert Herrick were of the class of 1890, but Du Bois met none of them. Having come to Harvard by way of Fisk, he knew what he knew. And he knew that to accept the social limitations that a still provincial college society imposed upon Negroes, Jews, Catholic Irish, and Chinese was not to excuse them.

Besides, he did not lack social life. In nearby colleges were other Negro students, and on one memorable occasion he joined with them to perform Aristophanes' *The Birds* in a colored church. He had other satisfactions too—in the semisocial relations of the Philosophical Club, where Josiah Royce sometimes dropped in for tea; in having his papers read or cited by Wendell in English 12, and his work publicly commended by William James, at whose home he was more than once a guest. Professor Hart also had him for dinner. These giants in the Harvard faculty endorsed his application for a Rogers graduate fellowship.

But after two years of Harvard College and two years as a graduate fellow there, Du Bois was still unsatisfied. He had far more education than most young white men, but he felt that he had not had enough. At work on his master's thesis, *The Suppression of the Slave Trade*, he had conceived, however vaguely, a notion of his mission—that "mightier mission" of which he felt a part. He was going to raze the barriers of race. He saw this as "a matter of knowledge; as a matter of scientific procedure." His view of it seemed all the more valid in that day when the German ideal of scholarship was much sought after. Urged by their German-trained teachers, hundreds of American students rushed to Germany to acquire the laboratory habit of mind. Among Du Bois' own teachers, Palmer, Royce, and James had studied there. Du Bois was constantly reminded that German methods of investigating the phenomena of social existence were responsible for establishing such fields as political science, sociology, and history on a modern basis in America.

The Slater Fund "for uplifting the lately emancipated" had been established in 1882, and its income had been used to promote industrial and vocational training among Negroes. But in 1890 the chairman of its board had said: "If there is any young colored man whom we find to have . . . any special aptitude for study, we are willing to give him money from the educational funds to send him to Europe or give him an advanced education. . . . So far we have found only orators."

Whether or not this was a nasty oblique personal fling at him (since he had won prizes and attention for public speaking at Harvard), Du Bois rose as to a challenge. He applied to the Slater Fund. The chairman, ex-President Hayes, answered that he had been misquoted—that the fund had no plans for such aid. But Du Bois was not to be rebuffed. Gathering letters of recommendation from his most influential professors, and writing a clearly impudent letter of his own, he reapplied. Days of silence were followed by a fresh bombardment of letters from everyone he "knew in the Harvard Yard and places outside." Finally he was granted a fellowship "to study at least a year abroad under the direction of the graduate department of Harvard."

In 1892 he registered in the University of Berlin and was temporarily dizzied by a wealth of resources and dazzled by slants of intellectual light for which not even Harvard had prepared him. He was admitted to the seminars of Wagner and Schmoller in economics and the fiery Von Treitschke in history. The meaning of his knowledge underwent radical changes. The intellectual conformity and the conventional patterns of thought he had acquired at Harvard began to dissolve. Habitual premises were susceptible of revision; truth was not final. Having heard Von Treitschke—soon to be censured by young Wilhelm II—thunder that the European push into Africa should not be looked upon as "the advance of civilization and the tutelage of barbarians," Du Bois could no longer think of the little old woman of Windsor as a magnificent symbol of noble empire dedicated to guiding the colored peoples of the earth to Christianity and higher culture. New contours of thought began to form and alter the landscape of his mind, modify the perspectives of history. Perhaps above all he came to see the "race problem" as

a world social problem and to sense its connection with the politi-
cal-economic development of Europe.

Du Bois studied and also he traveled. Every break from books and
lectures found him going to some new place. He went to the south
of Germany, to Italy, France; east to Austria-Hungary, Czechoslovakia, Poland; north to Sweden, Denmark, Norway. In Holland he
talked with natives of Borneo, in France with Cameroon and Al-
gerian blacks, in England with Indians. The designation "colored"
came to mean "a greater, broader sense of humanity and world-
fellowship."

But two years of study and travel were all he could afford; were,
indeed, more than his fellowship allowed, and in 1894, sporting a
beard and carrying a cane, he came back from Europe. Harvard
granted him the Ph.D.

Now twenty-seven, he felt ready for his life's work, which he conceived as "putting science into sociology." He was going to face the
facts, "any and all facts . . . of the racial world," and study and
present them. His object was uplift and reform.

3. MIXED BLOOD

Robert Sengstacke Abbott was an altogether different breed. Though he was described as shrewd, calculating, and
"tight with guile," the facts dispute the estimate. His mind was not
equipped to deal with subtleties. The formal education he managed
to acquire was not of much use to him. In middle life he was called
a demagogue and dangerous—"like a monkey with a shotgun,"
Julius Rosenwald said, "who will hurt anybody." But he was more
hurt than hurting, and his demagoguery, if this is what it can be
called, had in it more of pathos than of calculating sense. He was
not the son of his father.

Born in a cabin on the crummy edge of a Georgia plantation,
Robert Abbott spent much of his life trying to live down the op-
probrious term "Geechee." It was an epithet that conjured up in the
Negro mind the storied attributes of the lowest slave type, the ig-

norant "field nigger," with a dull and stupid mind, gross habits, and primitive passions beyond control. And it was unfair. Robert's father, Tom, had been Charles Stevens' trusted boss house slave, the envy of other slaves for miles around. The esteem in which the Stevenses held him is attested by the fact that when freedom came they gave him a cabin and a plot of ground, and when he died in 1869 they buried him in their own graveyard.

And by that time, in the common opinion, Tom had deserved less. He had gone off to Savannah and abused his freedom. Nearly fifty years old and still unmarried, he had played city sport, lived by his wits and on his gracious white-folks manners, which attracted, among others, Flora Butler, a hairdresser and ladies' maid at the Savannah theater. But Flora was not a frivolous, easy woman. She would settle for nothing less than marriage to a man who had a job and "common decency." Tom pled and promised and, when they were married, took Flora to his cabin and plot of ground on St. Simon's Island. Farming, however, was beneath him. He converted the front room of his cabin into a store. In the room behind it Robert was born only five months before Tom died of "galloping consumption."

Flora was more durable. Free since childhood, she had become a skilled hairdresser and an expert seamstress, but no one on St. Simon's had a need for her services, and after the death of Tom she took her infant son and returned to Savannah, where she readily found employment among the wives of the German shopkeepers with whom she became a favorite by picking up a speaking knowledge of their language. This favoritism proved timely. She had been settled in the city only a few months when Tom Abbott's sister, alleging Flora to be an unfit mother, brought suit for the custody of the child. The Germans came to Flora's support, and one of them, John H. H. Sengstacke, engaged a lawyer who successfully defended her.

Sengstacke had had dealings with lawyers and lawsuits. His short history in America was thorny with legal tangles. White to all appearances, and German-reared, he was born the son of an immigrant father and a slave girl. When the mother died at the birth of a second child, his father took his two mulatto children to Germany to be reared by his sister. The father himself returned to the States in 1850, prospered in the mercantile trade, regularly remitted money for the support of his children, and died in 1862. He left a will that amply secured his offspring, but his white executors ignored it, for after his death no money from the estate, estimated at fifty thousand dollars, ever reached Germany. The son came to America to investigate in 1869.

John H. Hermann Sengstacke was an educated man, fluent in five languages—just the man for the job of translator for the Savannah *Morning News*. But in the course of pushing his claim to his father's estate he had to reveal the fact of his Negro blood. He was fired. Thereafter some of his father's old friends treated him with contempt. Completely unprepared for this betrayal of old loyalties and this ravishment of his personal dignity, by the time he was financially able to escape to Germany he had perforce identified himself with the Negro race, and he decided to remain. The experience of his Negroness left deep scars. Already there was something of the messiah in him, and something of the masochist. When the dwindled estate was finally settled he came to the conclusion—at once bitter torment and solace—that since he was a Negro he was lucky to salvage two or three thousand dollars, a small frame house, and a store-front building on a bluff in the western section of Savannah.

This was the man who married Flora Abbott in 1874 and gave his name not only to the seven children he begot but to his stepson as well. This was the man who, with the burning ardor of the ancient Christian convert, embraced with passion the scabrous cross of his Negroness and staggered under it with mad delight.

Ordained a minister of the Congregational Church and appointed a teacher in a rural Negro school, he also undertook to publish, edit, and sustain a Negro newspaper. As a preacher-teacher he earned altogether forty dollars a month. His church had few members, and these were so poor that they "could pay," he reported,

"only one dollar towards his whole year's salary." Yet he alienated
some of these and expelled others for belonging to secret societies.
His school had no books, no blackboards, no pencils, no stove. He
wrote his newspaper copy in longhand—all of it. "We labor under
great disadvantages," he informed a friend. And indeed he did.
Eventually the disadvantages became willful malignities offered to
him personally. He saw the grim red finger of malice pointing at him
from every quarter. He saw himself as a Negro persecuted not only
by society but by individuals. The world was against the Sengstackes. The world was against him.

4. "EVERYBODY ALWAYS PICKED ON HIM"

If this was the spirit of Robert's training at home
and in his father's school, it was given substance by his earliest
experiences at Beach Institute. This was a day school founded by
the Freedmen's Bureau but supported by the American Missionary
Society. In Savannah, as in other urban centers in those days, there
was a Negro color caste as rigid as iron. Mulattoes, as we have seen,
were generally the privileged and the exclusive. They had their own
churches, their own social clubs. Only mulattoes were normally
expected to go to school beyond the second or third grade.

Robert was as black as tar. The prejudice of his light-skinned
schoolmates at Beach was cruel to an extreme possible only to
adolescents. They dubbed him "Liver Lips," "Tar Baby," and
"Crow." Their malevolence undoubtedly generated the unconscious
self-hatred that was one of the twisted, ruling passions of Abbott's
life—that made him shun the color black even in clothes and cars;
that made him dun Negro fraternal organizations to use the white-
ball as the symbol of rejection, and plaster black Chicago with
slogans urging Negroes to "Go to a White Church on Sunday."

Only Joseph and Catharine Scarborough were not unkind to him
at Beach, and if this was more out of respect for their father's friendship with the Reverend John H. H. Sengstacke than friendly regard
for Robert, the latter did not sense it. Indeed, he fell in love with

Catharine—he was seventeen at the time—and courted her for nearly thirty years. In 1897 he asked her to marry him, but her father was "outraged" at the black man's presumption, and Catharine declined the honor. In 1918, when she had twice been widowed by ne'er-do-well mulatto husbands, Catharine finally agreed to marry him. He was by then a millionaire, but even as he prepared to go to her in Savannah she wrote that she had changed her mind.

But all this was in the future in 1886. What was in the present was the intolerable weight of obloquy and the crushing blows to his self-esteem. He did not cry out aloud. Instead he adopted a system of attitudes—not principles of conduct or principles of ethics —informed only by a defensive spirit, which served him the rest of his life. And the chief of these was patient meekness. In some ways it was as false as Uriah Heep's—and to much the same purpose.

To the disappointment of his stepfather, Robert retreated from Beach after less than two full terms. He dreamed of Hampton, in Virginia, but when his stepfather suggested Claflin University, a hundred miles from his home, he pretended enthusiasm for that place and agreed to work his way through that institution's equivalent of high school. He stayed six months. He was nineteen and still separated from his future by a vast ignorance. Another year went by before Hampton accepted him "conditionally" to study the printing craft.

At Hampton, it is reported, "everybody always picked on him." His hangdog mien and his genuine feelings of inferiority invited it. He was the butt of crude, practical, and sometimes vicious jokes. He probably resented them, but he was too patient, too hungry for acceptance, and too cowardly to protest. Driven to the other extreme at times, he tried to bluster through class recitations, but his dull mind was no help to him, and he invariably made a fool of himself.

He did no better socially. The same prejudice, though degrees milder, that plagued him at Beach prevailed at Hampton, and, inept to begin with, Robert had no success in the highly formalized and rigidly controlled social life of the campus. He was not asked to join the intimate bull sessions. He got no invitations to parties. Girls ignored him, and one of his classmates told him, half in jest, that he was "too black to associate with fair women."

Ironically enough, his black skin did bring him one distinction. Toward the end of his first year he was chosen as a member of the Hampton Quartet. But this was not because his tenor voice was the best that could be found. It was because "white people resented seeing light-complexioned boys in the group"; because Hampton's white administrators knew the emotional impact that "four black boys forlornly singing spirituals" had on white audiences; and because white audiences were the targets of the school's financial appeals. Abbott had a good voice, and he sang the sorrow songs with feeling, but not even the distinction of becoming a member of the quartet in his first year suggested that, next to Booker T. Washington, he would one day be the school's best-known graduate. It took some students five years to complete the four-year course. Abbott required seven.

He was twenty-seven when he graduated and accepted a teaching post in a school on the outskirts of Savannah. Soon he was supplementing his income with part-time work as a printer. He was not very good in either job, and both together did not provide enough for him to court Catharine Scarborough in the manner he thought she deserved. Rivalry for that lady's attentions was keen, and when she rejected his first proposal Abbott felt that the odds were against him. His rivals, though scarcely more affluent than he, were light-skinned. Perhaps if he could get money he could overcome the handicap of his color, equalize the competition. But how get money? His stepfather's example proved that money was not in teaching or preaching. Even the printer's craft offered scant returns to a black man in Georgia. Perhaps in another state—a city in the North—he could use his vocation as a steppingstone "to higher things." After presenting Miss Scarborough with a handsome gold watch in the summer of 1897, he still had enough money to support himself while he explored.

He went to Chicago. When the Hampton Quartet had sung there at the World's Fair four years earlier, Abbott had been awed by the conspicuous display of Negro wealth and achievement. Now almost at once he wrote home, "I will stay out west and try to make a fortune."

But fortunes were not easily made, and he did not know how to begin. He managed to obtain part-time employment as a printer, but earning "real money" at his trade looked no more promising in Chicago than it had in Savannah. It did not take him long to discover that the men to emulate, the men whose names were spoken with deference along State Street and Dearborn Street, were either independent businessmen or professionals. Daniel Hale Williams was a physician and surgeon, Charles Smiley a caterer, Edward Morris a lawyer, and John Jones, who was still remembered as the first Negro to hold public office in Chicago, had been a wealthy merchant tailor. These men were of the status to which Abbott aspired. His ambition was uninformed by any idea of service or any dedication to large purposes. He wanted simply to "accomplish *something* noteworthy"; he wanted—as a later phrase had it—to be a big shot.

He tried to find ways into the closed circle of the elite. He joined the Grace Presbyterian Church where the elite went. He sacrificed necessities to buy admission to the charity balls given for the benefit of Provident Hospital and the Institutional Social Settlement. No one paid the slightest attention to him. For all that he had been a member of the Hampton Quartet and had a better than passable tenor voice, his bid to join the choir of Grace Presbyterian Church was rejected. He was black, and his speech gave him away as one of those "new-come Southern darkies" who were "spoiling things" for long-time residents of the North. Every rebuff fed his passion to "show them" and increased his torment to "make his mark," no matter how. He wrote his mother, "Tell father if he will back me, I will . . . run a paper. . . . Let me know his intentions before I begin to make up my mind as to what steps to take."

The Reverend Mr. Sengstacke, undoubtedly recalling his own costly experience, advised against the newspaper but seemed willing enough to back his stepson in another line, for in the fall of 1898 Robert enrolled in the evening classes of the Kent College of Law.

Now for the first time he dropped Sengstacke as a surname and put himself on record as Robert S. Abbott. It is reported that when his stepfather heard of this he wept.

If Robert S. Abbott also wept, it was for other reasons. He had a better than average capacity for self-pity, and later he was to write of this period that he "probably would have starved to death but for the generosity of some folk who would loan me a dime now and then. Even when I did work I did not earn enough to pay back rent, repay loans and eat. . . ."

Somehow, though, he managed to get through law school, only to be advised by the light-skinned lawyer Edward Morris, to whom he went for encouragement and help, that he was "too dark to make any impression on the courts in Chicago." As a matter of fact, Abbott failed to pass the Illinois bar. He was told that Indiana was easier, and he moved to Gary. He went on to Topeka, Kansas. The story was the same. When he returned to Chicago in 1903, all he had to show for five years of painful effort was a contract as Chicago distributor of the national Negro weekly, the *Kansas Plaindealer*. He was thirty-three, and all the pathways to fulfillment seemed blocked against him, but he was as obdurate as stone.

He did not look like a man in whom the fires of worldly ambition burned with corroding intensity. Stubby, dour-faced, he affected semiclerical garb, poor but neat: patched white shirt with celluloid collar and white string tie, a blue suit turning green with age, shoes lined with paper. Indeed, he seemed the exact copy of a pastor of a small, earnest fundamentalist sect. He did not play cards, or smoke (though he was to acquire the habit of fifty-cent cigars later), or drink.

Excluded from the "best" society, he shunned the worst, and made his acquaintances among that emerging middle class of decent domestic servants, small tradesmen, part-time lawyers, and night-time doctors who were becoming extremely vocal on such subjects as race discrimination, Negro rights, and Negro solidarity, and who, under the leadership of Louis B. Anderson and George Hall, were learning the uses of political power even as they slowly acquired it.

Abbott joined their social groups, earned a part of his precarious living doing their printing jobs on borrowed presses, and took part in their discussions. They liked him, and he liked them. Among them he did not have to live down his blackness; he had rather to live up to it. Other qualities began to peep from beneath the cloak of his patient humility. He had gratitude. He could be depended on. He had insinuating kindliness of spirit. He counted among these people—counted enough for them to exert their political influence to get him a job in a printing firm that did the work of the city government.

It was among this middle-class-in-emergence, too, that he again broached the idea of starting a newspaper. The more intelligent could not see it, and would not help him, and told him so. There were already three Negro newspapers in Chicago—the *Conservator*, the *Broad Ax*, and the *Illinois Idea*—and none of them was a financial success. There was no need for yet another paper. But Abbott thought otherwise, and he backed his thinking with an inspired argument—his friends and acquaintances had no voice. The social historian, Roi Ottley, notes that existing papers "were primarily vehicles for the editors to expound their views . . . and advance their personal political ambitions." Abbott's acquaintances were never mentioned in them. Their births, their weddings, their deaths were unheralded. Their churches, their clubs, and their community activities existed in a murmurless limbo. Abbott would give them a voice. This was the idea that drew nourishment from the subterranean depths of personal frustration, and around it his fumbling intelligence, his oceanic patience, and his legendary stubbornness fixed as inexorably as fate.

So, his only capital twenty-five cents and a tongue ready with promises, Robert Sengstacke Abbott launched the first issue of the paper for which he did not even originate the name. The date was May 5, 1905, and the Chicago *Defender* would not miss a weekly issue for fifty years. At the age of thirty-seven Abbott had at last found his métier. His manner, his methods, and his mission would evolve and change with time.

5. RACE WAR

Meanwhile, although W. E. B. Du Bois' purposes had lengthened and his pace accelerated, he had not changed the direction he took in 1894. He still believed that "the Negro problem was . . . a matter of systematic investigation and intelligent understanding," and that "the world was thinking wrong about race, because it did not know."

But investigation, no matter how systematic, was not enough. The experience of two years as a teacher at Wilberforce, a third year spent on a study of Negroes in Philadelphia for the University of Pennsylvania, and seven years on a more comprehensive study at Atlanta University, where he had gone to join the faculty in 1897, taught Du Bois that. The world was thinking wrong, but the South itself compounded the error in action. In growing indignation, even while the "Atlanta University Studies" were being distributed and quoted among scholars throughout the world, Du Bois watched the spread of the very evils his studies were meant to expunge. Jim Crow laws, spreading disfranchisement, and swollen lynching rates aroused him to passionate protest and then to organized opposition. The year and the month the Chicago *Defender* was founded, Du Bois issued a call for "aggressive action on the part of men who believe in Negro freedom and growth." Twenty-nine colored men responded. They met in Niagara Falls, Canada, in July, and demanded free speech, a free, unsubsidized press, manhood suffrage, and an end to distinctions based on color and race.

Though these demands were as germane to American idealism as the Constitution itself, a cannonade of criticism roared through the press, white and Negro. While the *Outlook*, then the most influential weekly magazine, barked of radicalism and hinted at subversion, and the New York *Evening Post* spoke of a congregation of "malcontents," sections of the Negro press, largely controlled by Booker Washington, boomed forth a personal scurrility calculated to riddle the reputation of Du Bois. He was accused of being "ashamed of his race," and "wanting to be white," and "envious" of Booker Washington.

These attacks were renewed the next year when the "men of Niagara" met at Harper's Ferry, and the year after that, when they met in Boston. Snarled the dean of Howard University, Kelly Miller, who might have gone along with Du Bois had he been invited to, "We may expect a further session at Appomattox, so prone is the poetic temperament to avail itself of episodal and dramatic situations."

But there were to be no further sessions of the Niagara Movement, though dramatic situations seemed to explode everywhere— and they were not "episodal," and in no way digressive. They were of a trend that had proved increasingly dynamic since the Spanish-American War. They resulted from clashes of personality, of ideas, and especially of social forces that seemed beyond the control of men, and certainly beyond the control of any one man, even though that man should be Theodore Roosevelt, President of the United States.

Well into his second term Roosevelt's attitude toward the race problem grew callous. The evidence was that he not only permitted the civil degradation of Negroes to proceed without protest but, taking his cue from Booker Washington, emphasized the Negroes' shortcomings and put the blame for their condition on themselves. Thus the vast slums that fouled the air of cities were not even in part the result of segregation, unemployment, and the venal exploitation of landlords, but of Negro shiftlessness. Negro family disorganization, juvenile delinquency, and crime were not in part the natural consequence of the neglect of public agencies to do corrective social work and to provide parks, playgrounds, and swimming pools such as could be found everywhere for whites.

In Roosevelt's second term only a few Negroes realized that the President's "friendship was neither consistent nor sustained," but many were to realize it in 1906, when, scorning to hold a hearing, he discharged without honor a battalion of the Negro 25th Regiment on the charge that it had "shot up the town" of Brownsville, Texas.

Taken on the word of one lone army inspector, this action was so arbitrary and unfair that Senator "Pitchfork" Ben Tillman, as rabid a racist as ever pounded the hustings, defined it as an "executive lynching."

Senator Tillman's sensibilities were not as shocked as he pretended.

On a strumpet's false charge that she had been raped by a Negro, the white people of Springfield, Illinois, went surging through the Negro section of the city setting fires to dwellings, looting stores, and howling, "Abraham Lincoln may have freed you, but we'll show you where you belong!" For three days the arson, the mayhem, and the murder went on to the encouraging shrieks of a thrice-convicted female criminal named Kate Howard, even then at liberty under bond. Seventy people were killed and injured. Two hundred Negroes fled to Chicago, and an equal number to places unknown.

Ben Tillman did not say a word.

But a distinguished journalist named William English Walling did in "Race War in the North," an article that appeared in the *Independent*. ". . . Either the spirit of Lincoln and Lovejoy must be revived and we must come to treat the Negro on a plane of absolute political and social equality, or Vardaman and Tillman will soon have transferred the race war to the North. . . . Yet who realizes the seriousness of the situation, and what large and powerful body of citizens is ready to come to their [Negroes'] aid!"

Though the body of such citizens showed neither so large nor so powerful as it was later to be, the spirit of the abolitionists was revived in the grandson of one of them. Wrote Oswald Garrison Villard, "We call upon all believers in a democracy to join in a National conference for the discussion of present evils, the voicing of protests, and the renewal of the struggle for civil and political liberty." Jane Addams, John Dewey, William Dean Howells, Mary White Ovington, Joel Spingarn, Moorfield Story, and the men of Niagara answered that call, and the Niagara Movement was absorbed in the first meeting of what came to be known as the National Association for the Advancement of Colored People.

Du Bois, who had complained of the throttling and the buying of the Negro press, now had a sounding board. It was called the *Crisis*. Ostensibly the organ of the NAACP, Du Bois was its first editor, and soon there issued from it words of such clarity and sense, thunders of such wrath, and screeches of such derisive laughter that its audience of one thousand quickly grew to ten, then fifty, then one hundred thousand.

"Sympathize with the great Peace movement . . . sympathize with world-wide efforts for moral reform and social uplift, but before them all we must place those efforts which aim to make humanity not the attribute of the arrogant and exclusive only, but the heritage of all men. . . ."

"Let every black American gird up his loins. The great day is coming. We have crawled and pleaded for justice and we have been cheerfully spit upon and murdered and burned. We will not endure it forever. If we are to die, in God's name let us perish like men and not like bales of hay."

"In Virginia eighteen counties celebrated *Colored Tuberculosis Day*."

But neither Du Bois nor the organization he represented was content with words, however sensible, or angry, or droll. Far from it. Believing that the denial of rights was not only unjust but, as Du Bois wrote, "a menace to our free institutions," the NAACP first set up a Legal Redress Committee. Within six months its lawyers, headed by Arthur B. Spingarn, were in court fighting the disfranchisement of Negroes in Maryland, the "grandfather clause" in Oklahoma, and Negro peonage in Georgia and Alabama. Within a year it had defended Negroes accused of crimes ranging from petty larceny to rape and murder. Within that length of time also the NAACP had opened branches in seven cities, where officers and members busied themselves "to widen industrial opportunities for Negroes, to encourage the law-abiding spirit, and to cooperate in civic improvements." By 1911 its voice was heard overseas, where Du Bois was sent to the International Congress of Races, and where he took the opportunity to smudge the rosy picture of American

race relations that Booker Washington had painted for foreign gal-
leries the year before.

"The keynote of Mr. Washington's propaganda for the last fifteen
years [has been that] it is not well to tell the whole story of wrong
and injustice . . . but rather one should emphasize the better aspects. . . . It is a dangerous fallacy into which Mr. Washington
and his supporters fall. They assume that the truth—the real facts
concerning a social situation at any particular time—is of less importance than the people's feeling concerning those facts. There
could be no more dangerous social pragmatism."

Nor was it only "radicals" like Du Bois who saw it this way.
With such conservative names as Mrs. W. H. Baldwin, W. T. Schieffelin, and L. Hollingsworth Wood behind it, the National Urban
League was far from radical, but its officers saw it this way. When
it was formed in 1911, its purpose was to press for opportunities
for Negroes that had too long been denied them. Its slogan was
"Not Alms but Opportunity." The Urban League exerted itself to
open the doors of Northern industry, to pry loose the lid of segregation and discrimination in Northern housing and recreation, and it
dared to challenge Northern civic and economic management on
the issue of Negro employment.

Booker Washington was listed among the League's sponsors, but
it was apparent that he was not pleased with its activities in the
North. He had caused to be reprinted in his own paper, the
Tuskegee Student, an editorial from the Beaumont (Texas) *Enterprise:* "Negroes can do more for themselves and for humanity by
working in the fields of the South. . . . The Negro who will work
and who will keep his place can find more real happiness in the
South than he will ever find in cities of the North." And he had
sent Robert R. Moton, the man who would eventually succeed him
as principal of Tuskegee, throughout the South to urge Negroes "to
remain with the white men of the South."

But the truth was that Washington's "soft-speaking conformity
and sheer opportunism" had not paid off in solid gains. In Washington's South, 2,000,000 Negroes were still illiterate farm hands

and sharecroppers. While the Negro population in the rural South had increased to 6,250,000 by 1910, only 90,000 owned farms. Only 50,000 held membership in national and international unions, and in unions of common labor—in which category Negroes were mostly employed—there were none at all. Fifty-one and four tenths per cent of all Negro women and 49.3 per cent of all Negro children between the ages of ten and fifteen worked, but only 16 per cent of white women and 22.5 per cent of white children were employed. The death rate of 34.2 per 1000 was twice the figure for whites. Of every 10,000 Negroes, 98 were annually convicted of crime, compared to 12 of every 10,000 for whites.

Failing to show the results claimed for them, the soft conformities met opposition, solid and implacable, and there seemed to be little the conformists could do about it. It is true that Washington seduced and brought over to his side some Negro newspapers, including the New York *Age*, the Chicago *Broad Ax*, and, as we have seen, the Chicago *Conservator*, but his touch was noxious. No sooner had a paper come under his influence than it began to wither and die. No sooner had he deflated opposition in one place than it ballooned in another. As the election of 1912 approached, there was no holding down opposition any place.

It was not a good time for Mr. Washington. Formerly straw boss for Roosevelt and currently messenger boy for Taft, Washington was obligated to both the Progressive Republican and the Old Guard candidate. He had strong reasons for attempting the impossible job of supporting both men—Taft because he was the choice of the monied interests who donated so liberally to Tuskegee; and Roosevelt because he proclaimed himself on the side of the Negro majority, and Washington could not resist a majority. But there were those Negroes who could not see either candidate. Taft had played "safe and silent" on the question of civil rights. Roosevelt had turned his head while the representatives of eight million Negroes were barred from his splinter convention.

Du Bois and the "radicals" did not hesitate. "We sincerely believe," said Du Bois' *Crisis* editorial, "that even in the face of promises disconcertingly vague, and in the face of the solid caste-ridden South, it is better to elect Woodrow Wilson President of the United States and prove once and for all if the Democratic Party dares to be democratic when it comes to black men. It has proven that it can be in many Northern states and cities. Can it be in the nation? We hope so and we are willing to risk a trial."

There followed, naturally, attack and defense. The Indianapolis *Freeman* declared, "Because a man comes from Harvard and Heidelberg [sic] to boot, does not mean that he is prepared for leadership in a general way. . . . We make a mistake in trying to have him [Du Bois] as a leader of the race." The Richmond *Planet* believed that "Dr. Washington's policy is to move in the line of least resistance. The colored people do not believe that Dr. Washington has the fortitude or inclination to bare his breast to opposition. . . ." Galled because it had been accused of selling out to Booker Washington, the New York *Age* printed without comment a letter to the editor:

". . . [Dr. Du Bois'] greatest public work has been the publication of 'The Souls of Black Folk,' which has been rightly styled by the white press as the 'lamentations of a black man who wants to be white.' . . . 'Deeds! not words,' was the cry of Clarius Marius before the Nobles in the Roman Senate. . . . 'Deeds! not words,' was the cry of Abraham Lincoln at the dedication of the National Cemetery at Gettysburg, and the theme of Booker T. Washington in all his writings and all his lectures has been the tradition of all those whom he has proven himself worthy to succeed: 'Deeds! and not words.'"

As befits a minister, the Reverend Dr. William Moses was more temperate. "In my opinion, the colored people of America can, and should, and are slowly uniting under the unquestioned leadership of Dr. Du Bois. . . . He never sounds a false note on any question; nor gives any uncertain sound. He rings out clear and true. And American prejudice and racial discrimination shudder at his very name."

But the editor of the Atlanta *Independent*, who was also the Negro Republican boss of Georgia, did not agree.

"He [Du Bois] is a former citizen of our town. We know the man. . . . He never took time to register or vote and to put into practice what he advocated until 1908. . . . The Negroes of this country would like to know whether he voted [in 1908] for the party of disfranchisement against the party of enfranchisement for money or principle. . . . The Negro people would like to know and have him explain how he expects to cure disfranchisement, Jim Crowism and race proscription by voting for the Democratic party. . . ."

Even some sections of the white press entered the controversy.

6. MOODS OF DESPAIR

One Negro editor, however, stayed conspicuously aloof. Robert S. Abbott had not made up his mind on this and many other issues, and until his mind was made up not even the persuasive powers of his friend, Dr. George Hall, could move him. Abbott refused to be bought. As a matter of fact, when Hall tried, not too subtly, to buy into the *Defender* in the interest of Booker T. Washington, he was repulsed with an asperity that threatened their friendship. Abbott was slow, Abbott was stubborn, but he was not, he said, "a pure-born fool." In truth, the growth of the *Defender* in both circulation and influence bore him out.

Contrary to the belief of some, not all the credit for this growth was due to the often questionable and always sensational ways and works of J. Hockley Smiley, whom Abbott had hired in 1910. Though meagerly gifted himself, Abbott knew talent when he saw it, and he could make talent work for him. He used this knack to advantage so long as he lived. Smiley had the talents and the techniques of a Hearst. It was he who introduced the glaring red headlines, who thought up the slogans ("With Drops of Ink We Make Millions Think") and the elaborate, circulation-pulling hoaxes. It was Smiley who departmentalized the paper into theater, sports, and society sections, and he who recruited Pullman porters, dining-car waiters, and performers on the Negro vaudeville circuit to carry weekly bundles of the *Defender* east to New York and Boston, south to Atlanta and Birmingham, and west to Seattle and Los Angeles.

But the editorial page belonged to Abbott, and much of the credit for the *Defender's* growth must go to the editorials. This is not to say that Abbott wrote them. He seldom wrote them in their final form, for his prose was often ungrammatical and clumsy; but his ideas informed the editorials, and in them his consciousness, it might be said, prevailed.

It was a consciousness that was cunning without being the least subtle. It did not work from design but through instinct, and often, therefore, it plunged—like a man falling through space—past all the levels of logic to plop at last against the bedrock of personal experience. Whatever position he took, he took on this bedrock ground, and whatever position he took, he held tenaciously. He was almost never known to change his mind, even when he was demonstrably in error.

For instance, when he was a member of the Chicago Commission on Race Relations it was brought forcibly home to him that the *Defender's* campaign to lure Negroes from the South was doing more harm than good. The facts with which the commission dealt showed clearly that the hysterical South–North migration caused a great leap in all the depressing statistics—unemployment, delinquency, crime—and a tragic upsurge of anti-Negro feeling North and South. Mentioning the *Defender* by name, the commission itself urged "greater care and accuracy in reporting incidents involving whites and Negroes, the abandonment of sensational headlines and articles on racial questions, and more attention to means and opportunities of [Negroes] adjusting themselves and their fellows into more harmonious relations with their white neighbors. . . ." But, in 1914, Abbott had taken the position that migration to the North was the Negro's salvation, and in 1919 he refused to abandon it. When disastrous riots flared up all the summer and fall of the latter year, Abbott "did not view them as unmitigated evil."

If he seldom changed his mind, even more rarely did he change his heart. He was emotionally rigid and complex. He felt his black skin to be not only a severe handicap in the Negro world—which, of course, it was—but a source of personal shame. In spite of the most concrete evidence to the contrary—his wealth, prestige, and influence—he was convinced that his intrinsic worth as a person could be certified only by the acceptance of mulattoes. Nevertheless, he felt an obsessive loyalty to blackskin people per se. He reflected their moods instinctively and their minds so perfectly that they saw their composite image in the pages of the *Defender*. He was "for the masses, not the classes." He wanted them to "solidify, throw off the shackles. Rise!" and any small instance of rising—a high school graduation, a black boy on a white athletic team, a Negro victory in the prize ring or in any other contest against a white opponent— any immaterial instance was enough for columns of praise and joy.

Yet—strange duality!—no instance whatever was testimony to his own intrinsic worth. Only intimate social concourse with mulattoes could provide that; only, say, a light-skinned wife could make him worth while and respectable in his own eyes. When finally he married at the age of fifty he took to wife a woman whom he did not love but who was indistinguishable from white. When this unhappy affair ended in divorce he took a second wife who was "white in fact," and who, accompanying him to "white" places of entertainment, did not seem to mind the ridiculous gibberish he spoke in the impossible hope of being mistaken for a foreigner. It is strangely characteristic that, though he gave only casual and token assistance to the black Abbotts and completely ignored them in his will, he contributed regularly to the mulatto Sengstackes, was for years a dependable source of income for their white relatives in Germany, and saw to it that some of the white direct descendants of his father's master were educated.

Though these abiding indices to his character were evident in 1912, Abbott had at that time made up his mind on no public issues and on only one policy for his paper. The *Defender* would not fight Negroes and the editor's own private enemies. It would concentrate its fire on the common foe, the whites. Abbott wanted to unify "the black population for aggressive counter-action," and if this required him to vilify even well-meaning whites, then he would vilify. Of course this was wrong on the face of it, but "give the skunks hell," Abbott would say, and in his book of rules nearly every white man was a skunk, including the good philanthropist friend of the Negro, Julius Rosenwald, who was not the only white man to think that Abbott was a mindless "monkey with a shotgun, who will hurt anybody."

Anybody, that is, except Negroes—who certainly were hurt enough by the white press; and anything except the struggle in which even the semiliterate masses believed themselves engaged. Week after endless week the *Defender's* slogan for that struggle was "American Race Prejudice Must Be Destroyed." The proof of its destruction would rest, Abbott himself wrote (with a habitually greater regard for sense than syntax), in "the opening of all trades and trade unions to blacks. . . . Representation in the President's Cabinet. Engineers, firemen and conductors on all American railroads, and all jobs in government. Representation in all departments of the police forces over the entire United States; Federal legislation to abolish lynching and full enfranchisement of all American citizens."

Though Du Bois probably had the *Defender* in mind when he said that "some of the best colored papers are so wretchedly careless in their use of the English language . . . that when they see English they are apt to mistake it for something else," it is highly unlikely that he also included the *Defender* in his condemnation of those colored weeklies that did not "stand staunch for *principle.*" That year, 1914, nearly every Negro paper in the country blasted Du Bois at one time or another, but not the *Defender.* Abbott hated and feared divisive argument among Negroes, and Abbott realized that he and Du Bois were fighting the same war on the same side.

Many Negroes did not realize, except sporadically, that Du Bois was on their side. The man had an unhappy predilection for making enemies. He was impatient, especially of ignorance; he was temperamentally unsuited to mingling with the masses. He was called "race traitor" more than once because it was thought he sounded like one. He was as caustically critical of Negroes as of whites. "Jeremiads were needed to redeem [the Negro] people," he said, and jeremiads he gave them. Abbott on the other hand gave them panegyrics and made excuses for their wrongdoing. Neither man realized that he reflected a deepening mood of frustration and despair.

There were reasons for this mood.

7. EXODUS

No sooner had Woodrow Wilson been inaugurated than it became apparent that a constant progress in demagoguery in the South had led to a recovery of those extremes of sectionalism and race hatred that were thought to have been buried with Reconstruction. Within months Cole Blease was shouting to wild applause, "Whenever the Constitution comes between me and the virtue of the white women of the South, I say to hell with the Constitution!" No sooner had Congress convened than it put into the legislative hopper a confusion of bills brazenly designed to prohibit Negroes from holding commissions in the armed forces, to choke off immigration of Negroes from the West Indies, and to facilitate the segregation of Negroes in the civil service. Indeed, segregation in the civil service was accomplished without legislation, by executive order of the President. If this was in the pattern of "absolute fair dealing" and an example of "advancing the interests of the Negro race" that Wilson had promised before his election, it was not testified to by Negroes. A few liberal white papers in the North deplored this "perfidious action," but the South, which had a political-power potential three times greater than the North's, applauded it. And went beyond. Curfew laws, applicable only to Negroes, were revived in Georgia, Alabama, and Florida. Police brutality and mob law took over.

Then, in 1915, Booker Washington died. Washington's influence among Negroes had waned of late, and Du Bois probably spoke for thousands when he said, "In stern justice we must lay to the soul of this man a heavy responsibility for the consummation of Negro disfranchisement, the decline of the Negro college and public school, and the firmer establishment of color caste in this land."

Nevertheless, Washington's death was an incalculable loss. Whether he spoke well or ill in Negroes' behalf, he did speak—and in councils of influence. Whether Negroes agreed or disagreed with his policies, and even though many of them scorned the uses to which he put his intelligence, they believed that in his heart Washington meant his people well, and they knew that only when they came from his mouth might their appeals be heard. If Washington's "imperturbable good nature" had inclined him to keep silent on the subject of their rights, it had all the same won them time and leniency in which to go on fighting for those rights. As the New York *Times* said, "Washington was far from being the Negroes' acknowledged leader," but he was still the only Negro leader the whites acknowledged. "Who now will speak!" lamented the Richmond *Planet*. Who indeed?

And speaking, what say—either as advice or in exhortation? For not only did the race problem grow more complex, but its complexity was compounded at its very heart in the South when the guns began to yammer along the Marne and when natural disasters brought in their train a load of economic tensions and uncertainties.

First of all, the war-stimulated European demand for cotton in 1914 had seemed the knock of opportunity for which the South had listened vainly since 1853. When it came cotton acreage was recklessly expanded forthwith. Cotton mills were thrown up everywhere. White tenants, sharecroppers, and small farmers, their wives and children swarmed to the mill towns like plagues of locusts. For the first time since the Civil War the surplus of Southern white labor was absorbed.

Then in 1915 the boll weevil came again in clouds, and apparently to stay. What the weevil left, floods destroyed in two tragic years in succession. Destruction of the cotton crop wiped out collateral, and planters' credit dwindled. For want of cotton, mills closed down.

Rural Negroes, the vast majority, were caught in this squeeze, and what they did to extricate themselves set a current flowing toward consequences that might have been foreseen. They crowded into Southern cities, where they were soon in such numbers as to make the laboring poor whites, traditionally committed to enmity for blacks, fearful of a glut on the labor market and the debasement of their wages. Tensions rose and registered their rise on the most sensitive of social barometers. In 1915 sixty-seven Negroes were lynched, thirty-two of them within the corporate limits of Southern towns.

When the boll weevil was brought under subjugation and the re-covery made from floods, was there a reversion to the former state of things, to that peace—uncongenial, uneasy, uneven though it was —that, putting the best face on it, might be said to have prevailed since the demise of Reconstruction? Not at all. When cotton could grow again (and in a twinkle soared to forty cents) and the gins were ready to roar and the mills to pound, it was discovered that growing cotton and running mills needed Negroes, and needed them more desperately than Negroes needed "soft air, sunshine and sow-belly." And Negroes in thousands were gone—north!

The earliest realization of their departure brought a sigh of relief in some Southern quarters. The Negro's going, the Nashville *Banner* said, would "rid the South of the entire burden and all the brunt of the race problem, and make room for and create greater induce-ments for white immigration." Like many another Southern paper, the *Banner* was not expert in analysis. How could the South, where wages averaged only twenty-three dollars a week, lure white migrants who could earn three times as much in the North? How, even—and this was soon to be the crucial question—could the South keep its Negro field hands and laborers when word was being whispered among them of the big money in the North? In "Chi," in "Dee-stroy" and in Pittsburgh eighty dollars for a six-day week was quite common, and time and a half for Sundays. Add also the fact that each week there passed from black hand to hand copies of the Chi-cago *Defender*, haranguing:

". . . For the same reason that an unchecked rat has been known to jeopardize the life of a great ship, a mouse's nibble of a match to set a mansion aflame, I've concluded to carve a slice of liver or two from that bellowing ass who, at this very moment no doubt, somewhere in the South, is going up and down the land, telling the natives *why* they should be content . . . to remain in that land—to them— of *blight*; of *murdered* kin, *deflowered* womanhood, *wrecked* homes, *strangled* ambitions, *make-believe* schools, raving 'gun parties,' *midnight* arrests, *rifled* virginity, *trumped up* charges, *lonely* graves, where owls hoot, and where friends dare not go! Do you wonder at the thousands leaving the land where every foot of ground marks a tragedy, leaving the graves of their fathers and all that is dear, to seek their fortunes in the North? And you who say their going is to seek better wages are insulting the truth, dethroning reason, and consoling yourselves with a groundless allegation."

Surely the language and the order of its elements were Abbott's.

Though Du Bois was calmer, he too knew how to harangue, and he did month after month. "We might as well face the facts squarely: if there is any colored man in the South who wishes to have his children educated and who wishes to be in close touch with civilization and who has any chance or ghost of a chance of making a living in the North it is his business to get out of the South as soon as possible. . . . The same reasons that drive the Jews from Russia, the peasants from Austria, the Armenians from Turkey, and the oppressed from tyranny everywhere should drive the colored man out of the land of lynching, lawlessness and industrial oppression. . . . The only effective protest that the Negroes *en masse* can make against lynching and disfranchisement is through leaving the devilish country where these things take place."

Given the whole course and context of Southern history, it is no wonder that the common white men of the South, seeing their dreams of wealth threatened by this disaffection, should again resort to those measures they had hitherto employed to control the Negro. If the common men did not pause to consider that these means might frustrate the end they sought, there were those uncommon white men who did. "There is no secret about what must be done if Georgia would save herself from threatened disaster," wrote the editor of the Atlanta *Constitution*. "There must be no more mobs. . . . We must be fair to the Negro. We have not shown that fairness in the past, nor are we showing it today, either in justice before the law . . . or in other directions." The Montgomery *Advertiser* warned, "While our very solvency is being sucked out from underneath we go on about our affairs as usual—our police officers raid poolrooms for 'loafing Negroes' . . . keep them in barracks all night, and next morning find that many [are] valuable assets to their white employers: suddenly [the Negroes] have left and gone."

This response to the logic of the circumstances came too late. By 1916 a half million Negroes had "left and gone." By that year, too, even some of the more stable minds of the South had moved from hope to frustration and from restlessness to despair. The organs through which these more stable minds spoke did not make a complete about-face to the common man's reactionism, but they did praise *The Birth of a Nation*, a film infamous for invoking the common white man's hatred of the black; and they kept silent while United States marines killed blacks in Haiti; and they were alarmingly unanimous in their refusal to say that the burning alive of an "impudent Negro before thousands of men, women and children" in Waco, Texas, was anything but an enlightening spectacle calculated "to teach Negroes a lesson."

The South was soon brought to the discovery that the Negro was learning other lessons from other teachers. Ray Stannard Baker, writing in *World's Work* in 1916, first brought it to attention: ". . . There are more than four hundred and fifty newspapers and other publications in America devoted exclusively to the interests of colored people. . . . The utter ignorance of white Americans as to what is really going on among the colored people of the country is appalling—and dangerous."

Until then most white people were unaware of themselves and their public policies as Negroes saw them. When they did become aware, they reacted in several ways, all of them predictable. Early in 1917 an Associated Press dispatch, datelined Pine Bluff, Arkansas, informed the public that "Chancellor John M. Elliott today issued an injunction restraining John D. Young, Jr., Negro, and 'any other parties' from circulating the Chicago *Defender*, a Negro publication, in Pine Bluff or Jefferson County. The injunction was granted at the instance of Mayor Mack Hollis. . . ."

At the same time Du Bois began receiving so many letters of the substance of the following that his office kept a file of them:

"I would be glad to continue to serve you as agent as willing, but you are aware of the fact that the crackers or the Ku Klux will beat a colored man for giving the *Crisis* away in some sections of this country. I wish to stop here a little longer as I make good wages in railroad service. . . . As long as I can stay in peace I decided I would discontinue. . . ."

Scattered here and there were Southern Negro editors, too, who in order to "stay in peace" did what one of them in Tennessee confessed to doing: "I went straight to the white folks in this section and knocked on the door of their conscience and they received me, and assured me of their loyal support."

Aggressive Negro leaders believed the attitude expressed by the Tennessee editor to be more harmful than the opposition of white people. With Booker Washington dead, they decided the time had come to forgo the luxury of divided opinion and to weld Negroes into a unity that had seemed impossible so long as Washington lived. To achieve this, they called a conference at Amenia, New York, in 1916 and resolved, among other things, "that antiquated subjects of controversy, ancient suspicions and factional alignments must be eliminated and forgotten if [the] organization of the race and [the] practical working understanding of its leaders are to be achieved."

If both Abbott and Du Bois were overoptimistic as to the unity brought about by the Amenia conference, and if the organization of the race did not immediately result, there was no way of telling from the Negro publications, which more and more white people were reading and which presented an unbroken front of social disaffection, of defiance to established custom, and of racial militance. The monstrous aspect of this phenomenon, undeniably in view by the spring of 1917, inspired fresh fears in the majority of Southerners who were still committed to the old beliefs and habits and to the conviction that unquestioned submission to them was necessary to the safety of the South and the well-being of the country.

So it was not surprising that a Southern sheriff named Moon, armed with a pearl-handled pistol and papers certified by the attorney general of Georgia, should journey from Waycross to Chicago, burst unceremoniously into the office of the *Defender*, and claim the authority to arrest its editor. But Abbott knew just enough law, and he was surrounded by just the right number of hard-bitten men of his staff, to disallow this.

It is not surprising either that James F. Byrnes, mantling his native section in the seamless robes of patriotism, should declare in Congress that "would-be Negro leaders . . . are antagonistic to the United States"; that he should be the prime mover in trying to get one of those leaders, A. Philip Randolph, sentenced to two and a half years in prison; and that, eventually, he should call upon the United States Attorney General to institute sedition proceedings against W. E. B. Du Bois and Robert S. Abbott.

It was already a crime in South Carolina, Mississippi, and Georgia to read the *Defender*. It was almost as much as a Negro's life was worth to be caught with a copy of the *Crisis* in a Southern community. And in at least one instance it was death to be discovered a "migration agent"—as many Negroes, in the pay of Northern industry, were—even if one paid the license fee, which ran to a thousand dollars in Birmingham and Jacksonville.

The pump and heave of racial animus was not confined to the South. Some ten thousand Negroes had been invited, some as strike-breakers, to East St. Louis, Illinois, in 1916, and then had stayed on to become non-union laborers in the city's war-swollen industries. The whites did not like it or them. After a series of "racial incidents" throughout the spring came an explosion of such violence as to leave at least a hundred Negroes dead, a half million dollars in property damage, and six thousand Negroes homeless. A young Russian Jew who witnessed the three-day riot commented, "The Russians at least gave the Jews a chance to run while they were trying to murder them. The whites of East St. Louis fired the homes of black folk and either did not allow them to leave the burning houses or shot them the moment they dared attempt to escape the flames."

Two months later, disarmed, as one official report put it, "when it was feared that they would use their weapons to defend themselves" against the attacks and insults of Houston's citizenry, Negro soldiers of the 24th Infantry seized the forbidden arms and in one wild night killed seventeen whites. The trial of these soldiers was a farce that ended as it was bound to end—with fourteen Negroes hanged for mutiny and murder and forty-one imprisoned for life.

Du Bois wrote that "there was never a period in the history of the American Negro when he has been more discouraged and exasperated."

The fact was not evident from the record of Negro registration when America entered the war.

8. WALK TOGETHER, CHILDREN

The record was made in the face of persistent rumors that President Wilson had said that the war was "a white man's war." Negroes rushed to volunteer in such numbers that within five days of the declaration quotas of Negro military outfits were oversubscribed. There were ten thousand Negroes in the four Regular Army units, and another ten thousand in the National Guard when the War Department ordered a halt to Negro enlistment. "No more," it said, "need apply." This in itself was enough to make the President's rumored remark seem painfully credible, but then a few days later Colonel Charles Young, the highest-ranking Negro officer and a graduate of West Point, was summarily retired. "High blood pressure," the army medical board declared. "Prejudice. A miserable ruse," the Negroes said. Ruse or not, it worked to prevent Young's promotion to general rank. To prove his health, the colonel rode horseback in full field equipment from his home in Ohio to Washington, D.C. Abashed by this evidence, coupled with Negro protest, the army recalled him. But he was not destined to wear a general's star. He was assigned as military attaché in Haiti, where he fumed out the war.

The President's remark, if he made it, was bitterly modified after registration for the draft began in July. It quickly became apparent that something was wrong, and whatever it was had this final result: 51.65 per cent of all Negro registrants were placed in Class 1, as against 32.53 per cent of whites, and 30 per cent of Negro registrants were actually inducted, as compared to 26 per cent of whites. It looked very much as though draft boards were guided by the forthright precepts of Willard D. McKinstrey, editor of the Watertown (New York) *Times*, who had written:

"It seems a pity to waste good white men in battle with such a foe. The cost of sacrifice would be nearly equalized were the job assigned to Negro troops. . . . An army of a million could probably be easily recruited from the Negroes of this country without drawing from its industrial strength or commercial life. . . . We will be sacrificing white blood . . . and drawing our skilled labor when unskilled labor was available."

Given this thinking, which, though it did not operate to the extent some might wish or Negroes thought, operated flagrantly enough to draw repeated protests and to lead, finally, to the dismissal of the whole Atlanta draft board, to whom the equitable percentage of exemptions was thirteen for Negroes and seventy-two for whites—given this thinking, it seemed to a conclave of Negro leaders something less than reasonable to deny "the right of our best [Negro] men to lead troops of their race in battle, and to receive officers' training in preparation for such leadership."

Already in April the government had said that such training would not be given to Negroes, since "it was illegal under the law to train them in camps with white officers," and since there were no camps for Negro officers. Speaking, he thought, out of the new unity of Negroes, Joel Spingarn proposed the establishment of a separate camp, but there were objections to this—and from an unexpected quarter. Not only did a cadre of Southern whites inveigh against a waste of funds in training a "people who cannot make good officers," but Robert S. Abbott declared himself against "this Jim Crow officers' camp." Du Bois rebuked him.

"Where in heaven's name do we Negroes stand? If we organize separately for anything—'Jim Crow!' scream all the Disconsolate; if we organize with white people—'Traitors! Pressure! They're betraying us!' yell all the Suspicious. If, unable to get the whole loaf we seize half to ward off starvation—'Compromise!' yell all the Scared. If we let the half loaf go and starve—'Why don't you *do* something?' yell these same critics. . . . Just now we demand Negro officers for Negro regiments. We cannot get them by admission to the regular camps because the law of the land, or its official interpretation, wickedly prevents us. Therefore give us a separate camp for Negro officers."

Abbott fell into line.

Du Bois was not alone in wanting to know where the Negro stood. State and federal governments asked the same question. German propaganda and intrigue were at work, and, though the government's fear of Negro disloyalty had no basis in fact, it had every justification in reason. Just where did Negroes stand, then? Just what were their objectives? the Attorney General of the United States wanted to know. "We are seeking to have the Constitution thoroughly and completely enforced," answered Du Bois. "We are not trying by this war to settle the Negro problem," said the Secretary of War. "True enough," replied Du Bois, "but you are trying to settle as much of it as interferes with winning the war."

The War Department yielded to the pressure and set up a Negro officers' training camp at Fort Des Moines, Iowa. A thousand "college-trained and college-worthy" Negro men were sent there under the command of Colonel C. C. Ballou. One of this officer's first official acts was to call the Negro officer candidates together and tell them that they "need not expect democratic treatment." To add insult to willful injury, when the Negro 92nd Division was organized

Ballou, raised to the rank of major general, was given command. He promptly issued a bulletin that read, "White men made the Division, and they can break it just as quickly if it becomes a trouble-maker. . . . Don't go where your presence is not desired."

The presence of Negroes seemed not to be desired anywhere. The very month the Des Moines camp was set up, special trains were run to a place in Tennessee called Macon Road Bridge, five miles east and south of Memphis, and five thousand men, women, and children looked on while a Negro was burned alive. The Memphis *News-Scimitar* reported, "This is the first time in the record of lynching that the mob lynched in broad daylight and did not seek to hide their identity or wear masks."

Seventeen other Negroes were lynched between May and September.

And in October, the very month when six hundred and thirty-nine Negro officers were commissioned at Fort Des Moines, the drum major of the 15th New York Infantry was severely beaten because he did not think or know enough to remove his jaunty field cap when he tried to buy a paper from a white newsdealer in Spartanburg, South Carolina. The 15th, camped on the edge of the town, seethed. This was not the first incident, or the most outrageous, or the last; but it was the one that focused the attention.

Noble Sissle was no ordinary drum major. He was a music maker —as public to Negroes as an advertising calendar, and almost equally so to a sophisticated segment of Northern whites, who were just beginning to appreciate "jig bands playing nigger jazz." Sissle was one of those who had brought this jazz from God-knows-where to the East, and from the Renaissance in Harlem to the Rondo in the Village he had played its strange, inverted chords and compounded its earthy rhythms, as inscrutably sad and yet as profoundly unsentimental as Shakespearean tragedy, in a musical vernacular as fluid and far-ranging as dreams, defiance, and irony could make it. Though scarcely understood, Sissle's music was known, and was, indeed, beginning to be celebrated by a sizable coterie of Northern whites. The news of his unprovoked beating made headlines in the press.

The country was already in a condition bordering on hysteria. The war clouded everything, so that nothing was clear, nothing was simple. Hate rode hard upon the heels of fear. Negro soldiers especially were touchy. Already they had rioted and killed in other places, and now, though several days had passed since the beating, reports said they proposed to riot in Spartanburg. Colonel William Hayward, commanding the 15th, reported to the War Department his fear of "a violent eruption." The War Department felt that something should be done.

Actually it could make one of two choices, neither of them good. It could keep the regiment at Spartanburg and thus invite the eruption so much feared; or it could send the regiment, half trained, overseas. Secretary of War Baker chose the second. Redesignated the 369th Infantry, the 15th sailed from Hoboken in December 1917.

Du Bois wrote: "Close ranks! . . . Let us, while this war lasts, forget our special grievances and close our ranks shoulder to shoulder with our own white fellow citizens. . . . We make no ordinary sacrifice, but we make it gladly and willingly with our eyes lifted to the hills."

His syntax as clumsy as ever, Abbott wrote: "I say with absolute certainty that without a shadow of a doubt . . . we are Americans always!"

The men of the 369th Infantry were destined to be the first American troops to move up to the fighting front.

CHAPTER EIGHT

African Fantasy

1. LES ENFANTS PERDUS

THE REALLY big offensive that would plow through the Vosges Mountains, carry to the west bank of the Rhine, and end the war began on the night of September 25, 1918. At six-thirty in the evening of that day the 1st Battalion of the 369th New York Infantry moved out of the first line of Sous Secteur Beauséjour. It was the last of the three battalions to move, and it moved out in groups of half a platoon, in single file, with a distance of fifty paces between each group. The move was not particularly hazardous. There was still some artillery fire, but the German attack of seven infantry divisions, which was the last such attack of this war, had been temporarily discouraged and repulsed, and the 2nd and 3rd Battalions of the 369th had moved out in broad daylight three hours earlier.

The 369th was fighting as an organized part of the 161st French Division under General Lebouc. Its morale was high. The men were proud of the name the French had given them, *Les enfants perdus*. Just before they had gone into the front line of Sous Secteur Beauséjour on September 12 they had seen copies of Lincoln Eyre's dispatch in the New York *World* describing the "Battle of Henry Johnson." This event had occurred nearly five months before and had been headlined in the American press at the time, but the men of the 369th had been at the front for one hundred and thirteen days and had seen no newspapers. They were proud that Henry Johnson and Needham Roberts—men of their own outfit, Negroes —were the first Americans to be awarded the Croix de Guerre.

Now as the 1st Battalion, Major Arthur Little in command, slogged out in the dark toward the new front, the half-platoon groups closed, still in single file, on the shoulder of the road. They made a line nearly a tenth of a mile long, and in this order they threaded their way through the gummy jam of men and vehicles all bound for various rendezvous close behind the new front. The rendezvous for the 1st Battalion was Ravin des Pins. They were due at ten o'clock, and they made it only because an afternoon reconnaissance had uncovered a trail that led off the road and across the mutilated country. Even so, it was a tough three-hour march. No sooner were they disposed on the sheltered slope of their ravine than the great guns spoke. It was 11:00 P.M. The Battle of the Meuse-Argonne had started.

The artillery engagement, which lasted six hours, seemed to go well. At 5:00 A.M. the first assault teams started over. These teams consisted of several Moroccan battalions of the 161st French Division, and the 2nd and 3rd Battalions of the 369th. From where the 1st Battalion waited, it looked like a black man's war, but men in battle or about to go into battle can know very little, and all they could see from the south bank of the Dormoise River was the steep slope of the hill rising on the north bank and, finally, 3rd Battalion men crawling up the hill, silhouetting suddenly against the sky line, and disappearing instantly, as if by magic. It was evening before they saw the last line go up and over, for German artillery had pinned the first groups down for more than ten hours.

Not until it crossed the river on the night of September 26 did the 1st get its orders. At dawn it was to begin an advance in a northeast direction to Bellevue Ridge, a hill rising abruptly from the plain of the Argonne country, there to relieve a French battalion positioned somewhere on the crest and along the north face of the hill. As soon as practicable after making the relief, they would go in alone on the town of Sechault, take it, reorganize, and then, supported by the 2nd Battalion, press through the woods called Petits Rosiers. They were to dig in north of the woods and await further orders. The whole distance of their advance from the Dormoise River was to be just over seven kilometers. It did not look bad on the situation maps, and it did not sound bad in the orders.

It continued to look good as the 1st came down the hill on the north bank of the river and out onto the flat ground. But appearances were deceptive. Initially pinned down for nearly eleven hours, the Moroccans and the 2nd and 3rd Battalions had broken through the night before and had thereby incurred the risk of all night infantry attacks—they had by-passed some German positions. Before the 1st could penetrate the plain to the depth of half a kilometer the by-passed pockets put up a stiff resistance, and it required a half day's dogged fighting to clean them out, while, meantime, German artillery pounded the plain. The 1st lost eighteen of its two hundred and sixty men in this mop-up, and ten more in the broad light of early afternoon as it relieved Favre's battalion on Bellevue Ridge. From here Sechault was still more than a kilometer away, and enemy artillery raked the area that stretched before it.

But the 1st was under orders to take Sechault on September 27, and this was the afternoon of that day. At three o'clock they started down the ridge that they had relieved at two. From the northeast came a constant pounding of artillery. They went down in companies, each company with a section of two machine guns, at fifteen-minute intervals. This took an hour. If the town was to be won by dark they had not more than three hours to accomplish it. There was no artillery support. The only cover in a kilometer of flat land was a drainage ditch a scant fifty yards from the southern edge of the town, and before they could take this they would have to drive the enemy out of it and subdue a German gun mounted just behind it. The gun, shooting canister, had a clear field of fire.

The men wriggled forward on their bellies. A few yards in, the first man was hit. He rose, was hit again, turned slowly, took one eternal step, and then fluttered down, arms flaying, like a stricken bird. Other men rose by reflex and some of them were hit. A battery of Austrian 88s drummed fire from beyond the woods four kilometers north of the town. They were guns without courtesy, and they were not called Whiz-Bangs for nothing. When you heard their shells they had already arrived and exploded. At 4:40 P.M. Major Little sent back a request for artillery support. It never came.

And even before he could have expected it the major got support of another kind. He had decided to send in Company C as an assault wave to overrun the ditch and the gun and after a two-minute interval to pile the other companies in on the right and left. He so informed Lieutenant MacClinton, who commanded Company C. The German outwork, which ran from east to west, was not two hundred yards long, and the three companies of the 1st Battalion were on a line that overlapped each end of the outwork by a city block. There could not be many Germans in the ditch. Major Little counted on a rush creating an element of surprise.

He had just sent Sergeant Davis crawling across the plain with this advice to the company commanders when he looked up to see staggering from the rear through that field of fire the remnants of a company of the 2nd Battalion. It was a completely foolhardy thing to do, but in their dazed and disorganized condition—their commander, Captain Clark, having been killed—they could not be expected to realize this. Ordered held in support until the town should be taken and the assault on the woods begun, they had bivouacked on the eastern spur of Bellevue Ridge. Here an enemy plane had spotted them and enemy artillery found them. Within minutes their strength had been reduced by nearly a third. It seemed better to move up than to be chewed up without a chance to resist. And here they were, a hundred and fifty men loping drunkenly into a spattering rain of fire toward a place they were not supposed to be. The major cursed in amazement.

The enemy must have been amazed too, for suddenly there was

no fire at all from the ditch, only the sound of artillery growling overhead. The cessation of fire probably would have lasted only a moment, but in that moment the major ordered Company C in. Bayonets fixed, they rushed in yelling, and the enemy, numbering about fifty, swarmed pell-mell out of the ditch and into the nearest streets of the town.

From the shelter of the ditch, where the men were packed like sand, Major Little ordered a detail to search for the wounded and sent forward three two-man patrols. Only one of these six men returned, but on the basis of the report this man gave the major sent a dispatch to regimental command. It was 6:00 P.M. "The town [Sechault] is filled with M.G. snipers. . . . Cannot tell you how soon we can go forward. Shall we halt when too dark to see?"

Halting did not depend on the descent of night alone.

Sechault was just a small town in the center of a great plain, but it had been designed as if for the special advantage of the enemy. The north–south streets, some nearly as wide as Parisian boulevards, ran straight through without a break. The Germans had set up machine guns to command these streets. Three hundred yards north of the town they had established machine-gun posts protected by sandbags. Two and a half or three kilometers beyond this defensive line a thick woods darkened the horizon. The woods swarmed with the enemy and trembled with the roar and recoil of artillery. Altogether there must have been a dozen guns, some of them 155s, in and north of the woods. The enemy meant to contest every foot of ground. If they could not blunt the edge of this spearhead in this sector it would be all over, and they knew it.

At six-twenty two companies of the 1st began a house-to-house advance through the eastern and western edges of the town. They pressed to take advantage of the remaining daylight. Company B met little resistance, and within less than an hour occupied a house on the northeast edge of Sechault. But it was slow, hard work for Company D and fifteen men were killed doing it. Every house in the western section had to be flushed from cellar to attic, and some of the cellars were saturated with gas. At seven thirty-five Major

Little reported again to regimental command: "Appearance of a counter attack from the north. . . . Forming to meet it."

But this meant getting through the town in force and finding cover beyond it. In the only unhit stone house in the center of the town a command post was set up. Here the major got bad news. He was isolated.

The 163rd and the 363rd French Infantry were to have been echeloned to his left and right rear and to come in support when needed. But the Frenchmen had simply got lost, disappeared. Two hours of scouting failed to find them. Informed of this situation, the regimental commander, Colonel William Hayward, sent Major Little the following message: "You will have to exercise your own best judgment on the spot." He had lost half of his own battalion and another third of the men who had staggered onto the field before Sechault. What was his own best judgment?

At a few minutes past eight o'clock the bombardment started again. The enemy lobbed shells over the woods and into the town. It was a creeping barrage that raked the town from south to north. The only way to meet it was to move forward, dig in, protect a makeshift line with outposts, and hope for the best. By the major's reckoning, the outpost farthest from the enemy's machine guns would be a scant hundred yards. It was dark, and darker as it began to rain.

"We are not conducting a holding action, men," the major told his officers. "This is an offensive. Let's go."

They went. They began to find ditches. An irregular pattern of unconnected ditches was all around the north side of the town. A flare caught some of the men as they advanced and machine-gun fire whanged into them. Lieutenants Holden, Hutley, and Winston were wounded. Captain Cobb and twenty-two men were killed. Some of the ditches were refuse pits, stinking of human offal, but the living men lay tight in them—a dozen here, fifteen or twenty there, and so on. The enemy tried to coax them to expose themselves. As soon as one flare drifted down, another swooshed up. At 2:00 A.M. a patrol from the lost 163rd French Infantry stumbled into one of the outposts a quarter of a mile northwest of the irregular center, and liaison with support had been established at last. The rain, the flares, and the enemy fire kept up more or less continuously all night.

In the morning General Lebouc himself took personal command of the action in this sector of the northwest front, the arc of which the Germans had extended for a distance no one on the Allied side had estimated. The 3rd Battalion was now sent up to join the other two battalions of the 369th. They were to take the woods and march on to Les Petits Rosiers. They tried. From the 7:00 A.M. H-hour until 2:00 P.M., when the first line reached the edge of the woods, they tried. Major Little reported: "Cannot get through woods without artillery." This time he got artillery, and reported later: "The French artillery fire referred to consisted of about a half dozen shots. The 1st Batt. has about 137 men and 7 officers. The 2nd Batt. has about 100 men and 3 officers. The 3rd Batt. has about 300 men and 9 or 10 officers. . . . I hope that a relief can be made."

The 363rd French Infantry came as relief the next day. At six on the morning of September 30, artillery gave the woods a shelling that lasted two hours. At eight o'clock the 363rd started an advance that carried through the woods and reached Les Petits Rosiers that afternoon.

For five days more the 369th New York stayed alerted at Sechault, after which they moved to the rear and camped in the vicinity of Minaucourt. Too weary to be jubilant at the rumored news that Austria and Turkey had demanded an armistice, they rested for a week. On October 14 they started fighting their way through the Vosges Mountains and down again to Belfort Gap and Bischwiller and the front-line trenches of Secteur Collardelle, which they reached on October 16. Twelve days later they fought their last fight in the war and lost three killed, eight wounded, and one missing. The missing man was later found buried in a grave the Germans had dug and marked. On November 5, with the war sputtering out, they withdrew to Belfort, and on November 12 a document, addressed to Headquarters 369th Infantry U. S. Army, reached them and was read:

"After having boldly stopped the enemy, you have attacked them for months with indefatigable faith and energy, giving them no rest.

"You have won the greatest battle in History and saved the most sacred cause, the liberty of the world.

"Be proud of it.

"With immortal glory you have adorned your flags.

"Posterity will be indebted to you with gratitude.

"The Marshal of France, Commander in Chief of the Allied Armies, Foch."

It sounded fine, and the ceremony of pinning the Croix de Guerre to the regimental colors of the 369th New York Infantry was a fine and impressive sight. But only seven hundred and twenty-five officers and men of the original three thousand were there to see it. The rest were either wounded or dead.

2. BLACK STAR'S ZENITH

The boys came marching home again to Harlem, Brooklyn, and the Bronx. To the music of a dozen bands they marched under the Victory Arch, up Fifth Avenue to 110th Street, and then west to Lenox Avenue. Now the head of the column was approaching 135th Street. At every dozen paces after 116th, some mother saw her son, some woman her man, some child its father, and rushed into the street, there to clasp and cling and hang in the ranks like burrs. But it was a parade still. Though it cast off its pomp, it kept the spirit and the starch. The men stepped jaunty as ever. Their rifles kept the proper angle. Their grins were wide.

Unnoticed on the curb as the parade swept by stood a little, rotund black man whose quick-darting eyes glistened like a captive bird's. Jerking a crumpled handkerchief from his coat pocket, he took off his gray velour hat and wiped his forehead. The weather was cold. Indeed, February 17, 1919, was one of the bitterest days of the year, but the little man's face dripped with perspiration. He wiped his eyes, for they too were wet, though whether with perspiration or tears he could not have said. He trembled visibly at one moment, but the very next he stood rigidly tight, breathing in short, quick gasps, lest the emotions that surged and rocked so painfully in him should tear him apart. He had the bitter, ironic sense that even if this happened, no one would notice. Almost no one had noticed him since he left the British West Indies three years ago. And he wanted notice. But now all eyes were fastened on the marchers. Heroes, he thought sarcastically, returning from the white man's war. All throats except his own were shouting a joyous welcome home.

The little man grunted. Home! They had no home. Where was their government? Where was their President? Where their ambassadors, their army, navy, men of big affairs? Fools, fools! he groaned. If Europe is for Europeans, then Africa shall be for the black peoples of the world. The other races have countries of their own, he thought, and it was time for the four hundred million blacks to claim Africa as theirs.

Quite suddenly the ugly little man, whose name was Marcus Garvey, felt tired. His face was dripping sweat again. He must get away. Pressing, elbowing, kneeing back through the crowd, he apologized to no one, though he was conscious of barking shins and smashing toes. People were packed from curb to building line. Black people were everywhere, leaning from windows above the street, gawking and shouting from fire escapes, peering down from rooftops. Boys clung crazily in the bare trees in the center of the avenue.

Marcus Garvey fought his way to the corner of 135th Street and turned west. The street was empty. A few steps brought him to the door of a crumbling brownstone house from which a flag fluttered on a staff at a second-story window. He looked up at the black star centered in a red and green field. This was the flag *they* should be marching under, and not that stupid and alien bunting representing a white man's land. This was *their* flag.

Africa for the sons of Ham! Up, you mighty race!

Garvey climbed the stairs to the second floor, unlocked a door, and went in. The neat and crowded room was hot and stuffy and smelled of stale food, but he did not open a window. The less he heard of the shouts, the music, and the marching feet from Lenox Avenue, the better. Slowly, as if fearing he might break, he lowered himself into the chair at the big desk. He dropped his head and wound his arms about it on the desk top. When Amy Ashwood, his secretary, came in an hour later, she found him sitting thus, his thick shoulders heaving with sobs.

3. "OH, KINSMEN!"

Marcus Garvey was born in the tiny town of St. Ann's Bay, Jamaica, British West Indies, in August 1887. There he grew up under as obdurate a full-blooded black man as ever cursed his enemies and in a tradition as proud as history and folk myth could devise. His father's father had been a Maroon, had shed his blood and spilled the blood of others for freedom, and had bequeathed to his descendants the prestige of his deeds and station. Marcus Garvey's father had kept that prestige intact; indeed, had added to it. The only master stone- and brickmason in the town, he acquired a small fortune. He owned the only private library in St. Ann's. Even the white schoolmaster and the Anglican priest borrowed books from him. Though he lent, he scorned the borrower. Most blacks, however, had no use for books, and for them he felt harsh pity. Even after a series of disastrous court actions had lost him nearly everything except his homesite and reduced him almost to the level of the other blacks, he pitied them. For the whites and mulattoes, who had brought the actions, he mixed hate with scorn. He died when Marcus, his youngest son, was sixteen.

The boy had got a start by then. He had been to school and, he claimed, was graduated from the Church of England High School. He had also learned the printer's trade, and at the age of seventeen he went to Kingston to follow it. His mother died very shortly afterward. In the seven or eight subsequent years, unencumbered by family responsibility, Marcus Garvey followed his trade in Costa Rica, Panama, Ecuador, Nicaragua, Honduras, Colombia, and Venezuela. In Limón he worked briefly for the United Fruit Company and learned something of the plight of Negro field workers. He started a newspaper, *La Nacionale,* protesting that "no white person would ever regard the life of a black man equal to that of a white man." The paper failed. In Colón he started another, *La Prensa.* That failed. "Sickened with fever and sick at heart," his wife wrote later, "over appeals from his people for help," he returned to Jamaica. Less than a year later he was off to London.

England was the bright sun of the colonial world, but already in 1912 there were those who could discern sunspots—though the magnetic storms they presaged would be many years abrewing. African and West Indian, East Indian and Egyptian students and workers, all of them extreme nationalists, were Garvey's friends. He learned a great deal about his "heart's people" and his "native land."

Reading at Birkbeck College and at the British Museum ended his systematic education, but he continued to learn, and particularly from Duse Mohammed, a Nubian-Egyptian who published the *Africa Times and Orient Review* and made speeches in Hyde Park advocating Egyptian home rule. Garvey too made speeches in Hyde Park. In London he met American Negroes who told him that their lot at home was poor. He read Booker Washington's *Up from Slavery*—"and then my doom . . . of being a race leader dawned upon me." Seeing the war clouds gather and congeal over Sarajevo in 1914, he hastened home to Jamaica. He did not intend to fight the white man's war. He itched to start the black man's.

That summer he organized and issued the first manifesto for the Universal Negro Improvement and Conservation Association and African Communities League:

"To establish a Universal Confraternity among the race; to promote the spirit of race pride and love; to reclaim the fallen of the race; to administer to and assist the needy; to assist in civilizing the backward tribes of Africa; to strengthen the imperialism of independent African States; to establish Commissionaries or Agencies in the principal countries of the world for the protection of all Negroes irrespective of nationality; to promote a conscientious Christian worship among the native tribes of Africa; to establish

Universities, Colleges and Secondary Schools for the further education and culture of the boys and girls of the race; to conduct a world-wide commercial and industrial intercourse."

But obviously Jamaica was not large enough for such ambitious undertakings. An unknown foreigner, Garvey went to New York in March 1916. Three years later, though he had made speeches in thirty-eight of the states, founded a paper, the *Negro World*, harangued from a stepladder draped in red, green, and black from every street corner in Harlem, and claimed a membership of two thousand for UNIA, he was still relatively obscure.

He had erred badly, partly from ignorance, partly from passion. In Jamaica he had grown up under a color-caste system in which the blacks were separated from the mulattoes by a wider social and economic gulf than that between mulattoes and whites. He had felt as great a resentment of mulattoes as of whites, and his experiences in Central America had not modified it. He carried his resentment to England; he brought it to the States.

Here he tried to exploit it, but no such dipartite Negro race structure operated—or at least was not acknowledged to operate—here. Garvey, therefore, attracted only Harlem's West Indians and a tiny core of the utterly dispossessed in the hinterlands. And even among these he had the doubtful status of a curiosity.

But, by the winter of 1919, Garvey had seen his error and had modified his resentment enough to take steps to correct it. He employed William Ferris, a mulatto graduate of Harvard, to edit his paper. Ferris brought in Hubert H. Harrison, William Pickens, John Bruce, and Eric Walrond, the first three of whom had been identified with race-uplift movements long before Garvey left Jamaica.

Both the tone and the character of the paper changed radically. It outdid the Chicago *Defender* with a program of race pride and unity, and the *Crisis* with a program of race redemption. It was printed in Spanish and French as well as English, and soon it was going to subscribers in all the Caribbean Islands, in Central America, and in British and French possessions in Africa. It proclaimed "One Aim, One God, One Destiny" for the Negro race, which, said

J. A. Rogers, one of the paper's writers and an incurable mythologist, included not only Dumas, Pushkin, and Browning, as the world generally knew, but Beethoven ("the world's greatest musician was without doubt a dark mulatto"), Ethiopians ("that is, Negroes, who gave the world the first idea of right and wrong"), and Jean Baptiste Bernadotte ("a colored man, founder of the present royal house of Sweden. Enlisting as a private in Napoleon's army he rose to be field-marshal. In 1818 he ascended the throne of Sweden as Charles XIV").

Facts or myths, Negroes were ready to believe them. They were ready to believe anything that would seal up the seepage of dignity and pride that "the brave exploits of colored soldiers" in the war had raised to a high level. A fresh outbreak of mass intolerance was draining it off. The Ku Klux Klan—its body and its spirit—had come back to life with greater vitality than ever. By the spring of 1919 it was active in every Southern state except Virginia. Exploiting war weariness with talk of "dangerous entangling alliances," the Klan's Americanism program attracted citizens in Massachusetts, Connecticut, and New York. Indiana, Illinois, and Michigan knew the like. It was against Catholics, Jews, and all foreigners.

In the North it circularized a proposal that "agents be sent among the colored population to emphasize the desirability of returning to the ancestral homeland [Africa]." In the South the official word was, "We would not rob the colored population of their rights, but we demand that they respect the rights of the white race in whose country they are permitted to reside." They tried to enforce respect by means of the knout, the torch, the gun. Seventy-six Negroes, some still in the uniforms of the United States Army, were lynched in 1919. In the awful "red summer" of that year Negroes and whites did each other to death in Longview, Texas; Elaine, Arkansas; Chester, Pennsylvania; and in the nation's capital. A twelve-day riot in Chicago left twenty-two Negroes and sixteen whites dead and more than five hundred of both races injured.

The high toll of whites in affairs of this kind was a new thing altogether. A new kind of Negro was exacting it. Wartime experiences had changed him. He had held jobs from which he had formerly been restricted. He had won at least a legal victory over residential segregation. His children had gone to school with white children, and he himself had had his choice of seats on streetcars and trains, in theaters and some restaurants in the North.

But especially had the army experiences abroad scoured new contours in his mind and reshaped the patterns of his thought. He had seen white boys from Dixie salute Negro officers. He had discovered that white men die, whether cravenly or bravely, as easily as black. In France and Belgium he had broken the taboos, even the most sacred, and the world had not collapsed about his head. And either abroad or in the North he had heard of a thing called Bolshevism—or so Congressman James F. Byrnes seemed to think. Speaking before the House in August 1919, Byrnes declared it palpable that Negro leadership "appeals for the establishment in this country of a Soviet government" and the "incendiary utterances of would-be Negro leaders . . . are responsible for racial antagonism in the United States."

Byrnes succeeded in moving Attorney General Palmer Mitchell to action and to words. Three months later the Justice Department reported that "there can no longer be any question of a well-concerted movement among a certain class of Negro leaders . . . to constitute themselves a determined and persistent source of radical opposition to the Government and to the established rule of law and order." And this, apparently, was satisfactorily documented by, "First, an ill-governed reaction toward race-rioting. Second, the threat of retaliatory measures in connection with lynching. Third, more openly expressed demands for social equality. . . . Fourth, the identification of the Negro with such radical organizations as the I.W.W. and an outspoken advocacy of the Bolshevik doctrine."

In the first three instances the Attorney General was almost as right as weather, but in the final instance he was as wrong as Byrnes. Bolshevism was not for Negroes. It was godless. It was supported by a dogma and explained in a jargon that the common run of Negroes made no effort to understand. It advocated ideas—among them the idea of a forty-ninth Negro state—abhorrent to Negroes. But first of all and most of all Bolshevism was not democracy, and American Negroes were possessed of an abiding faith in democracy.

This was true even of those who seemed deeply moved by the promises of Communism. And there were promises. A group of American Negroes went to the Third Congress of the Third International to hear them. When Claude McKay, the Negro poet, addressed the Fourth Congress of the International, some Americans doubtless recalled a poem he had written in the desperate dog days of 1919:

> If we must die, let it not be like hogs
> Hunted and penned in an inglorious spot,
> While round us bark the mad and hungry dogs,
> Making their mock at our accursed lot. . . .
> Oh, Kinsmen! We must meet the common foe;
> Though far outnumbered let us still be brave,
> And for their thousand blows deal one death blow!
>
> . . . .
>
> Like men we'll face the murderous cowardly pack,
> Pressed to the wall, dying, but fighting back.

Vengeful and radical this may have been, but Communist it was not, as even Congressman Byrnes should have known. The bitterness could not hide the simple human impulse behind it or obscure the fact that the bitterness itself was the consequence of the abnegation of those principles under the aegis of which the war had been fought and a million men had died. "Make the world safe for democracy!" But what world—and whose?

4. BLACK STAR'S DECLINE

Marcus Garvey thought he had the answer. Almost nightly the curious gathered to hear him shout it out in the big auditorium he had bought in Harlem. "We will draw up the banner of democracy on the continent of Africa!" Garvey was flamboyant and dramatic. He could whirl like a dervish and beat his breast like a Jeremiah. He wept on occasion, but not now from personal frustration: he wept publicly from fullness of spirit. The crowds that came to hear him swelled in number and in pride. They were no longer simply curious. From one branch with a handful of members, UNIA grew to twenty branches with, Garvey claimed, two million members scattered throughout the whole colored world.

"We have died for five hundred years for an alien race. The time has come for the Negro to die for himself," Garvey shouted. "Race is greater than law! Wake up, Ethiopia! Wake up, Africa! Let us work toward the one glorious end of a free, redeemed and mighty nation. Up, you mighty race! You can accomplish what you will."

Money poured in, ten million dollars in the three years from 1919 to 1921, his widow reported later. "Africa for Africans," cried Garvey, and "Back to Africa," the headlines of his paper screamed. In the pages of the *Crisis*, Du Bois cautioned, "Do not invest in the conquest of Africa. Do not take desperate chances in flighty dreams." A relative newcomer named A. Philip Randolph called Garvey "charlatan" and "fool," and the best-known Negro leaders agreed with him.

But Garvey now had the ear of the great dark host of the naïve, the disillusioned, and the dispossessed. He filled the air with obloquy of the NAACP, the Urban League, and similar organizations, which, he warned, belonged to upper-class Negroes whose leaders were "weak-kneed and cringing . . . sycophant to the white man." These " 'Uncle Tom' Negroes must give way to the 'new' Negro, who is seeking his place in the sun." His followers cheered.

They cheered even more when Garvey projected an all-Negro steamship company, incorporated it as the Black Star Line, and with their money bought a rusty ship. No matter that on her first voyage to Cuba the ship foundered just off Newport News and jettisoned her cargo to keep afloat. There were other things to cheer about: the organization of the Negro Factories Corporation "to build and operate factories in the big industrial centers of the United States, Central America, the West Indies, and Africa to manufacture every marketable commodity"; the recapitalization of the Black Star Line for ten million dollars, and the purchase of two other ships.

The Factories Corporation built no factories and the ships plied no trade routes, but this did not matter either to a people caught up in a roaring vortex of race consciousness.

For by this time, 1920, Garvey had founded the African Orthodox Church and created the Court of Ethiopia. Though the first rejected the concept of a white God and soon had its Primate, priests, catechists, and seminarians, and its images of God, Christ, and the Virgin Mary shaped to Negro likeness, the second was more spectacular. Garvey himself assumed only the modest title of Provisional President-General of Africa, but the ranked orders of the Court's nobility glittered with titles and glistened in the barbaric splendor of royal garb. There were dukes and duchesses, lords and earls and dames, high potentates, knights commanders of the Distinguished Order of the Nile, magnificoes, and squads and squadrons of lesser folk—the African Legion, the Black Eagle Flying Corps, the Universal Black Cross Nurses, and the Universal African Motor Corps. All these made a brilliant show at the first UNIA convention, which attracted, the New York *Tribune* estimated, "25,000 Negro delegates from all parts of the world."

But if Negroes were attracted by the show, certain elements in the white race were attracted by something else again.

Garvey had long since taken the position that "political, social and industrial America will never become so converted as to be willing to share up equitably between black and white." He believed that "as long as the white population was numerically superior the blacks could never hope for political justice or social equality." In effect he recommended that they forgo these goals. The step from this to African resettlement and race nationalism was logical enough, and on this ground he was content to rest for a while.

Then as one by one, and finally in concert, the leaders of the less infectious Negro organizations attacked him for opposing his isolationism to their integrationism, the anti-mulatto bias he had learned as a boy and had never comfortably suppressed broke out anew. He publicly scorned and reviled mulatto leaders, who were "always seeking excuse to get out of the Negro race." They were "time-serving, boot-licking agencies of subserviency to the whites," the "pets of some philanthropists of another race."

Such aspersions, at first merely retaliatory, inevitably suggested a logical progression of their own, and Garvey made conscious drift toward it. "It is only the so-called 'colored' man who talks of social equality," he said late in 1921. "Some Negroes believe in social equality. They want to intermarry with the white women of this country, and it is going to cause some trouble later on. Some Negroes want the same jobs you have," he admonished whites. "They want to be Presidents of the nation."

He was now poised for the last short jump. In 1922 he made it. "I believe in a Pure Black Race. . . . It is the duty of both the white and black races to thoughtfully and actively protect the future of the two people, by vigorously opposing the destructive propaganda and vile efforts of the miscegenationists of the white race, and their associates, the hybrids of the Negro race."

No one can pick the point at which a man's destiny first joins with his will to move him toward the end the gods have ordained, but this seemed to be the point for Garvey. His sentiments—the complete abdication of Negro rights in America, the espousal of race purity—won him the applause and the support of organized white reactionaries. More than once the platform of Garvey's Liberty Hall was graced by the presence of Earnest Sevier Cox, faithful champion of white supremacy. John Powell, organizer of the Anglo-Saxon Clubs of America, spoke there. In January 1922, Garvey went to Atlanta, Georgia, to confer with the most powerful of all Klansmen, Edward Young Clarke, and shortly thereafter issued the following statement: "I regard the Klan, the Anglo-Saxon Clubs and the White American Societies as better friends of the race than all other groups of hypocritical whites put together."

Hitherto Negro leaders had tried to ignore or merely to belittle Garvey, but they could no longer afford the luxury of silent contempt. He was the Nemesis of all they stood for—widening opportunities, equality, integration, the fulfillment of American democracy. Also it was soon apparent that Garvey had made enemies of men who but lately were his friends and followers. Thus while the Negro leaders bombarded the little Jamaican from editorial page and platform, former Garveyites, led by Edgar M. Gray and Richard Warner, not only aroused fear in some of the faithful for their investments in the Black Star Line but went to New York's district attorney, Edwin P. Kilroe.

It seems that the business affairs of the line were, as George Schuyler punned, "on the shady side." It seems that the line's funds were sometimes used to pay the debts of the UNIA, a different concern altogether. It seems that capital was indiscriminately deposited to the personal accounts of various officials, that stock had been diluted with water, and that the mails were used to defraud. Kilroe was sufficiently impressed to confer with the postal authorities. Toward the end of February 1922, Garvey and three of his associates were indicted on twelve counts of using the mails to defraud. This was the first blow in a barrage so persistent as finally to beat Garvey back to the obscurity of Jamaica. He had scarcely rallied from it when the second came.

James W. H. Eason, once a high official in UNIA but now broken with Garvey, was known to be organizing a nationwide opposition movement. Never a good one for tolerating his enemies, the Jamaican went all out against Eason. Garvey's paper and Garvey's agitators railed at this "arch-foe" for months. In New Orleans to address a chapter of his anti-Garvey group in the first week of January 1923, Eason was beaten, stabbed, and shot to death. Two of Garvey's minions—his "chief of police" and a "patrolman" in the premature Universal Police Corps—were charged with the crime.

It was never proved that Garvey had ordered this murder—and, indeed, his policemen were eventually freed—but few of his growing crowd of enemies seemed to doubt it, especially when a day or two later his wife, pushing a long-pending divorce action, published "lurid charges of cruelty and misconduct" against him. The anti-Garvey papers, which included the most influential Negro papers, made the most of both affairs. A. Philip Randolph and Chandler Owen, editors of the *Messenger*, drummed up their slogan "Garvey

Must Go" to such effect that Harlem street meetings and Negro gatherings generally demanded the alien's deportation. A highly respected Episcopal minister, known as a temperate man, the Reverend Dr. Robert Bagnall, described Garvey as "a sheer opportunist and demagogic charlatan . . . egotistic, tyrannical, intolerant, cunning, shifty . . . avaricious, without regard for veracity, a lover of pomp and tawdry finery and garish display."

On January 15, 1923, a group of prominent Negroes who called themselves the Committee of Eight, but who spoke for many others, addressed an open letter to the Attorney General of the United States, Harry M. Daugherty. The letter charged Garvey as an "unscrupulous demagogue, who has ceaselessly and assiduously sought to spread among Negroes distrust and hatred of all white people," and respectfully pleaded that the Attorney General "vigorously and speedily push the government's case against Marcus Garvey for using the mails to defraud."

Garvey was brought to trial in May. Whether because a little reading of law in England had given him an exaggerated notion of his own legal competence, or whether it was simply that the irrepressible showman in him took over, Garvey dismissed his attorney at the end of the first day of trial. Thereafter for nearly a month he strutted and fumed under the indulgent eye of Judge Julian Mack and before the jury in a courtroom packed with his admiring followers. It was a megalomaniacal display of spectacular interest, but it had the effect of strengthening the government's case, which was so weak that any able lawyer might have destroyed it. Judge Mack urged Garvey to employ counsel. Even unfriendly newspapers warned him that it was foolish to "add his strength to that of his enemies." But Garvey was hardheaded, and he ignored advice. Though his final address to the jury was very moving, he had done himself too much harm, and on June 18 he was sentenced to five years in federal prison.

He seemed, however, a greater, more commanding hero than ever to his die-hard followers. Their fortunes and their numbers, too, were low, and it took them three months to raise twenty-five thousand dollars' bond. Nevertheless, they showed their spirit when, the night after Garvey's release, at a monster rally in Liberty Hall, they pledged a hundred thousand dollars for his defense.

Garvey's own spirit had never faltered. A few weeks after his release on bond he opened complicated negotiations for a resettlement scheme with the Liberian government, but these were hampered and finally shut down by the objections of both Britain and the United States. Next he organized yet another steamship line, the Black Cross, and bought yet another ship, the *General G. W. Goethals*. But on its first voyage it was impounded in Kingston, Jamaica. Garvey had lost his touch, his time had run out, his luck had changed. A federal grand jury indicted him for perjury and income-tax evasion. In February 1925 the appeal from the mail-fraud conviction was disallowed. Shackled like a common felon, he was sent to Atlanta Penitentiary. From there he tried to direct the vital force that he perhaps more than any other man had brought into being. But it was hopeless. That force was already finding other channels, already boring its resistless way in a dozen directions through the Negro psyche.

When he was pardoned by President Coolidge after two years, Garvey re-entered a world that had all but forgotten him, but through which his spirit still blustered like a germinating wind. He went back to Jamaica, but the West Indies were still too small. He went to England, where in 1940 he died, too wretched to remember how profoundly he had stirred the race consciousness of colored people throughout the world, and too senile to realize how firmly he had anchored the pride and passion of America's "new" Negro in the hurrying wave of the future.

5.   JAZZ AGE

Dating from Marcus Garvey there was a new Negro. He was far from happy to have things done to him, with him, and for him. He had jettisoned many of the old beliefs, the old attitudes, the old habits of mind—and particularly the habit of excusing himself *because* he was colored. His values and his standards of attainment had taken a great leap. In less than a decade he seemed to spring into manhood's full growth of initiative and self-reliance. It was this that marked the "Bolshevism," "incendiarism," and the "ill-governed reaction to race-rioting" so widely noted and deplored, and so greatly misunderstood to be the result of subversive influences.

This new sense of self and race, which the Negro philosopher, Alain Locke, described as a spiritual emancipation, found expression in a variety of dynamic ways in the years following the war.

Heretofore generally simple in their culture, and never having had any truly seminal principle of social and economic development, Negroes now reorganized and gave new direction to their lives in every area. The Friends of Negro Freedom functioned locally and nationally "to protect Negro tenants and organize forums through which to educate the masses." The American Negro Labor Congress was founded in 1925, the same year that A. Philip Randolph, at last irrevocably setting his own course, was joined by Chandler Owen to form the National Association for the Promotion of Labor Unionism among Negroes. In 1926 the Colored Housewives' League began encouraging Negro women to spend money only in places where there was some prospect that they or their men could also earn it. As early as 1927 in some of the larger cities boycotts operated sporadically against stores that refused to employ Negroes. Naturally the Colored Merchants' Association supported this activity, but it also served as an information and buying center for small business. Negro big business had its own informal clearinghouse, through which one could learn that such enterprises as Walker's Beauty Preparations, the Atlanta Life Insurance Company, the North Carolina Mutual Company, the Dunbar Theatre Corporation, and a small handful of other concerns were truly million-dollar institutions—and rated so by Dun and Bradstreet.

But setting up as independent of the white economy, though it would seem the strongest proof of self-direction, was illusory at best, and was but one side of the matter marking the ascendancy of race pride in the new Negro. There was also a bold and intellectually conscious reappraisal of the formula that composed the "old nigger" —the social and cultural mimicry, the conformity to white folks' presumptions, the responsiveness to white folks' thoughts, the artful aping of white folks' ways. Said Langston Hughes in 1928, "We are not any longer concerned with telling white people only what they want to hear." And if the truth, at once revealing and vindicating, was to come, Negroes could not afford to be so concerned.

And the truth would come, and did—in Du Bois' *Darkwater* (1920) and *The Gift of Black Folk* (1924), volumes of essays and poems that spoke of the Negroes' "own selves and the dwelling place of their fathers" and the "inner ferment of [their] souls." In *Survey Graphic's* special issue (1925) on "The New Negro" edited by Alain Locke. In the *Book of Negro Spirituals* (1926), edited by the Johnson brothers, who felt that at long last the spirituals could be rightly heard and sung and truly loved. The next year the younger brother, James Weldon, published *God's Trombones*, and the year after that a new edition of his novel, *The Autobiography of an Ex-Coloured Man*, treating boldly the theme of miscegenation, in which the miscegenate was neither fool nor beast. In the historical studies of Carter G. Woodson, *A Century of Negro Migration* (1928), and Charles Wesley, *Richard Allen: Apostle of Freedom* (1930), and in *What the Negro Thinks* (1929)—a book that did much to right the wrong uses to which Robert R. Moton, its author, had put his influence in the days before the First World War. In articles in the *Modern Quarterly*, *American Mercury*, *The Nation*, and *New Masses*; and in periodicals, pamphlets, and broadsides too numerous to mention by men too many to name.

And all this revelation and vindication elicited response from white academic circles in which the hereditary notions of what the Negro was had scarcely been disturbed for two hundred years—from Park and Detweiler at Chicago; Boas and Tannenbaum at Columbia; Dollard and Powdermaker at Yale; Seligman at N.Y.U.; and Odum, Vance and Woofter at Chapel Hill, North Carolina.

But most of all—and certainly with greater immediate impact—

this new Negro was revealed and vindicated by the race passion, bitter defiance, and hot-questing pride of the younger men. By Claude McKay's *Harlem Shadows* (1922) and Jean Toomer's *Cane* (1923), through which gushed a tide of love for a heritage too long despised:

> O Negro slaves, dark purple ripened plums,
> Squeezed, and bursting in the pine-wood air,
> Passing, before they stripped the old tree bare
> One plum was saved for me,
> One seed becomes
>
> An everlasting song, a singing tree,
> Caroling softly souls of slavery,
> What they were, and what they are to me,
> Caroling softly souls of slavery.

By Walter White's *Fire in the Flint* (1924) and *Flight* (1926), after which the author turned to writing of a factual kind, as in *Rope and Faggot: A Biography of Judge Lynch*. By Countee Cullen's *Color* (1925), and Langston Hughes's *Weary Blues* (1926), and Rudolph Fisher's *Walls of Jericho* (1928).

Also from the bold, cold, cynical music of a hundred jazz musicians, and from the subtle ironies and satire of the blues, which now could be heard performed by Negro stage folk in night clubs and in musicals on Broadway itself. In 1921, *Shuffle Along* opened at a downtown theater; then *Runnin' Wild*, which introduced the "Charleston"; *Chocolate Dandies*, with Josephine Baker, *Dixie to Broadway*, with the incomparable Florence Mills, and *Africana*, with Ethel Waters and Bojangles Robinson, followed quickly.

And all this, too, eliciting its appropriate response. For not only was there the sanction and encouragement of H. L. Mencken and Waldo Frank, and the serious criticism of Paul Rosenfeld and V. F. Calverton, but there was the creative use to which white writers, dramatists, and composers put the new Negro revelations. Eugene O'Neill wrote *The Emperor Jones* and *All God's Chillun Got Wings*. In 1927, Paul Green won the Pulitzer prize with *In Abraham's Bosom*, a play of Negro life. Marc Connelly's *The Green*

Pastures opened on Broadway in 1930 and ran continuously for five years. DuBose Heyward's novels, *Porgy* and *Mamba's Daughters*, were both successfully adapted to the stage. George Gershwin's "Rhapsody in Blue" began its eternal haunting of the world.

These men and others and their works established the Negro on the highest level of appreciation he had ever known. No wonder Alain Locke rejoiced that the new Negro "had attained an objectivity and an expressiveness" unthinkable to the old. No wonder Langston Hughes gloated that the Negro was at last liberated and now "stood free on the mountain top" of pride.

But eventually from his mountaintop the Negro came to see quite clearly encroaching on his new freedom and preying on his new-discovered pride the ancient fears, and he came to understand that the fears were conjured up by the very things designed to lay them—free inquiry and analysis, and new ideas that, assiduously pursued and applied, might conceivably upset the old status quo. Also he saw growing, partly in reaction to the exhausting psychological and economic demands of the late war and partly from disenchantment with the less than righteous peace, a kind of fateful involvement in the spectacle of the "new era of economy," which, nearly all agreed, the 1920s were. Though some warnings sounded and some consciences revolted at the crasser manifestation of economic progress, Babbitt did not seem a bad fellow to most. The calamity howlers, the dissenters, and the prophets of doom, like John Maynard Keynes, Roger W. Babson, and John Dos Passos, were simply interesting crackpots. Obviously the only calamity was a putting iron named "Calamity Jane," and the only doom—a pleasant one—that promised by the Four-Square Gospel as expounded by a charmer named Aimee Semple McPherson.

It was boom time. "It was sex time and drink time." The jazz age, which the new Negro fathered, named, and gave a voice, was an age of momentous trifles: the new Negro was a bauble in it. He became a commercialized fad. His talents were likely to be sold and his integrity rifled by slick gangster types who, for one thing, dominated a few of the theaters, more of the music outlets, and practically all of

Harlem—a place loudly trumpeted as "Nigger heaven." There could be found the exotic, the primitive, the virile. There life had "surge and sweep and pounding savagery." There Gaiety was king—but Harlem was not for Negroes.

> We cry among the skyscrapers
> As our ancestors
> Cried among the palms in Africa
> Because we are alone,
> It is night,
> And we're afraid.

Disillusioned and fear-driven, those Negroes fled who could. Langston Hughes set out by way of Russia to see the world once more. Alain Locke went to Italy, Paul Robeson to England, Cullen, Toomer, and McKay to France.

CHAPTER NINE

American Chapter

1. BUST

THOSE YOUNG "new" Negroes who fled were an infinitesimal and lucky minority of the race. Obviously the majority had no place to go save from the South to the North and perhaps back again—increasingly a two-way passage into frustration and futility. As early as 1926–27, when warnings of economic disaster seemed no more than faint whispers against the wind, thousands of Negroes lost the jobs to which industry had admitted them during the prewar boom. They were already in a depression, but it grew worse for them and gradually, almost imperceptibly at first, for everybody.

As the boom declined to bust, neither farm in the South nor factory in the North had places for Negroes. Even the employment traditionally theirs was taken away. North and South, labor unions generally excluded black workers and made common cause against them. One large Southern railroad, pressured by the Railway Brotherhoods, whittled down its Negro firemen from 80 per cent before 1918 to 10 per cent in 1930. Nearly half the skilled Negro workers in the country were displaced by August 1929, and by 1931

Negroes made up half the unemployed population in such cities as New York, Chicago, St. Louis, Memphis, and Atlanta.

In Southern cities it became common to see white men doing jobs they had formerly despised—digging gutters, cleaning streets, collecting garbage. Domestic service and service industries found less and less for Negroes to do and more and more of them clamoring to do it. By 1930 roughly a million Negroes were "on the turf," as they put it. At the beginning of the first full year of the depression the median income of Negro families in the North was less than half that of white families, and in the South the Negro city family earned $326 a year to the white family's $1339. The disparity widened as the depression grew.

As a natural consequence of this, the work of the old-line Negro uplift organizations began to fall off just at the time when that work was needed most. The depression increased racial tension. It sanctified the vaunted purposes of the Klan and the Anglo-Saxon League as nothing else could short of a holy crusade. In the eyes of many theirs was a holy crusade. They would save America from the Jews, who "controlled the nation's wealth"; from Catholics, whose chief American representative was a politically ambitious Irishman named Al Smith, who got "his orders from the pope"; from Negroes, who were "an inherently inferior people"; and from the Communists, who were again thought to be "making dangerous inroads" in the colored population.

The Klan and the Anglo-Saxon League would save America without ever realizing that among the forces that threatened to destroy her was intolerance, and that intolerance was most conspicuously in their employ. Discrimination increased at an appalling rate, and especially anti-Negro discrimination—partly no doubt because it gave many idle and ignorant whites something to do, and vicious whites a good excuse for doing it. In this time of double trouble the National Urban League, the NAACP, and the American Negro Labor Congress had fewer defensive resources. Membership in all these groups suffered drastic curtailment. The *Crisis'* subscriptions fell to thirty-five thousand from a peak of a hundred thousand.

Some Urban League centers closed. The American Negro Labor Congress shut down altogether.

Much of the little money Negroes managed to get was put to uses that gave greater emotional satisfaction at the same time that they promised more immediate practical returns than the long-range programs of the race leaders. Cults proliferated. Some were brazenly charlatan, offering in exchange for "consecrated dimes" the most esoteric nonsense. Others, like Father Divine's Peace Movement, set up free employment agencies and day nurseries, opened restaurants where substantial meals were served for ten or fifteen cents, established a chain of stores where food and clothing could be bought at cost, and provided communal living quarters for the faithful. All this was paid for under a system by which those of the cult's profession turned over everything they had and hoped to have to Father ("God" himself) Divine.

Such cults, however, were for suckers, in the common phrase, and the sophisticated black urbanite invested his pennies in the daily numbers lottery, which returned a fantastic 500 per cent to the lucky. Few were lucky except the numbers barons, who in the deepest trough of the depression as likely as not prowled the dark ghettos in Dusenbergs, Rolls-Royces, and sixteen-cylinder Lincolns, while their kept women, sleekly glittering with expensive baubles, sometimes managed to get a foot in and "almost to push through the doors to polite Negro society."

But life beyond those doors was mostly make-believe. Even by the middle of the second decade Negro polite society was less than it had been, and the impending economic crisis was to rend its standards of morality, manners, and taste almost beyond repair. It had once had an important function, authority, and support, but now its function was gone, its authority—thanks in part to Marcus Garvey—dissipated, and its support dried up. In the past several years its own emotional climate, "the dry rot of indifference and the mould of intolerance," had eaten away the communications the class had once maintained between the races. It had no skill to restore them. Though with thinner and thinner warrant its older elements continued to look upon themselves as saviors and benefactors of the race, the younger, more energetic and thoughtful of those born around the century's turn had long since begun to question the class's right to the immunity and privilege it claimed—immunity from the hazards of the day-to-day struggle, the privilege of pretending to direct it. The intensive social reshuffling of the postwar years and the spirit, more than the specifics, of Garveyism had created apostates from the class. Among them were Walter White, who had given up a financially secure career in a prosperous Georgia insurance firm to risk his future with the NAACP; and Lester Granger, who had left the sure if devious road to political preferment in New Jersey for the niggardly wage and obscurity of social work; and Asa Philip Randolph.

2. APOSTLE

A. Philip Randolph had come a long distance from Crescent City, Florida, where he was born in 1889, and a far way in thought since the days when he had "liked the prestige and sociability" of his father's calling. It had not been an easy journey. However commanding and sociable the position of a minister in the African Methodist Church, it was not financially rewarding. Young Randolph delivered papers, did odd jobs, and, as he grew bigger, worked summers as a railroad section hand to pay his way through high school at Cookman Institute in Jacksonville. In 1906 he went to New York.

Here appeared the first signs of what he would be later. He could not keep a job because he was constantly arousing his fellow workers to agitate for better labor conditions. He ran an elevator and was fired. He worked as a porter and promptly tried to organize the porters of the Edison Company, and was again promptly fired. On his third trip as a waiter on a coastal steamer he was overheard haranguing the steward's crew about conditions in their quarters. He was run off the boat.

At this rate it took him nearly a decade to finance and finish the irregular course of study he was taking at New York's City College, and even then he found no immediately receptive market for his training and his talents. He took up Shakespeare, employed a speech teacher who drilled him in the accents of Oxonian speech, and gave reading recitals in churches and clubs in and around Harlem. But this was only for a living. He became converted to socialism and was one of a small handful of Negroes so inclined who nightly could be found on Harlem street corners inveighing against the principles of private enterprise, the disease of capitalism.

Meantime he had met Chandler Owen, another apostate from the Negro upper class. Owen was brilliant, an intellectual dragonfly whose wit darted at likely surfaces with tongues of poisonous scurrility. He came later to be called the "Negro Mencken." Randolph, on the other hand, having abandoned the religious faith of his father somewhere along the way, apparently had no adequate leaven for the soul. He was heavy-spirited, humorless, "over-earnest." He lived a great deal within himself, and it was difficult to penetrate the formidable barrier of his reserve.

Owen, though, must have done it, for the two of them became intimate associates almost at once, and in 1917 founded a monthly magazine, the *Messenger*, which flaunted from its masthead: "The only radical Negro magazine in America." And so it seemed to most readers. "The principle of social equality," the editors declared in an early issue, "is the only sure guarantee of social justice." Within a few months of its founding the Justice Department indicted the magazine in these terms: "The *Messenger* . . . is by long odds the most able and dangerous of all the Negro publications." Randolph and Owen printed the condemnation as advertising.

Their magazine was fearlessly forthright, perhaps foolhardy. It turned topsy-turvy the standards of the black bourgeoisie. It preached socialism. The solution for the race problems, it said, "will not follow the meeting of white and Negro leaders in love feasts. . . . Industry must be socialized, and land must be nationalized. . . . The people must organize, own and control their press. The church must be converted into an educational forum. The stage and screen must be controlled by the people." And as if this were neither plain nor enough to effect their radical purposes: "*Lastly, revolution must come.* By that we mean a complete change in the organization of society. Just as absence of industrial democracy is productive of riots and race clashes, so the introduction of industrial democracy will be the longest step toward removing that cause. When no profits are to be made from race friction, no one will longer be interested in stirring up race prejudice. . . . The capitalist system must go and its going must be hastened by the workers themselves."

When America entered the war Randolph protested the "hypocrisy of the slogan 'making the world safe for democracy.'" He refused to serve in the war on grounds of conscience. "I am fundamentally and morally opposed to the war," he said. "I am a pacifist so far as national wars are concerned." He went about the country expressing these sentiments to Negroes.

In Cleveland in the summer of 1918 agents of the Department of Justice snatched him from the platform where he was speaking and threw him in jail. It was, plainly, a denial of his right of free speech, a persecution for conscience, and when Randolph was released he might have found the hair shirt of the martyr a becoming fit had he decided to wear it. But his instincts were right, and he passed up this opportunity for self-exploitation. He was not the man for "cheap personal note and glory." He was the man for a "true, good cause." If he was personally ambitious the fact was not apparent. Indeed, quite the opposite must have been the case. Years later it was said of him that he was "almost a god to the great mass of Negro workers."

In 1925 he found his true, good cause in the efforts of a small scattering of Pullman porters to form an effective labor union. These efforts had begun in 1909, but in spite of the common cause the Pullman conductors had made with the porters, the efforts had been dawdling and less than halfhearted. The company, naturally, did not favor unions, and the tradition of Negroes, unbroken since the days of Booker T. Washington, was to cultivate the favor of those who dispensed economic opportunities. Besides, the porters' contact with the upper-middle-class traveling public had steeped them in middle-class prejudices. It pleased them to serve "monied men," bankers, and industrial tycoons. It put little cash in their pockets, but it made them feel like moneyed men themselves, and even if one is only vicariously a tycoon he is likely to be against labor unions.

Thus the efforts to organize dozed and waked fitfully until 1918, when the War Labor Conference Board decided that Pullman employees had the right to organize and select their own representatives for collective bargaining. No sooner had the right been granted than the Pullman conductors formed their own separate union and bothered with the porters no more.

But by this time Booker Washington was four years dead and a new Negro spirit was in the ascendancy. By this time the slumbrous mass of old porters, among whom there were still ex-slaves, had been yeasted by younger men who were reasonably conscious of the benefits of collective bargaining. It was a matter of simple deduction. Unionized railroad workers got benefits. The "Big Four" Brotherhoods won victory after victory. The Order of Sleeping Car Conductors demanded and got shorter hours and higher pay. The company was no less anti-union, and particularly no less anti-Negro union. It did not recognize that a porters' union had any place or any necessity. "The laborer," it said, "can work or quit on the terms offered; that is the limit of his rights."

The terms offered were very poor. Whereas other Pullman carrier employees had a standard work month of two hundred and forty hours, porters worked four hundred hours. If they exceeded this before they had traveled ten thousand miles in a month, it did not count as overtime. Their work month was computed in hours plus miles. Even though they put in three to four hours in the yards preparing cars for trips, regular time did not begin for them until the train left the station. The highest wage they could hope for in 1918 was fifty-nine dollars a month, and this only after having worked forty-five years. The company expected them to eke out their wages with tips.

Nevertheless, Pullman porters were of the industrial elite and the economically advantaged among Negroes. They wore uniforms, not overalls; carried valises, not lunch pails. In the Negro social community they stood just below professionals, civil service employees, and businessmen. Their rank was important in the community and they were proud of it. Their place in the Negro community was strategic.

Pullman porters traveled. In the North and West they were the only Negroes with whom thousands of white people came into contact. If only some of them were conscious of helping to shape white opinion about Negroes, nearly all of them were careful to serve as models of the best Negro behavior. This was a social responsibility, which, having assumed, they generally lived up to. They were moral, upright, churchgoing. In short, they were self-consciously middle-class. But there was a hitch. Unions were for the laboring class. Some porters did join the Railway Men's International Benevolent Industrial Association in 1918, since it sounded less like a union— and was in fact much less than a union; but even the association suffered a severe loss of membership after the porters' wages were increased by an average of two dollars a month in 1920.

When in that same year Pullman presented its own company union plan, most porters were naïvely grateful. The company combined its union with the Porters' Benefit Association, a sort of picnic-outing group, and called it the Pullman Employee Representation Plan. Pullman gave it all the trappings of a fraternal lodge, including insignia, and promised the porters not only protection during illness and at death but bargaining rights as well. Indeed, Pullman went so far as to call for an election of delegates to a wage conference in 1924, where it soon became apparent that the new union's rights were paper rights, and the wage increase the company granted did not meet even the minimal expectations of the delegates. In conference the porter-delegates "suffered from a sort of psychological paralysis in the presence of white men." They feared that they might lose their jobs. They attributed the stingiest concession to the company's generosity and were extremely grateful. Only one of them, a man named Ashley Totten, who was already "in bad," spoke out. Only he realized that what the porters needed was a leader of courage and intelligence, preferably a man not employed by the company.

A. Philip Randolph was just the man. Already known for his activities on behalf of labor, he was deeply interested in the porters' problems. It seemed to him that they represented the problems common to all Negro labor. More, in fact. The porters' world was a microcosm of the Negro world, with its crosscurrents and dissensions. It had the same considerable though disingenuous identification with the white middle class. It too lacked the ability to appraise and therefore to modify its relation to the surrounding world. There was the same complex of relationships between the exploited and the exploiters; the same association of ideas; the same fairly definite patterns of thought.

If in his earlier years Randolph had believed that the solvent for all this was socialism, he had now apparently changed his mind and was on the side of orthodoxy rather than revolution. He had opposed Marcus Garvey on the grounds that Negroes were Americans, though black, and that America was their home, and that here they would have to live and work out their salvation. "If the Negro's American hope dies," Randolph was saying now, "then democracy's hope dies everywhere."

When the small founding core of porters asked him to become general organizer of the Brotherhood of Sleeping Car Porters in 1925, Randolph accepted. He was under no illusions as to the intensity of the struggle he faced. It began at once.

The company had all the advantages. It had experience in dealing with dissident labor groups. It had unlimited resources, a variety of methods. It had successfully publicized itself as the friend of Negroes, in proof of which it pointed to the fact that, with sixteen thousand on its pay roll, it was the largest single employer of Negro labor in the country. Unions were far from the order of the day even among whites in the early postwar years, and the company could count on a considerable anti-union sentiment among porters, and on at least a normal degree of perfidy, self-interest, and fear. Moreover, Pullman had an aggressive anti-labor policy, which it pursued adamantly in 1926–27, when an economic recession that cut into profits also increased the potential supply of Negro porters.

The company's initial strategy was to ignore the Brotherhood's existence. Under this cloak it called together its "bully-boy" district superintendents and secretly ordered them to find reasons to discharge any porter known to be affiliated with the new union. In exchange for assignments to choice runs, becoming welfare workers or other sub-officials in the Benefit Association, some porters were persuaded to turn stool pigeons. District superintendents in the Far West, in the Kansas-Missouri area, and in the Pennsylvania district were especially tough. Many porters were discharged without a hearing or the right of appeal. Some of these were replaced by Mexicans and Filipinos.

Still pretending to ignore the Brotherhood, the company attacked Randolph. His public record was not an impenetrable armor. He had not fought in the war and was called a slacker. In 1920 he had campaigned for Secretary of State of New York on the Socialist ticket and was therefore a "Communist." Since he was not and had never been in the employ of the Pullman Company, he was an "outside agitator."

It was easy enough to find anti-union employees to support these attacks. One of these wrote to the Chicago *Defender*, whose editor was, as usual, slow in making up his mind, "Mr. Randolph is a liar with a deceitful and seemingly fraudulent intent. I advise Pullman porters to beware of mere orators and scholars who bark but never bite and who belong to the correspondence school of labor leaders." Another, in a letter to the New York *Age* in 1928, deplored the fact that the preceding year "marked the dissolution of the Negro porter's monopoly," and went on to say that a "sinister influence has been hovering over this happy group of workers, preaching to them the doctrine of hatred and discontent against this Big Father of Industry that furnished employment to many thousands of

colored men and women. . . . Under his [Randolph's] leadership
we have been supplanted by 200 Filipinos and 300 Mexicans."

The mailed fist of the Pullman Company could also be felt in the
attack of a white group, the Industrial Defense Association, which
declared that Randolph believed in "miscegenation, free love, athe-
ism, and fermented class hatred by advocating an economic system
on the Russian plan . . ."; that he supported the idea of "having
Negroes use force and violence," and "the domination of black,
brown and yellow races in the world's affairs."

Randolph met these personal aspersions with as much dignity as
he could muster. "I knew that slanderers would attempt to blacken
my character with infamy," he said at one point. "I knew that among
the wicked, corrupt and unenlightened . . . I would be branded as a
disturber of peace, as a madman, fanatic, a Communist." But he
was mainly interested in defending the Brotherhood, in building its
membership, and in giving substance to the idea that the cause of
white labor and black labor was a common cause. Though he won
endorsements of the union from the American Federation of Labor,
the Amalgamated Clothing Workers, and the Big Four Brotherhoods, the Pullman Company still pretended that the Brotherhood
of Sleeping Car Porters did not exist, the Association of Railroad
Executives refused to recognize it, the Railroad Labor Board would
not protect it, and the Interstate Commerce Commission declined
to investigate its most pressing grievances.

An able writer, Randolph publicized the union's cause in the
Messenger, which he had made the official organ, and in more
widely distributed magazines like *Opportunity* and *Survey Graphic*.
He toured the country, explaining, protesting, defending. A clear
and logical speaker, he sometimes found it expedient to rely not
only on the arts of oratory but on a racialist appeal as well. "By all
the gods of sanity and sense, Brotherhood men are a crucial challenge to the Nordic creed of the white race's superiority. For only
white men are supposed to organize for power, for justice and
freedom."

When the Watson-Parker Bill creating a new Labor Mediation

Board became law in 1927, Randolph set to work to have the Brotherhood displace the Employee Representation Plan as the bargaining agency for the porters. Though the board found for the Brotherhood, the company claimed that there was nothing to negotiate; it "knew of no dispute between itself and its porters and maids."

But there was solid ground for dispute, as Pullman well knew, and by 1928, with more than half the porters and maids in membership, Randolph thought he had the means to bring the company to the forum. He would call for a strike vote. He did not want to strike. What he wanted was to make an indisputable show of union strength. What he hoped was that, at the simple threat to strike, the government's Mediation Board would step in, as the President could order it to do under the Railway Labor Act of 1926. It was in this hope that he had headed a delegation of union officials to call upon President Coolidge early in January. Though "Silent Cal" was as noncommittal as ever, the strike vote was taken in April. Of a total of 7300 union members, 6053 voted for and only 17 against. The results gratified Randolph.

Still the company took no official notice, and the government would not, since it did not see the strike vote as a threat to essential transportation. Indeed, Randolph himself contributed to this view. As days went by and the company made no gesture of recognition, the man's confidence was shaken. Persistent rumors reached him of porters backing off from the possible consequences of their vote, of their being afraid to strike under any circumstances. A strike by Negroes, Randolph realized, was a complete reversal of the psychology of a people who had got most of their industrial opportunities as strikebreakers. He began to hedge. "A strike vote is not a strike," he said, for the benefit of the disquieted porters, citing cases in which unions had "taken strike votes without striking."

He sensed how deep a conflict there was between his union ideas and the interracial labor pattern. The factors in the old amiable relationship between "master and man" were powerful still. Could he weaken them? Though the company held fast to the odd notion that it was entitled to gratitude for employing Negroes at all, perhaps the porters could be made to see that the company's obligations under the ancient tradition of noblesse oblige had been long abandoned, and that though they were absolutely dependent upon the company as the source of their daily bread, they should no longer be dealt with arbitrarily, by whim. Dare he call a strike? And how soon? Already Perry W. Howard, Republican National Committeeman, and other "prominent men of color [who] had hired their souls for Pullman gold to lie and deceive" were busy undermining the union idea. Would this first effort to win dignity and power for Negroes in the ranks of organized labor end only in outright defeat or bitter anticlimax?

Meantime, for all its official refusal to recognize that a threat existed, the company had not been idle. The firing of Negro porters increased. Quite suddenly Filipinos became a highly visible element in Pullman service even on the east coast. Pinkerton police were put on call to "avert trouble of any sort." Negroes who had wanted to be Pullman porters all their lives were easy to find, and the company not only found them but discovered them so eager that it could hold them on a stand-by basis without pay. As operating porters signed in for runs, they were required to say whether or not they intended to strike should a strike call come. Thus faced with the immediate prospect of loss of job and of dire consequences to home and family, even most of those who had voted to strike chose to stay with the company. No wonder that a few days before the strike date the company could issue a confident announcement: "The Pullman Company is prepared to maintain its service to the public, is not losing any sleep over the situation and does not anticipate that any of its patrons will be inconvenienced. The company is fully conversant with the activities of certain outside agitators to cause defection in the ranks of its porters, a large majority of whom are not in sympathy with the movement and will remain on the job."

President Coolidge maintained his silence; the Mediation Board sat tight. The conduct of both was "strange and unjustifiable." Though the President had had the board intercede in a dispute when only six hundred of the KC, NM & O Railroad's several thousand employees voted to strike, it was the board's declared judgment in the case of the porters, whose strike vote was all but unanimous, "that at this time an emergency . . . does not exist." Randolph thought it obvious that the board and "perhaps the President himself" had been warned that board intercession "was going to stir up the Negroes of this country and make them cocky, so that they would feel their power and that this would cause business interests to have trouble with their Negro workers."

The company seemed fully prepared to break a strike. Already weakened and its financial resources sapped by the company's summary dismissal of unionized porters, the union was further weakened by the defection of members right and left. A few days before the strike date Randolph, desperate and discouraged, asked advice of William Green, president of the AFL. The two men met in Washington. Green had the reputation of being a bumbler and, however sincere, frequently misguided; but on this occasion he came directly to the painful point. The porters were Negroes, he said, and by reason both of race and occupation in a "submarginal category." The public patience would not support a strike by such workers. Moreover, economic conditions did not favor it. Apparently Green had given the situation much thought, and he rumbled on, uttering opinions that, because of their inexorable truth, were all the harder to take. As the old labor leader talked, the distance that separated white men from black and black from the realization of their democratic heritage stretched before Randolph immeasurably, like an impassable morass.

"It is my firm conviction," Green said at last, "that the best interest of all workers concerned would be served through a postponement of strike action and the substitution therefor of a campaign of education and public enlightenment regarding the justice of your case and the seriousness of your grievances."

The word "postponement" fooled neither man. The strike was off.

The Brotherhood's retreat was the signal for its enemies to redouble their attacks. Internal dissension, repressed during the struggle with the company, broke out publicly. Porters who had voted to strike but who had also told the company bosses they would not strike began to say now that they would have struck—if. Already fear on the one hand and dismissals on the other had reduced the union's membership by half between the time of announcing the strike vote and voting to strike; and now what was left was cut in half again—to 2368 within six months. Word came from the Pullman Company that it would "probably look with more favor" on the union if Randolph, "a known Socialist, and an outsider," were dropped. But a hard core of union officials knew a trick when they saw one, and they knew, too, the integrity, the selflessness, and the courage of their man. They would not hear of Randolph's dismissal. Union morale dropped like a lowered curtain, dues dwindled. The official organ of the Brotherhood, the *Messenger*, was forced to cease publication. Union headquarters gave up its telephone; it gave up its electric light. It was said that the Brotherhood was dying.

And its funeral gift? A check for ten thousand dollars made out to Randolph and signed by a man Randolph suspected of acting for the Pullman Company, a man he scarcely knew. He could think of no other explanation. The check came in a letter, and the letter was too pat. It said that Randolph had "done all any person could be expected to do and now that the cause was lost," the writer urged him, Randolph, to take this gift as a reward and "take a trip to Europe." It must have been a great temptation. Office rent was coming up. His own house rent was due. Randolph returned the check by registered mail.

3. VICTORY?

Though as a matter of administrative necessity the union officials were made privy to what must be called—and was in fact commonly called—Pullman's attempt to bribe Randolph, the only public reference he himself made to it was general, even oblique. "Believing that money was all powerful," he said, "our detractors boasted glibly that we would soon be in the vest pocket of

Pullman. But they reckoned without cognizance of the force of the idealism of the New Negro. They knew not of the rise of a newer spirit within the race which placed principles, ideals, and convictions above dollars. Happily, the Brotherhood is demonstrating to black men and women, and incidentally to Pullman officials, that money is not everything, but that the spirit and the will of a people for justice is unconquerable."

Nevertheless, word of the incident got around and was added to until rumor became conviction that Randolph could live in velvet for the rest of his life if he cared to accept money for giving up the effort to organize the porters. But instead—and this was perhaps the greater part of it—he chose to stay on without an adequate or a regular salary and at great personal sacrifice to endure the fight. This belief helped, but not as much as it might have had Randolph's modesty allowed him to exploit it. And he needed all the help he could get if he was to make anything of Green's advice to wage "a campaign of education and public enlightenment."

For it soon became evident that the "respectable elements" of the Negro race did not like the idea of a labor crusade. Though the National Urban League favored unionization, local branches, more or less autonomous, shied away. Their drives for funds were directed at local corporations and industries, and these were naturally anti-union. The Chicago Urban League was especially hostile: Pullman contributed substantially to it.

The NAACP endorsed the union, and James Weldon Johnson, the NAACP's chief executive officer, persuaded the Garland Fund to give ten thousand dollars to the Brotherhood, but the NAACP membership generally was strictly class-conscious bourgeoisie and thought it had little in common with the laboring class. Several leading Negro newspapers, including the St. Louis *Argus*, the Chicago *Whip*, and the Pittsburgh *Courier*, opposed the union and attacked Randolph personally—and the company distributed free copies of these papers in its workers' quarters. But the lash of the *Whip* lost most of its sting when the only Negro congressman, Oscar De Priest, declared that he was an "eye-witness to the passing of fifty-five per cent of the *Whip's* stock to Daniel J. Schuyler, one of the attorneys for the Pullman Company." The *Argus* could scarcely claim impartiality of observation and judgment when in the same issue in which it carried an anti-porter-union blast it also carried a half-page ad for the Pullman Company. And the *Courier* was certainly suspect since, until 1928, it had staunchly supported the Brotherhood.

But the Negro church was the chief enemy of the union and of Randolph, and if the Negro masses were to be enlightened it must be brought about in part at least under the auspices of the church. No one knew this better than Randolph. Whatever the church's shortcomings—and they were many, of which an uneducated ministry was the first—it was the supreme cohesive agent; it was the base on which the Negro social structure stood. It had the oldest tradition, the largest following, the greatest power and prestige. But the great rout of the Negro ministry was ignorant of the union's functions, and it was against the union. It remembered that in his earliest days Randolph had criticized the Negro church, and that he was said to be an ungodly man. Something would have to be done to change or modify the church's attitude.

Though usually a direct man, Randolph knew that indirection had its uses. Nor had he been a minister's son quite for nothing. First he sought to awaken the church's awareness of its identification with the working class and to associate the principles of unionism with religious loyalties. Thanks to James Weldon Johnson and the Garland Fund, the Brotherhood now again had an official organ, the *Black Worker*. Its cover page blossomed with a biblical catch phrase: "Ye shall know the truth, and the truth shall set you free." Randolph's exhortations to labor action and labor solidarity bristled with religious admonishments:

"Let not your hearts be troubled neither let them be afraid, comes the injunction from the prophet of a new world brotherhood, and is a challenge and a promise to the work-weary, worn and oppressed millions by the heartless hands of capitalists, imperialists, in our modern industrial society. Fight on brave souls! Long live the

Brotherhood! Stand upon thy feet and the God of Truth and Justice and Victory will speak unto thee."

"Son of man, stand upon thy feet and I will speak unto thee. . . . Such a call to black men and women has come to fight for the cause of Truth and Righteousness. . . . We, as a great race, shall not fail, for the God of Power and Progress will aid."

Inelegant as these were, they came to be more and more effective.

Brotherhood officials did not overlook the fact that, for all its structural independence, the Negro church still looked up to the white church, still saw it as a model, still felt secure in following its lead. Moreover, Green's advice had not been to educate the Negro public only, for that was not the public that used sleeping cars for overnight trips and parlor cars for day trips. The white public, too, must be made to see the justice of the porters' case and the seriousness of their grievances.

Randolph enlisted the interest of the Methodist Federation for Social Science, and its *Social Service Bulletin* published a report on the problems of Pullman porters. In 1929 the Federal Council of Churches of Christ in America had its department of research and education make a study of the occupational status of porters and publish its findings in an official paper. The white Congregational Ministers Union of Chicago endorsed the Brotherhood. Powerful Catholic groups and various synods of the Lutheran Church did the same. The Negro ministry dared not let it be said that white churchmen were more helpful to a "race cause" than they. Influential Negro ministers began to fall into line. By 1932 there was scarcely a colored church in the country whose doors were not flung open to the union's program of education.

The program was pushed with determined vigor. The union held "labor institutes" up and down the country, and surprising numbers of people attended them—four hundred at Mount Carmel Baptist in St. Louis; fifteen hundred at the Metropolitan Community Church in Chicago, two thousand at the Abyssinia Baptist Church in New York.

The white press was beginning to find the activities of the Brotherhood worth news and editorial space. The *Nation* commented: "The men who punch our pillows and shine our shoes and stow our bags bear no little responsibility for the industrial future of the race." Randolph was widely reported to say, "The old policy of defending Negroes' rights is well nigh bankrupt and is of limited value. Fundamentally rights don't mean a thing if you can't exercise them. The solution, then, is for the Negro to take the offensive and carry the fight for justice, freedom and equality to the enemy. No minority group, oppressed, exploited and discriminated against, can win its rights and its place in the sun on the defensive."

If this sounded as if Randolph had forsworn the ideal of interracial unity in the labor struggle, it was because he had learned the strength of the biracial labor tradition. It was because he had to start where he could, which was with a challenge that his people could understand, and then go as far as he could, which was to affiliate his union with the AFL. In the Federation's yearly conventions, in its committees, and in private talks and public talks Randolph hammered away at the point: "Labor has paid dearly for its own lack of democracy, for capital kept labor weakened for decades by the use of masses of unorganized and 'unaccepted' workers. . . . Labor never can win fully until it opens its doors freely and equally to all workers."

In 1934 the Railway Labor Act was amended to outlaw company unions and to guarantee collective bargaining. It was the break the Brotherhood had waited for. With nearly a half million dollars put up by porters and maids, Randolph made a final great effort for members, and by 1935 more than eight thousand Pullman workers were paying dues to the Brotherhood. In that same year the union won a jurisdictional dispute with the Porters' Employee Representation Plan, now severed from the company, and Pullman, forced to it by the amended law, acknowledged the existence of the Brotherhood for the first time in the ten-year struggle.

Still the company was far from giving in to what it called the union's "exorbitant" demands. It delayed. It frustrated. It fought against the intercession of the national Mediation Board and, when this failed, it requested one postponement after another. The company reasoned that Negroes could be outmaneuvered and easily discouraged. But public opinion had been considerably modified by the pro-labor, pro-underdog policies of President Roosevelt's government, and both the public and the press were against the "vested interests." Pullman could delay only so long.

Finally in April 1937 it agreed to sit down with Randolph and the Mediation Board, but even then it stubbornly resisted negotiating a contract. Not until August 25—exactly twelve years from the day Randolph took up the fight—did the company sign an agreement. It called for an increase of two million dollars in annual wages, a reduction averaging one third in the number of hours a porter worked, and a cut in the distance he had to travel in a month from eleven thousand to seven thousand miles.

When news of this victory broke, Negroes all over the country celebrated at dances, dinners, picnics, boat rides. Only Randolph seemed preoccupied. Only he seemed to realize that this was at best a Pyrrhic victory. If it demonstrated the Negro's ability to organize on racial lines and move forward toward democratic goals, it proved as well the continuing necessity to do this, and it demonstrated that there were still goals that white America would never willingly leave undefended to the attainment of the race. It proved, in its final measure, that caste-class division was no less than ever a threat to the moral structure of democracy. Would nothing awaken the American people to the potency of this threat except a translation into physical terms—a physical "organization of the Negro people for power, for justice and freedom"?

These were the thoughts that preoccupied A. Philip Randolph. But he need not have brooded, for the organization of the Negro people for power and justice had already taken place in a few metropolitan centers, notably Harlem. And now such an organization was in development country-wide. Nor could one who watched closely fail to note the performance of a group intelligence and the operation of an entirely new spirit of calculation.

4. UNTROD PATH

It might be said to have started in the late winter
and early spring of 1933, by which time it was evident that Franklin
D. Roosevelt had brought to the White House a new concept of the
functions of federal government. With extraordinary moral courage
and (since he was no theorist or scholar) with an instinctive feel
for the empirical, he was testing his concept vigorously. There was
no lack of situations to test it in. When he took office on March 4
the banks of twenty-two states and the District of Columbia were
closed, and the nationwide banking system was at the point of collapse. On March 5, Roosevelt closed all the banks, and four days
later rushed a bill to Congress designed to allow the sound banks to
reopen and to furnish them with currency. Next he turned his attention to the agricultural situation, and within two weeks drew up a
singular bill for the relief of farmers. It was based on the unheard-
of principle of granting subsidies to farmers in return for crop re-
ductions. With this bill the President sent a message to Congress.
"I tell you frankly that it is a new and untrod path, but I tell you
with equal frankness that an unprecedented condition calls for the
trial of new means. . . ."

The message might well have been sent with all the bills that were
jammed through Congress in the first one hundred days, and it
might well have been blazoned on the office walls of all the ad hoc
agencies created to administer them. Before Roosevelt's first term
had run a year John Maynard Keynes, the British economist earlier
known to the American people as a calamity howler, wrote to the
President: "You have made yourself the trustee for those in every
country who seek to mend the evils of our condition by reasoned
experiment within the framework of the existing social system. If
you fail, rational change will be greatly prejudiced throughout the
world, leaving orthodoxy and revolution to fight it out."

But no matter how it might look to Keynes three thousand miles
away, to many people at home it began to look as though the

"framework of the existing social system" was already crumbling and revolution already triumphant.

At its base level the New Deal was a program of social reconstruction. Roosevelt himself was a reformist. He was a precedent breaker and an experiment maker in a big way. And of course he met increasing opposition—from Wall Street for revising the rules by which financiers played their amazingly intricate game; from industry for encouraging labor; and, most pointedly for our story, from the South for "wooing the Northern Negro vote."

It was a successful wooing. Even though the New Deal did not and could not keep all the glowing promises of the courtship, it did begin an equalizing process quite contrary to the will of reaction. "A minimum of the promises we can offer to the American people," Roosevelt said, "is the security of all the men, women and children of the nation."

He seemed to mean it. Wages and hours legislation worked to the advantage of a quarter of a million Negroes, half of them in the South. When an investigation revealed that the relief provided by the Agricultural Adjustment Administration was going to Southern farmers rather than to the workers and tenants for whom some of it at least was intended, the program was modified to permit checks to go directly to farm laborers, the majority of whom were Negroes. "Like any assistance to the Negro which is not controlled by the white landowners," wrote Thomas Woofter, a Southern liberal who helped administer the program, "this met with suspicion and some active opposition. . . ." What were those people in Washington up to?

Having first hailed the advent of Roosevelt as a Second Coming, the white South all at once began to find him and all he stood for bad beyond measure, and the South's spokesmen in and out of Congress were thunderously loud in saying so.

But it was quite otherwise with Negroes. Their vote for Roosevelt had been represented by only a few dissidents in 1932, but it rose to 65 per cent of the total Negro vote in 1944. In the years between, Negroes were reminded that the Republican party under Hoover had replanted the seeds of lily-white Republicanism, and each time they were reminded their impetus toward the Democratic party was renewed. In 1936 they sent to Washington from Illinois the first Negro Democrat ever to sit in the national government, and he has been followed by a Negro Democrat ever since. Adam C. Powell went as a Democrat to Congress from the 22nd New York District in 1945, and he has been in Congress ever since.

The revolutionary spirit of the New Deal encouraged surprising political and economic changes on the state and municipal level too, even in parts of the South. Though the changes were of little consequence numerically, they nevertheless indicated possibilities of greater change, and they helped further to document a circumstance that was to have ponderable effect in the 1940s and '50s—the circumstance of the physical organization of the Negro people for power and justice. Economic boycott opened job opportunities for Negroes in chain stores located in Negro neighborhoods in Durham, Memphis, and Atlanta. The Southern Bell Telephone Company and certain automobile agencies in Nashville and Louisville hired Negro salesmen. A dozen major Southern cities took on Negro policemen. Greensboro and Winston-Salem, North Carolina, and Richmond, Virginia, elected Negro city councilmen. Kentucky and West Virginia, Maryland and Missouri seated Negroes, only one Republican among them, in state legislatures.

But Wendell Willkie's wholly unexpected nomination as the Republican presidential candidate threatened to bring an end to what was called the "perfidious bond" between the Negro and the New Deal. Obviously a man of great sincerity and, for all his rural, rumpled presence, shining like Galahad, Willkie was almost as attractive to Negroes as Roosevelt was. Moreover, he was a Republican, a fact that had considerable weight with many Negroes in whom the memory of a traditional allegiance to the party of Lincoln was strong, and for whom rallying to the banner of the Democrats was an irritant to conscience.

Nor were Negroes, generally, unaware of the preponderance of Southern Democratic power in the Congress. Seventeen major committees in the Senate and twenty-five in the House were controlled by Southerners, and in both chambers they employed cynical devices to block legislation designed to benefit Negroes. So far as these latter were concerned, Byrnes and Smith of South Carolina, Cox and Russell of Georgia, and Bilbo of Mississippi were a pox pustulating on the fair body of the New Deal and polluting the blood stream of democracy.

Thus when Wendell Willkie told Negroes, "I want your support," they were attentive. "But irrespective of whether Negroes go down the line with me or not," Willkie said, "they can expect every consideration. They will get their fair proportion of appointments, their fair representation on policy-making bodies. They'll get the same consideration as other citizens."

The Democrats, though, could cite past performance. "Our Negro citizens," said the New Deal platform of 1940, "have participated actively in the economic and social advances launched by this Administration, including fair labor standards, social security benefits . . . work relief projects . . . decent housing. . . . We have aided more than half a million Negro youths in vocational training, education, employment. . . . We shall continue to strive for . . . safeguards against discrimination."

The New Deal's record on Negroes was in fact exceptional, and among those who helped to establish and publicize that record were men who somehow seemed to move in an aura of unassailable personal integrity—Harold Ickes, W. W. Alexander, Clark Foreman, and Aubrey Williams. Clearly if Negroes were discriminated against in some of the government-sponsored programs, it was the fault not of these policy makers but of local administrators in the South. In the North and Midwest there was little or no discrimination in the administration of FHA, CCC, and NYA.

Nor was this all. Perhaps of final, overriding importance was the fact that the New Deal guaranteed its consideration of Negroes by employing Negro officials whose duty it was to see that their people got consideration. It is true that some old-line Negro politicians and others criticized these race relations advisers as "vote bait" who "perform[ed] no useful service to the agencies in which they are employed or to the people whose special interests they are supposed to serve." But such strictures sounded like jealousy, and their effect—assuming that they had effect—was nullified by the fact that Southern whites also criticized the Negro consultants, though on other grounds, and by the circumstance that many race relations officers had given up secure and rewarding private employment for the headaches and multiple uncertainties of appointive posts.

It was in one of these posts that Ralph Bunche made an inconspicuous beginning to an illustrious career in world affairs. William Hastie, later the first Negro governor of the Virgin Islands, and later still (and now) a judge of the U. S. Circuit Court of Appeals, held one. Mary McLeod Bethune gave up the presidency of a college to direct the Negro work of NYA, under which some sixty-five thousand Negro youths were enabled to stay in high school and college. Frank Horne helped to create the liberal racial policies of the Federal Housing Authority. Robert Weaver, Ira Reid, Abram Harris, Rayford Logan, James Evans, Campbell Johnson—the whole catalogue would fill a page—deserved and got the gratitude of Negroes and the respect of the people with whom they worked.

By 1940 only three major departments—Treasury, State, and War —had no race relations officers, but even for these the pressure of events and the strength of a cohesive minority were soon to make them necessary.

Nevertheless, there remained an important area in which the race relations experts were completely ineffectual. As the country converted itself into the "arsenal of democracy" and American manufactory geared to the production of munitions, the anti-Negro bias of industry and organized labor reared almost as high and as implacable as Everest. Five million whites who were unemployed in 1939 were all absorbed by 1940, but a million and a half Negroes were still fretting under enforced idleness in 1941. NYA had trained eighty-five thousand Negro youths specifically for defense work, but that training was going to waste. The Office of Production Management set up a Negro employment and training branch, but the situation was not relieved. The National Advisory Committee decried industry's failure to hire Negroes. Secretary of the Navy Knox warned naval ordnance plants against refusing Negroes employment and against condoning anti-Negro attitudes of white employees, who, Knox said, should be "subject not only to immediate dismissal but may be prevented from obtaining employment in other establishments engaged in war production." In September 1940 the President's message to Congress cried shame on racial discrimination.

Yet in cities all over the country industry lamented "extreme shortages of skilled workers," while skilled Negro workers walked the streets. An official government report stated that between January and March 1941 the U. S. Employment Service placed 1066 workers in "selected essential occupations" in the electrical equipment industry, but only 5 were Negroes; 8769 workers in the aircraft industry, but only 13 were Negroes; 35,000 in machine shop and tooling, foundry and forging, but only 245 were Negroes. The report concluded, "Not only are non-white workers not receiving many skilled and semi-skilled jobs in a great many defense establishments, but they are receiving very few jobs of any type, even unskilled."

While Negro organizations such as the NAACP and the Urban League did what they could (which was not much, since their resources had not recovered from the drain of the depression, and since neither—one being legalistic and the other admonitory and educational in its approach—had a quick opening offensive against the old enemy in this new emergency); and while the race relations experts conducted surveys, wrote advices, and here and there cracked the shell of prejudice; and while the President addressed a memorandum to Messrs. Knudsen and Hillman, co-directors of OPM, declaring in strong terms that the government could not countenance discrimination against American citizens in defense production and that the doors of employment must be opened "to all loyal and qualified workers regardless of race"—while all this was building into a national issue with overtones of scandal, A. Philip Randolph brooded.

It was said that for hours and even days at a time, as 1940 clanked into 1941, he shut himself away in his office, saw no one save his secretary, answered no phone calls. He had been little in the public eye since 1937. That seemed to be the way he wanted it.

Then one day in the early winter of 1941 the clerical staff at Brotherhood headquarters and the knots of off-duty Pullman porters, who habitually congregated there, were startled to see Randolph burst from his office, stride swiftly through the hall, and, impatient of the creaking elevator, dash down the three flights to the street. Hatless and coatless in the freezing January weather, he hailed a cab. A few minutes later he entered the office of an old colleague, Frank Crosswaith, chairman of the Harlem Labor Union. To Crosswaith, Randolph outlined his plan for an effective new use of the "organization of a people."

The idea was not new. It had originated with old Jake Coxey, who in 1894 called up a host of the unemployed and marched to Washington to demand that something be done about their plight. It had been used again in 1932, when fifteen thousand veterans of World War I formed a "Bonus Expeditionary Force," part of which straggled into the national capital demanding immediate payment of a bonus of a thousand dollars a man. All the same, such a march was a bold thing for Negroes to contemplate.

For three months the Negro March-on-Washington committee of Randolph, Crosswaith, Walter White, Lester Granger, Rayford Logan, and Henry Craft went quietly about the business of making plans. But no matter that eventually was to involve so many could be kept secret for long. Before the committee had planned it, the March-on-Washington movement had a national press. Randolph was the spokesman. "The administration leaders in Washington will never give the Negro justice until they see masses—ten, twenty, fifty thousand Negroes on the White House lawn! . . . July first is March day." The number that was prepared to march from all sections of the country, he said, was a hundred thousand.

Washington was only mildly apprehensive at first, but as the scope of the plans for the march gained definition in the press, apprehension increased. Fiorello La Guardia, mayor of New York and head of Civilian Defense, was sent to deal with the march committee, and he was quickly followed by Aubrey Williams, director of NYA, but since neither man had the authority to make concessions, both failed. Then Mrs. Roosevelt herself came to New York. "You know where I stand," she told Randolph, "but the attitude of the Washington police, most of them Southerners, and the general feeling of Washington itself are such that I fear that there may be trouble if the march occurs." But Randolph was resolute. Nor did his resolution falter when the emissaries, each having failed singly, came back as a group; nor when President Roosevelt, grown properly disturbed now, summoned him to a conference in which the Secretaries of War and Navy also sat.

Randolph wanted firm assurance that positive steps would be taken against discrimination, especially in defense production. He argued that there was no time to send legislation grinding through the Congress, even if that body could be supposed to support it. He suggested an executive order, though no such order affecting Negroes had been issued since Lincoln's time. Mr. Stimson reasoned. Mr. Knox bellowed. Mr. President hemmed and hawed. Mr. Randolph gave courteous thanks and left.

Just a week before "M-day" the President sent for Randolph and the March-on-Washington committee and showed them the draft of an executive order. The committee rejected it. The order outlawed discrimination in defense industries only: it must outlaw discrimination in government as well. After a conference lasting several hours a satisfactory draft was drawn, and the next day it was issued.

Executive Order 8802 decreed that "there shall be no discrimination in the employment of workers in defense industries and in Government because of race, creed, color, or national origin. . . ." It set up a committee on fair employment practices to investigate violations of the decree. The order drew heated opposition from the South, where it was called an "insidious social fiat" and interpreted

as an encroachment upon the most cherished of Southern patterns—
segregation. Governor Dixon of Alabama said it was a "meddling
with the racial policies of the South," and promptly attended a meeting where it was proposed to create a League for White Supremacy.
"The time to act is now," the Supremacists declared. "An organization should be formed, so strong, so powerful, so efficient, that
this menace to our national security and our local way of life will
rapidly disappear. It can be done. It should be done. Alabama must
lead the way."

If in the circumstances these sentiments were so extravagant as
to seem burlesque, one of the original members of the Fair Employment Practices Committee adopted them and added to them. "All
the armies of the world," said Mark Ethridge, "both of the United
Nations and the Axis, could not force upon the South the abandonment of racial segregation." Then he resigned.

The South simply went on ignoring Executive Order 8802.

But not only the South. Defiance of the order was widespread.
Though the Fair Employment Practices Committee lacked enforcement powers, anything it did was thought to be politically damaging
to the New Deal. Eventually the President was prevailed upon to
take away the committee's status as an independent agency responsible to himself and to make it responsible to the War Manpower
Commission, which was dependent upon a Southern-dominated
Congress for funds. A punctured balloon could have withered no
faster. Randolph protested to President Roosevelt once, twice, re-
peatedly—in vain.

Early in the summer of 1942 he issued a call for a mass gathering
of New York Negroes—this to be "the first of a series . . . to be
duplicated in every city in the North having a considerable Negro
population." Twenty thousand people flocked to Madison Square
Garden to hear speeches by Walter White, Lester Granger, Frank
Crosswaith, and "Mother Mary" McLeod Bethune, all of whom received loud and sustained applause. Randolph spoke not a word,
"although the thousands had been drawn by his magnetism." But
in the end, when he rose to dismiss them with a gesture, a silence

fell deep as night. "It was a moment of reverence," one who was there said later; and later still a white observer, Edwin R. Embree, wrote that Randolph was "almost a god to the great mass of Negro workers."

But "almost a god" was not enough for a people who wanted heroes.

Nor were the angers and dissatisfactions with the world at large the only conducements to the physical organization of the Negro people that already was beginning to seem inviolable. Angers and dissatisfactions are but negative after all, and they cannot of themselves supply a people's will to do and to be. Because not one Negro in, say, ten thousand would ever know the meaning of accomplishment and success, the need was all the greater (and the gratification, when it came, scarcely less) to identify with the positive personal triumphs of one of their own kind, and to see in this rare one the apotheosis of all they themselves could never be.

5. A BIG MAN GOES FAR

For this a giant of a fellow named Paul Robeson seemed to have the potential. He had been known to Negroes and the country at large since 1917, when syndicated sports writers began putting his name in headlines: "Dashing Robeson . . ." "Rutgers Blanks Fordham; Robeson, Giant Negro, Plays Leading Role for Jersey Eleven." He was nineteen years old at the time, a junior at Rutgers, and about to be elected to Phi Beta Kappa. In his senior year he was on Walter Camp's All-American.

For a while after that the headlines in the white papers disappeared. Robeson graduated from Rutgers and went on to study law at Columbia. He supported his studies and, later, a wife by playing professional football. The Negro papers found his exploits with the Milwaukee Badgers excellent copy.

There were two brief flurries of headlines in the national press during this period. One came when it was rumored that a group of sportsmen had "confidentially pledged a million dollars" to back

Robeson as the "prospective heavyweight champion of the world." But Robeson was not interested in the prize ring, so nothing came of this. The second came when, having graduated at the top of his law school class, and having been urged on by a wife forceful and ambitious in ways not easy to explain, he accepted a position in a prominent white New York law firm. The white press's reaction to this was mixed. The Negro press was jubilant.

But writing briefs for cases involving railroads, banks, and hundreds of thousands of dollars hardly seemed calculated to help Robeson fulfill the "service to his people" of which his father had used to speak. The Reverend William Drew Robeson had been a great influence in the lives of his three sons, the eldest of whom was a physician and the middle one a minister. Paul told a friend of those days, "I want to plead the case of the misunderstood and oppressed peoples before the highest courts of the land. I want to help create laws which will guard their homes and children; I want to legislate those laws. I want to speak out so the whole world will hear!"

There were ways of pleading the case of the oppressed, but Robeson seemed in no hurry to find them. He had, he admitted, a lazy streak. He seldom sought for things to do, but he could work with great concentration and brilliance once he was committed. In the law firm he felt as he used to feel in his college classes and on the athletic field—the need to excel *because* he was a Negro. He prepared brilliant briefs, but white associates were chosen to defend them in court. He knew why this was so: a Negro lawyer simply did not represent important white clients before a court of law. He began to experience real frustration for the first time in his life, and he had not developed the equipment to deal with it.

His wife sensed his bafflement. She was blindly ambitious in many directions, but experience had taught her discernment, and she had inherited from her Jewish-Negro stock a passionate sense of reality. She knew her husband, knew his temperament, knew his talents. She was too ambitious to entertain the prospect of his frittering his life away in a picayune civil practice, which was the fate of so many Negro lawyers; too realistic to encourage him to resign with nothing else in view; and too sensible not to cast about for a means to his greater fulfillment. Meantime she drew him into the fields of her intellectual and social interests—amateur politics, amateur music, amateur theatricals—where she roved with all the inquisitiveness of a scientist and the ardor of a votary.

By now 1924 had come and, as we have seen, the viable interest in the Negro and in Negro life as subjects for serious art was beginning to flower. Eugene O'Neill had already had great success with *The Emperor Jones* and was currently at work on *All God's Chillun Got Wings*. *Porgy* and *Scarlet Sister Mary*, novels of Negro folk life, were soon to climb high on the best-seller lists, but not quite so high as those books about Negro life in Harlem, *Nigger Heaven*, *Home to Harlem*, and *The Blacker the Berry*.

Much of Harlem was as synthetic as bathtub gin, but there were some genuine people living there, and the cultural tide of the 1920s washed more than flotsam and jetsam onto the banks of the Harlem River. Writers and artists and actors came in on that tide, bringing new and sometimes wild ideas, and an abundance of life.

The James Weldon Johnsons gave a party for Claude McKay just before he sailed for Russia in 1922. McKay had recently published a book of poems of which Johnson was to write, "There is nothing in American literature that strikes a more portentous note than these sonnet-tragedies. . . ." But the party itself struck a portentous note. McKay had been Max Eastman's associate editor of the *Liberator*, and until lately the executive editor with Michael Gold. He had had white friends and associates of the Mike Gold stamp for some time, and he had been in the habit of taking "some of them up to the cabarets and cozy flats of Harlem. I did not invite my white friends to the nice homes of the Negro elite," he wrote later, "simply because I did not have an entree."

The Johnsons gave him and his friends that entree. Soon no party given by the Negro elite was complete unless it included half a dozen white guests, liberals of one stripe or another. And the more liberal the better. And the more active in the arts the better still. The Eastmans, Carl Van Vechten, Eugene O'Neill, Cleon Throckmorton, Susan Glaspell, and Theodore Dreiser were quite active indeed.

This, then, was the eclectic and dynamic circle into which Eslanda Robeson drew her impressionable husband. Her lively energies were not dissipated in the circle's gay party life. They bubbled up in community activities and in volunteer social and charity work, which she pursued in that spirit of noblesse oblige that is so conspicuous an element in the home learning of upper-class Negroes.

Paul too could be counted upon for work of the same sort, in the same spirit. All through his boyhood and four years of college he had given recitations and "rendered" solos in his father's church. He had a notable flair for dramatic reading, he had a superb but untrained bass voice, and he could be counted on to use them in some struggling mission church's crisis of money raising. He refereed basketball games in parish houses and at the YMCA. He sponsored a neighborhood boys' club. In 1924 he found himself committed to act in an amateur production of Ridgely Torrence's play, *Simon the Cyrenian*, at the Harlem YWCA.

Mrs. Robeson was not one for hiding her husband's light under a bushel. She was convinced of the range of his untrained talents. At one party or another she had met members of the Provincetown Playhouse coterie, and she brought some of them to watch her husband perform in Torrence's play. Later Kenneth MacGowan said, "Some magic emanated from the man," and James Light spread the word in MacDougal Street that Robeson was "a born actor." Before Robeson knew what was happening to him, O'Neill the playwright, Light the director, and Robert Edmond Jones the scene designer had fixed upon him to play Jim Harris in *All God's Chillun Got Wings*.

The announcement of this brought on a wind of controversy and a rainfall of protest. *All God's Chillun* was that kind of play. It dealt in somber, realistic terms with the melancholy married life of a mixed couple. The papers protested playing a Negro opposite a white actress. O'Neill issued a statement to the press. "Prejudice . . . is the last word in injustice and absurdity. . . . All we ask is a square deal. A play is written to be expressed through the theater, and only on its merits in a theater can a final judgment be passed on it with justice. We demand this hearing."

Robeson was once again in the headlines of the white press. He was to stay in headlines almost continuously for the next twenty years.

In the spring of 1925 he gave his first concert of Negro spirituals at the Greenwich Village Theater, and Alexander Woollcott lauded him as "the finest musical instrument wrought by nature in our time." Later that year he went to London and played *The Emperor Jones* to great applause at the Ambassadors' Theater. He returned briefly to the States and found himself a much-sought-after celebrity, courted by whites and feted by Negroes—practically all of whom identified with him as he identified with them. He was one of them. He was, he said in a public speech at the time, their "instrument."

Back in Europe again, he saw a lot of Claude McKay, who had just returned from his second trip to Russia full of enthusiasm and unstinting of praise. "Russia now has her opportunity. Russia has had the courage to tear down old rotten walls." It was the kind of thing many Western intellectuals were saying in the 1920s. The Robesons heard it on every hand.

Robeson made a triumphant concert tour of the States in 1927 and then went back to England, which was to be his home for the next four years. From here his music and his personality radiated all over the Continent. He gave command performances. Always and everywhere he sang the sorrow songs of his people. Indeed, they were all he knew at the time. The London *Daily Express* proclaimed him "more than a great actor and a great singer. He is a great man, who creates the soul of a people in bondage and shows you its true kinship with the fettered soul of man. We became like little children as we surrendered to his magical genius."

This piece and others in the same vein were widely reprinted in the United States. American Negroes were strengthened in their belief that Robeson was their "instrument," their ambassador to the world.

When he sang "Ol' Man River" in the first American revival of *Show Boat*, Edna Ferber, the author of the book, wrote, "I have never seen an ovation like that given any figure of the stage, the concert hall, or the opera. . . . That audience stood up and howled. They applauded and shouted and stamped. . . . The show stopped. He sang it again. The show stopped. They called him back again and again. . . ."

That was in the spring of 1933.

Meanwhile, though it was evident that something had happened to the social climate of America because of the depression of the 1930s, a far subtler change had been occurring in the intellectual atmosphere since the lush days of the 1920s. In that boom time some intellectuals had found the American environment uncongenial and, rather than "suffer death on the cross of American industrial-materialism," fled to Europe. But the world-wide depression had driven them home again, where, in an air now acid with poverty, their ideas were even less viable than before.

They were a lonely lot, as all idealists and utopia-seekers are likely to be, and now also they were deprived of the sense of a commonly shared intellectual adventure they had known in the bistros on the Left Bank of Paris. Playwrights without producers, writers without an audience, artists without a market, they were sharply aware of the illness of a society that thwarted their creative drives. They had a heightened perception of the "dreadful deficiencies of capitalistic democracy"—in witness to which were the shut-down factories, the staggering bread lines, the millions of unemployed. They felt helpless to effect a cure, and they were certain that it could not cure itself.

Could socialism? For a time a few professed to think so. Technocracy? Some flirted with the idea of it until it was pointed out that technocracy was merely "mechanistic positivism reorganized." Then quite suddenly the intellectuals discovered the brilliance of dialectical materialism. Here was a new adventure! If in the final analysis Marx's dialectical materialism could also be defined as mechanistic positivism, it should only be remarked that American intellectuals had not come—and in the early 1930s were still years from coming—to the final analysis of Marxism. For the present it was enough that it recreated a sense of sharing in an intellectual excitement of a kind a dying capitalistic democracy could not supply. Moreover, at least in their imaginings, it identified them with the dimly felt aspirations of the voiceless millions for whom they, the idealists, had always felt concern. Marxism was a saving grace.

Especially did it seem so to the Negro intellectual, to whom it appealed with special force. His deprivation was more than the chance result of a capitalistic democracy in its death throes. His deprivation and isolation were of the very structure of that democracy. His emotional heritage, transmitted through a long line of dissenting radicals and newly incremented by every generation, was a compulsive will to a comradeship of struggle, to abolish differences of caste and class and, above all, race.

And Marxism offered that and more. It offered not only liberation but brotherhood. Richard Wright was "amazed to find that there did exist in this world an organized search for the truth of the lives of the oppressed and the isolated. . . . It was not the economics of Communism, nor the great power of trade unions, nor the excitement of underground politics that claimed me; my attention was caught . . . by the possibility of uniting scattered but kindred people into a whole. . . . I felt that . . . it linked white life with black, merged two streams of common experience."

Like Wright, the Robesons were "impressed by the scope and seriousness" of the Communists' activities. They were certainly active. They had formed Leagues for the Defense of this and that. They were for the survival of "the people's art," for the Negro Youth Congress, for James Ford, a Negro, as Vice-President of the United States. Their efforts seemed so all-out and self-denying that Wright, even before he joined the party, resolved to tell "the common [Negro] people of the self-sacrifice of Communists who strove for unity among them." Soon the Robesons were attending those hot little

gatherings where the outraged compassion of fellow travelers confessed to impulses so ennobling as to seem the doctrines of a new
and great religion.

The Robesons returned to England and the Continent in 1934
and remained abroad five years. Again Paul saw Claude McKay,
who was still inexhaustible on the subject of Russia, and who took
him to meet Max Eastman in Nice, Glenway Wescott in Ville-
franche, and Frank Harris in Cimiez. Mrs. Robeson settled down
to study at the London School of Economics, and, probably through
her, Paul became acquainted with Harold Laski and some of his
like-minded colleagues.

As the guest of the Dean of Canterbury one weekend, Robeson
was treated to a strange and impressive discourse on Christianity,
the one brotherhood of man, and the USSR. "All I hear of the Russian program grips and inspires me," said the Very Reverend Hewlett Johnson. "If what we hear is true, it is majestic in range, practical
in detail, scientific in form, Christian in spirit. Russia would seem
to have embarked upon a task never yet attempted by modern or
ancient State."

A week later Robeson was in Russia, and within that same year
he returned there as a guest of the Russian state. Meanwhile he
had learned the language. He had read avidly—Exupéry, Gide's play
Oedipe. He made a picture in Russia. He made proper speeches:
"All I can say is the moment I came here I realized that I had
found what I had been seeking all my life. . . ." "All the people
of this portion of the globe must be proud when Stalin speaks of
the cultures of the different nationalities of the Soviet Union as
'socialist in content and national in form.'"

After this second visit to Russia, Robeson was not the same. He
seemed much older. At thirty-six there had been about him still a
boyish charm, a natural ease and grace of manner—the mark, one
supposes, of a mind that, however troubled, is innocent and free. At
thirty-seven he seemed plundered of innocence and of things native
to his spirit. The zestful geniality that had characterized his relations with the world was strained. He was no longer the "magnificent

primitive" pictured by Alexander Woollcott. He seemed to be enduring a torturous conflict of conscience and a harrowing obliteration of the ideas by which he had lived—the ideas that were embedded in the structure of his character and that had had no little influence on his personal success. He was like one struggling toward a reconciliation with himself.

Forsaking his old haunts and giving up the great financial rewards of London's fashionable West End theaters, he joined the Unity Theatre group, which, its brochure said, was "open to all members of the Labour and Trade union movement and to those who are in sympathy with our aims and objectives." He was no longer interested in being merely an entertainer. A way "to plead the case of the misunderstood and oppressed" had found him. He attended various "progressive congresses" and supported groups promoting cultural relations with Russia. He was taken up by the London *Daily Worker* and the *New Statesman.*

In his spare time he acquired a smattering of Chinese, competent Spanish, and a thorough mastery of Yiddish. Sometimes for expense money, but often for no money at all, he gave concerts for "workingmen's gatherings" in Birmingham, Glasgow, and Dublin, in Manchester and Marseille. He was always at the service of the British Negro colony in Camden Town. In Stockholm, Copenhagen, and Oslo his converts "developed into anti-fascist demonstrations." He sang not only Negro spirituals but the Jewish "people's" songs in Yiddish, the Chinese "people's" songs in Cantonese, songs expressive of "the new spirit of Soviet Russia" in Russian, and the songs of the Spanish Republic in Spanish. In 1938 he went to Barcelona and to the Madrid front to sing for the soldiers of the Republic.

These activities were faithfully reported in the American press, and especially in the Negro press, and they had the stamp of American approval. Fear and hatred of fascism were growing, and Negroes felt they had greater warrant than most Americans to hate fascism. Robeson himself had said that "fascism is no less the enemy of colored peoples than of Jews." He was in England when Mussolini's

THE LONESOME ROAD

Fascist legions invaded Ethiopia. In Germany he had seen the Nazi Brown Shirts when they were as yet but local bully boys, but in the summer of 1936 he saw them again—a force disciplined in terror —in Lisbon on their way to join Franco in Spain. In 1938 came Munich, and after Munich only the thoughtless and the blind did not see that fascism was a threat to freedom everywhere.

The imminence of war in Europe forced Robeson to return to America in the summer of 1939. He arrived just in time to subscribe to the sentiments of a letter addressed to "All Active Supporters of Democracy and Peace." Though dated two weeks before the Hitler-Stalin Pact, it was published the very week the pact was announced, and it bore the signatures of four hundred names well known in American intellectual and artistic circles. It rejected "the fantastic falsehood that the USSR and the totalitarian states are basically alike." It said that the Soviet Union "continues as always to be a bulwark against war and aggression, and works unceasingly for a peaceful international order." Just weeks later Russia attacked neutral Finland.

Robeson did not act like one of those whose idealism had been betrayed by the Hitler-Stalin Pact. He was not one of the thousands who publicly questioned or criticized the Russian turnabout. Perhaps an ironic sensibility, or an urge to sacrifice in some aberrant act of atonement his moral consciousness as well as his privileged position, operated in him. When the Nazi-Communist pact was broken and Hitler marched against Russia in 1941, Robeson delivered a speech in which he said, in part, "I am awfully happy and optimistic because fascism has at last come to grips with the one power [Communism] that will show it no quarter."

What he thought when America too came to violent grips with fascism is not recorded, but to be pro-Russian then was not to be anti-American democracy. Robeson was generous of his talents on the home front. He sang to thirty thousand people at the Watergate in Washington, D.C., to the workers of the American Aviation Plant, to a convention of the National Maritime Union, which, incidentally, bestowed an honorary membership on him. His programing was different from what his American audiences were used to. He sang the spirituals still, though not so many, and principally he sang pieces like "Joe Hill," "Peat Bog Soldiers," "Cradle Song of the Poor," and the "Song of Kazakstan."

Imperceptibly, in the way the mind is slowly shaped or altered by the accidents of day-to-day perception and experience, a peculiar estrangement had developed between Robeson and his people. They still flocked to hear him sing, still believed he was fighting their fight, still told themselves he was one of them. But he was no longer their instrument. He was sincere, but his sincerity seemed striving to overreach itself, to be more than it was, to be a substitute for every other moral and personal force. His human warmth was gone, his sense of humor was gone, or shut away. This was not *the* Robeson. This was another man bearing the same name.

He opened in the Theatre Guild production of *Othello* in October 1943. It was a great artistic success, though Michael Gold, who reviewed it for the *Daily Worker*, made it sound like a political rally of the proletarian left. Before the Broadway run ended, Robeson was honored by the National Federation for Constitutional Liberties for his "outstanding contribution toward building international unity within our country and throughout the world." The NFCL had been certified subversive. Before the Broadway run ended, an organization that Robeson had helped to found, the Council of African Affairs, was placed on the government's list of Communist-front organizations. Before the play left Broadway another organization with which he was connected, the National Negro Congress, was brought under suspicion when Mrs. Eleanor Roosevelt, ordinarily so generous of her patronage, refused to sponsor a concert in its behalf. Later the National Negro Congress was added to the government's list.

By the time the play's provincial tour ended in June 1945 the war in Europe was over, and in Asia nearly so, but, said Frederick Lewis Allen, "no sooner had America started to relax" than it was "borne in upon us, with increasing ominousness, that Soviet Russia in her turn was bent upon world conquest" and that "Communism was a deadly threat to institutions at home."

By the time the play's tour was over Paul Robeson had become co-chairman of the National Committee to Win the Peace, and a member of the national executive committee of the Independent Committee of the Arts, Sciences and Professions, both of which the New York *Times* reported "linked with left-wing and Communist activities," and both of which also went on the government's subversive list.

Accused of belonging to thirty-four Communist-front groups in 1946, Robeson was called before a Joint Committee on Un-American Activities of the California legislature. He testified, "Real racial equality is almost not an American conception. . . . If Mr. Truman is going to raise the underprivileged one-third of the nation, or the Negro one-tenth, he'd better establish a dictatorship in the South." He testified, "I think the best country in the world to test the principles of Marxism might be the America of today."

Edgar G. Brown, director of the Negro Council, appeared before the same committee the next day. He had no great importance as a race leader, but he spoke the troubled mind of Negroes. "Ninety-nine and nine-tenths per cent of the Negroes in the United States believe in the American system," he testified. "Any implication in yesterday's testimony by Paul Robeson that American Negroes would welcome an authoritarian regime to insure equalitarianism as in Russia is the biggest lie." He testified, "I do not consider Paul Robeson as a real spokesman or representative campaigner for Negroes. He is no hero now."

6. THE BETTER MAN WINS

One night in the early summer of 1935, the year the Russians were entertaining Paul Robeson as a guest of the state, a tawny Negro boy sat awaiting the end of the ceremonious preliminaries that would send him into his first important boxing match. He sat quietly, his shoulders slouched, his face hooded by a towel draped over his head. Opposite him in the ring sat his opponent, a man six and a half feet tall and weighing close to three hundred pounds, grimacing and fidgeting on his stool as if he itched in places he could not scratch. The Negro boy seemed completely unaware of him, of the blaze of lights, of the sixty thousand people who packed the vast stadium, of the several million who, the papers would say, sat huddled over radios across the great land.

Celebrities were now being introduced from the ring. Flash bulbs popped. Fight officials and trainers and seconds passed back and forth along the apron of the ring. The Negro boy, who had just turned twenty-one, and whose ring name was Joe Louis, scarcely stirred. "You lis'nin' to me, Chappie? Now you hear me good," his trainer said softly into the boy's ear. The boy grunted. "A tree liak this here you got to chop down," the trainer went on. "Cain't do no fancy whittlin'. No knife work. Ax him. You hear me, Chappie?" The boy grunted again and now, as the announcer moved to the center of the ring and reached for the suspended microphone, stood up, suddenly, marvelously alert.

Harry Balogh, the announcer, had been carefully instructed and rehearsed. Powerful segments of the American press had not wanted this fight. The Scripps-Howard chain of newspapers had opposed it from the beginning, and lately William Randolph Hearst, whose wife's pet charity, the Milk Fund, stood to benefit from it, had urged calling it off. Trouble was brewing between Italy and Ethiopia, and that "trouble could find focus in the prize ring at Yankee Stadium." American Negroes had already formed the Council of Friends of Ethiopia and had sent a delegation to denounce Italy before the League of Nations. It was foolhardy at this time, Hearst felt, to match a Negro against an Italian, especially when the Italian seemed certain to lose. The bout would exasperate passions, and "among whites there was talk of an aftermath of rioting."

"Ladies and gentlemen," the announcer said into the microphone, "tonight we have gathered here to watch a contest of athletic skill. We are Americans. That means that we have come from homes of many different faiths, and that we represent a lot of different nationalities. In America we admire the athlete who can win by virtue of his skill. Let me then ask you to join me in the sincere wish that regardless of race, color, or creed, the better man may emerge victorious. Thank you."

It is estimated that fifty million people listened to the blow-by-blow broadcast of the Louis-Carnera fight. When it ended in the sixth round, with the Italian a bloody, stumbling hulk, ten million Negroes heard for the first time a voice that when it spoke hereafter would quicken all the numbness of their patient years and sound through all the ranges of their hope. It said, "I glad I win." It was a coarse, thick voice unused to speech. On the night when they first heard it Negroes in Harlem, as in every ghetto in the country, sent up a "terrific roar. . . . Pandemonium broke loose. Tens of thousands marched through the streets." They laughed and sang and wept for joy. Some went to church to pray.

7. FOLK EPIC

The life of Joe Louis has something of the quality of an American folk epic. A mingling of three old indigenous strains —peasant-class black, master-class white, nomadic red—he was born on an Alabama tenant farm in 1914, the fifth child of his illiterate parents. By the time the seventh was born the father, Monroe Barrow, was breaking under the strain of never ending debt and wrenching less than a living from a worn-out cotton farm. He crumpled up completely while Joe was still a toddler, and the sheriff came and took him to the home for Negro feeble-minded near Mobile. Neither his wife nor his children ever saw him again. There was no money for sentimental journeys.

There was no money period. Mrs. Barrow seldom saw a dollar from one year to the next. She and the older children worked the land, and Joe was helping at the age of four. The cotton they raised was just enough to keep them poorly housed. They raised collard greens and beans and a stand of corn for food. Relatives scarcely more prosperous donated salt pork. The Barrows lived in the pattern prescribed by early postbellum history—matriarchal family, poverty, illiteracy. Though on Sundays they went regularly to church, where Mrs. Barrow renewed her trust in God, on weekdays there was little time for school. Joe did not learn to talk till he was six, or read till he was nine. The Barrows were so ragged that their clothes whistled in every wind.

Things got a little better when a widower began to call on Lillie Barrow. Patrick Brooks had several children of his own, but he was hard-working and ambitious, and he had it in his mind to "leave out for Dee-stroy" as soon as he was able. There was money there and a man had a "better go" for it. While he nursed this dream toward reality he wooed, and when word came that Monroe Barrow had died in the distant asylum Lillie married Patrick Brooks. After her son had become heavyweight champion of the world she was horrified to learn that she had been misinformed about Monroe's death. He did not die until November 1938. Joe wired money for a costly funeral.

Leaving his own younger children with his new wife, Pat Brooks went to Detroit and got a job at Ford's. He was following a pattern that was by then classic in its simplicity. He would send for his family when he had saved enough. This took two years. All the Barrows and Brookses reached Detroit in 1924. Joe was ten. He just could write his name, and his speech was so thick that he had difficulty making himself understood. Four or five years in elementary school helped some, but not much. The kind of learning he went there to get simply confused him and strangled the expressions of his personality. He switched to a vocational school. At the end of one marking period his teacher noted on the report card that Joe was "good in manual training. This boy should be able to do something with his hands."

Joe was already doing many things with his hands, and with his whole lithe, handsome body. For one thing, he was protecting himself in the human jungle where the Barrows lived. Also he worked after school delivering ice, selling papers, and collecting scrap metal. There were a lot of Barrow-Brookses, and they were poor—though far from poverty-shocked—and Pat Brooks's job at Ford's went "a-glimmering" when the depression struck. For almost a year they were on relief, incurring a debt that Joe Louis felt morally bound to repay in 1935. He thanked the Welfare Board, but he said, "They's others you can he'p now." He was living up to the family code of poor but decent. "I wants all my chil'ren to be decent," Mrs. Brooks used to say. She worked at decency, she embellished it and made it shine. She kept the children in school as long as she could. She even had Joe taking violin lessons on a pitifully cheap violin once a week.

One day when Joe was going for a lesson he met an ex-schoolmate. Thurston McKinney, who was two or three years older, had long since quit school and had become the amateur light heavyweight boxing champion of Michigan. He fought for merchandise checks, and when the merchandise turned out to be something he did not need or want, he sold it for cash, pocket money. He was in search of a sparring partner the day he met Joe. He joshed Joe about the violin—"It ain't nothin' for a man to do"—and persuaded him to fill in as a sparmate. They went to the Brewster Center Gymnasium. Joe was completely ignorant of the fine points of boxing, and McKinney toyed with him for a while; but Joe's reflexes were perfect, and his body seemed to have an intelligence independent of his mind, a sentience that never registered in his face. Suddenly he caught McKinney with a right and the older boy would have fallen had not Joe rushed in to hold him up. "You way too good for school, man," McKinney said.

It was summer, and in the fall Joe did not return to school—was, in fact, already working as a six-dollar-a-week lathe operator at Briggs. Jobs of any kind were scarce in 1931, and Joe knew he was lucky. The day after the encounter with McKinney he gave up the violin too, and joined the Brewster Center Boxing Club. There was a little racket about this at home. "But, Ma," Joe said, "a guy kin be decent an' a fighter both."

Joe was both. For the next three years, during which he got a job at Ford's, he fought for merchandise checks. His wages went to his mother for the common pool. In 1932 he won the Detroit Golden Gloves. In 1933 he barely missed becoming national amateur light heavyweight champion. In 1934 he made it.

That was the year a man named John Roxborough first took an active interest in Joe Louis. A mulatto lawyer, physically as glossy-smooth as new chrome, but mind-scored and complicated beyond belief, living professionally on the slippery edges of the under-world, Roxborough was an American archetype machined by those attitudes that operated to exclude him from sharing in the decenter large prospects society offered to white men of half his talents, train-ing, and ambition. He was cunning, he was callous, and he was in-volved in transactions that were shady.

Still he could not quite put down or cast off a hundred years of careful breeding, or uproot all the thousand precepts planted by his forebears. He had scruples still, and particularly strong ones on matters of race. If in privacy he lived beyond the reach of them, he, nevertheless, was very careful that other Negroes should not. He sent—that is, financed—many worthy Negro boys through college, ad-monishing them, "You've got to help the race." He donated to Ne-gro social welfare. He did boys' work at the Negro Y. He found jobs for worthy Negro youths either with friends or in one of the legiti-mate enterprises—insurance companies, real estate—he controlled. Not the least complex thing about John Roxborough was a romantic sense of mission. This was strangely wedded to an instinct for the main chance.

In pursuit of his interest in Joe Louis, Roxborough called in a friend from Chicago. He had a habit of employing fronts, even in legitimate affairs, and Julian Black was to be a front. "I've found a boy, a fighter," Roxborough said, and began laying down the rules for a game Black did not even know he was going to play. "No fakes, no falls," Roxborough said. "Joe's not to have bouts that aren't con-tested strictly on merit."

But Black knew about Negroes in boxing, he had managed sev-eral, nearly all of whom, he knew, had been asked at one time or another to fake or fall. Otherwise they did not last long as fighters;

or if they were really good and lasted, they were never allowed to reach the top of the heavyweight division. Jack Johnson had spoiled that. Black spoke of this, and called the names of Langford, Godfrey, and Wills.

Though Roxborough had never managed fighters, he knew all this too, but the difference was that he thought this knowledge could be put to redeeming use. He remembered that when Jack Johnson won the world's heavyweight championship Jack London, reporting that fight from far-off Australia, expressed the hope that "somewhere in America might be found a man to crush this impudent black." There was a frantic search for a "white hope," and Jim Jeffries came out of retirement to meet Johnson in what was advertised to be "the greatest battle of the century." Jack London reported that fight too for the New York *Herald*. "Fight?" he wrote. "There was no fight. . . . It was a monologue delivered to twenty thousand spectators by a smiling Negro." The New York *World* commented: "That Mr. Johnson should so lightly and carelessly punch the head off Mr. Jim Jeffries must have come as a great shock to every devoted believer in the supremacy of the Anglo-Saxon race." This was raillery, of course, but next day, when rioting broke out country-wide, it seemed something else again. The New York *Herald* reported, "Half Dozen Dead as Crowds Attack Negroes. Reign of Terror Here."

"This fighter's a good boy," Roxborough said. "Not smart-alecky. Modest."

"I've never seen a good fighter yet who was modest, especially a spook," Black said.

"This boy is. We've just got to make white people know it."

"The way things are, that's going to take some doing."

"I know the kind of boy he is," Roxborough said. "I've watched him. I've asked around. You find out what Jack Blackburn thinks of him as a fighter."

"I don't think Blackburn'll be for training a colored heavyweight in earnest," Black said.

"See," Roxborough said. "And, Julian, I want him trained for real, in earnest. I've got plans."

Though a Negro himself, and once a great welterweight, Jack Blackburn objected at first, for reasons he considered overwhelming. Negro heavyweights earned little money; they were used mainly to help build the reputations of white fighters; and "*They* ain't never goin'a let another colored boy wear 'at crown." But he consented at last, and Joe Louis was trained for real. Julian Black became the manager of record. Behind all three stood Roxborough, putting his lawless cunning to work for the furtherance of an altogether lawful, proud, and beneficent end—the making of a Negro boy into an American hero.

There was plenty to work with. Joe Louis had the physical equipment of all great boxers. His "rhythm," Jack Blackburn said, "showed he was jus' nat'ally a fighter." His timing and co-ordination were flawless, his strength and power exceptional. But Jack Johnson—and Sam Langford and Joe Jeannette—had all these too, and in great degree, and they were not enough. Joe Louis had something more. He had traits of temperament, of personality, and of character so different from those usually ascribed to figures in the world of sports as to make him seem a strange mutation. Even after his private life was largely absorbed in his public career he retained a quality so modest and guileless that some of the keenest observers called him "dumb," "stupid," and "insensitive."

But Joe Louis was none of these. He was not articulate, but he was extremely sensitive—and especially to those nuances of fear and rage and hope that sped like messages of doom or redemption through the air his people breathed. Toward the end of his first year as a professional boxer, when it was quite evident that Negro fans were already rearing him to the status of race hero, a reporter talked to him. Joe had just knocked out Charley Massare, "one of the greatest heavyweight prospects since Dempsey," and in his dressing room in the Chicago Stadium he was cooling out, while a squad of policemen guarded his door against a mob of Negroes clamoring to see him. "Joe," the reporter asked, "do you hear that?" "Yeah,"

Joe replied impassively, "I hears it." "Well, what do you think, Joe? They're calling for you." There was a moment's silence. "I thinks if I evah does somethin' to let my people down, I wanna die."

Certain constellations in his mind and character were fixed. Probably without being aware of it, he had assumed a responsibility for discharging some of the burden of obloquy and shame and struggle his people bore. He was—or, thanks to John Roxborough, was made —perceptive to the least change in the running current of race relations. In 1935, when anti-Jewish feeling, whipped up beyond control by unscrupulous race baiters in Harlem, exploded in a riot that destroyed more than two million dollars' worth of Jewish and white property, Joe Louis was mindful to point out that the promoter who "brang me to the big-time" was Mike Jacobs. Already a man to be seen (and more to be seen than heard, since he was after all what he was), Joe appeared at many race-uplift rallies, including one for Philip Randolph's Pullman porters.

Finally, unlike many of limited learning and an even more limited experience of the right to self-respect, Louis was sensitive to the demands of human dignity and pride. In the very last fight of his first professional year he knocked out Lee Ramage, who was the latest "greatest heavyweight prospect." Joe had been a three-to-one underdog in the fight. When it was over he spoke on a local radio hookup. He said, "He [Ramage] was sho' a tough customer. I never seen so many gloves flyin' at me as he sent to my face. I tried to box him, but I soon learn . . . he knows too much boxin'." Later he said, "I wanna win good an' lose good."

The proof of losing good came sooner than Joe Louis and almost everyone else in America expected. To say that the Carnera fight had made him overconfident and even somewhat cocky is to point out that Louis had at least a normal complement of frailties. He was young, he took pride in his prowess. He had had twenty-six professional fights and had won all of them, twenty-three by knockouts, when he climbed into the ring against Schmeling in 1936. Sports writers like Grantland Rice, Allison Danzig, and Bill Cunningham had hung enough superlatives on him to founder the humility of a saint. Even the New York *Times* seemed to concede that Louis was invincible. The Schmeling fight proved that he was not.

The German was anxious to regain the heavyweight title he had lost three years before. Joe Louis stood in his way. He was determined to crush Joe Louis. Having once lost to Max Baer, a Jew, Schmeling was in disgrace at home, where Hitler was already beginning the most wicked persecution of a people the world has ever known. But few Americans then understood the mad emotional structure of Nazism—the satanic hate and rage with which it inspired its disciples; the will to discipline it imposed. When Schmeling, training at Napanoch, made typical Nazi racist remarks about "superior" and "inferior" peoples, few sensed behind them the dark power of the German's psychological commitment. Twice, meantime, he had watched Louis fight, and he had studied for hours all the Louis fight pictures. He declared that he had found a weakness, and he planned and trained with cold, grim efficiency to exploit it.

Louis, on the other hand, apparently thought of the German as just another fighter and the match with him as just another fight. He trained routinely. Self-complacency had crept over him so gradually that he did not realize how careless he had become, how dull his fighter's instincts, how negligent his fighter's mind. He behaved as though he believed the newspapers, none of which conceded he could lose. He had his twenty-second birthday at his training camp in Lakewood and he celebrated it with a party. He played a lot of golf with Joe Williams, a sports writer assigned to the camp by the *World-Telegram*. Williams reported admiringly that it was "amazing any man could be so unconcerned . . . as Louis" in the weeks before an important fight.

Joe was unconcerned—and that was the way he remained all through the training period. He seemed not to realize how much of the pride of his people depended upon his skill and power; that he was their very symbol of equality. For the first and only time in his professional career his emotional machinery failed to respond to the spark of his Negroness and to the goad of his racial experience.

So Max Schmeling defeated him the night of June 17, 1936. The

German *had* found a weakness. In the fourth round his right fist, zinging over Louis' lowered left, crashed against his opponent's chin. The "Brown Bomber" went down. Though he was up at the count of three, and though he still had enough to keep the German wary, he fought in a daze. His defense was as thin as tissue paper. He took a terrific beating. Round after round Schmeling's right fist did its methodical work of destruction until that work was done. In the twelfth round Louis was knocked out with a punch as clean and true as a rifle shot. He had "lost good." But the German would not even concede him this. In an article in the *Saturday Evening Post* some weeks later, while pictures of the fight were being billed in Germany as *The Typical Nazi Triumph* and *The Great Nordic Victory*, Schmeling accused Louis of deliberately hitting low.

No one recorded what Schmeling said in his German-language broadcast to the Fatherland immediately after the fight, but all remembered that it had ended with an exuberant "Heil Hitler!" Turning from the microphone to the writers who crowded his dressing room, Schmeling upbraided them in a heavy accent. "You should have known better. I would not have taken this fight if I did not think that I, a white man, could beat a colored man. *Ja?*" A few minutes later he had a felicitous cable from Goebbels, and he waved it over his head.

Meanwhile Joe Louis lay still half dazed in his dressing room across the corridor. His managers, Roxborough and Black, his trainer, and a few still incredulous newsmen were with him. He could remember little about the fight, and as his head cleared he kept asking over and over, "What happen'?" It was Jack Blackburn, the trainer, who told him, trying to make the telling neither less nor more than it should be. "You got tagged, Chappie. An' when you git tagged right, that's all—there ain't no more." There was a deeper silence in the quiet room. "You got in a low one too," Blackburn said, "but you didn't know what you was doin'." Louis struggled upright then. "Roxy," he said, "you go tell him I'm sorry. I don' wanna foul nobody." Without a word Roxborough left for Schmeling's dressing room.

An hour later, when Louis and his handlers were leaving the stadium, a reporter asked whether they would protest the blow Schmeling landed after the bell ending the fifth round. "He beat me fair," Louis said, and that was that.

The Negro race went into mourning. That night the bars and restaurants in Harlem closed early and many cabarets did not open at all. South-side Chicago stayed indoors. It was said that Paradise Valley, Detroit's Negro section, "whimpered like a runned-over puppy." Everywhere in the colored world Joe Louis' defeat was felt to be a calamity as tragic and as irrevocable as a sudden, unlooked-for death. Indeed, it was a death—the death of a hero. The ideal attributes of the hero—imperious skill, indomitable strength, invincible courage—could no longer be vested in one of their own. They believed that they had fastened their hopes on unattainable goals. They were thrown back—or they felt thrown back, which was much the same thing—to an acceptance of the white man's evaluation of the race. Pride could not anchor in attributes they had, but only in attributes they aspired to have. Schmeling's shattering fists, they felt, had smashed more than the body of a black man: they had crushed the pride of a race.

But at the very time when Joe Louis seemed least so, he was most heroic. He was back in training before the bruises were gone from his body. By mid-July, scarcely a month after his defeat, a match had been arranged with Jack Sharkey, who had once beaten Schmeling for the title. The Schmeling fight, the newspapers said, had "exploded the Louis myth." The German, the newspapers said, had "taken it out of him." Watching Louis train, sports writers commented that the defeat had "affected Louis badly." He was slow, he was deliberate, he was self-conscious even against sparmates in the training ring.

The newspapers reported many things about him, including the fact that he gave but grudging support to the American Olympic Committee, who solicited him for funds to help American athletes travel to the games in Germany. He was changed. He was now, Paul Gallico wrote (and implied much more) in the Reader's Digest, "a mean, mean man." He was also a "has-been." Ten days before the match with Sharkey, Allison Danzig reported that "Almost to a man, they [the fight experts] agree that Louis is trying his comeback far too early and against far too shrewd a campaigner in Sharkey."

Louis knocked out Sharkey in three rounds. He won three more fights in that year and three the next before he defeated James J. Braddock for the heavyweight championship in 1937.

Though these victories had much to do with restoring Louis to public esteem, his character and deportment in and out of the ring had everything to do with keeping him there. The things he did and the things he refused to do became, more and more, the subjects of editorial comment. He fought for charity more often than the four previous heavyweight champions combined. Before a fight his silence was impenetrable; his post-fight remarks were without presumptuousness. "I was lucky"; "I glad I win"; "I know I been in a fight."

He had no disdainful words for an opponent, "no matter how pitiful [the opponent's] exhibition or how dirty his fighting." He refused to endorse a nationally advertised brand of cereal because he did not eat it, and he turned down five thousand dollars to endorse a cigar because he did not smoke. Roi Ottley, a well-known newsman, tells of overhearing the following dialogue between two Negroes. "If we had more Negroes like Joe Louis," said one, "things would be better for us." "Sure 'nuff," replied the other, "but if we had more white folks like Joe, things would be better still."

But if Joe seemed once more a paragon to his own people, he was scarcely less a model to whites. All the latter had seen and heard and read of him, quite aside from his athletic prowess, added up to those ennobling moral characteristics—honorableness and honesty, modesty and generosity—with which men will endow their heroes when heroes give them half a chance. Joe Louis gave them better than half a chance, and whites, too, took pride in him—in the oft-repeated boast that only in this country was such a career possible for him; in the belief that the American environment alone could

imbrue him in the "American" virtues. Joe Louis had achieved that
rare metamorphosis from Negro to American.

So—save perhaps a few scattered colonies of Germanophiles, who
were extremely confident—all of America came up to the night of
Louis' return match with Schmeling in 1938 in a state of high, apprehensive excitement. Some of the excitement was patriotic. It
was not that the seventy thousand people who packed Yankee Stadium already recognized German National-Socialism as an international evil. No doubt some had read in *Mein Kampf* Hitler's
exhortations to a "Germany, mistress of the globe by the victorious
sword of a master race." Though at least two hundred Jews bearing
anti-Nazi slogans picketed the stadium, and though only three
months before Hitler had begun the occupation of Austria, not
many in America took Hitler and his rantings seriously until after
Munich, and Munich was still three months in the future. No. The
excitement of patriotism amounted to this: the heavyweight championship of the world was a national possession, and Joe Louis,
American, was to fight Max Schmeling, German, to keep the title
here.

But it was not quite that simple for Joe Louis and fourteen million Negroes. They were very much aware of the new racism and of
the moral sickness with which Germany seemed bent on infecting
the world. Negro newspapers had recently reprinted their hot con-
demnations of Hitler's and Goebbels' refusal to shake hands with
the American Negro athletes who had "swept to scintillating victories" in the Olympic games in 1936. Negroes were reminded, too,
that Schmeling had accused Louis of deliberately fighting foul, and
had scorned him as a "black fellow" and a "stupid amateur" in
such a way as to sear all colored people in the acid of his contempt.
To Negroes, Schmeling was not just a German; he was Nazism's
embodiment, and when Joe Louis stepped into the ring against
him the outcome would somehow prove whether the concept of
superior-inferior races or the concept of racial equality would
prevail.

Considering the mixed emotions, the apprehensive excitement, the vague but real sense of crisis, the jingo atmosphere (a thousand German nationals were present in a body), the fight itself was an anticlimax.

Just as the referee finished his instructions to the fighters someone shrieked, "Joe, remember Hitler sent him! Hitler sent him!"

The bell rang. Scarcely had the fighters met when Joe Louis' left hand flashed out and sent Schmeling reeling against the ropes. A right hand crunched against the German's jaw and he went down. The crowd rose instantly. Far out in the dark reaches of the stadium, among the cheaper seats, a cry went up, "Oh, Joe! Oh, Joe! Oh, Joe!" and as Schmeling rose, blood streaming from his mouth, the whole stadium seemed to take up the cry. "Oh, Joe! Oh, Joe!" There was another drumfire of blows so vicious that the German whimpered in pain and many at the ringside winced to hear him. The German went down again. The shouts changed. "Back to Hitler! Back to Hitler!" The mixed emotions were now one emotion, the seventy thousand voices one voice. Schmeling struggled to his hands and knees, rose swaying and glassy-eyed. The punch that sent him down for the last time spattered blood over the press row.

Nat Fleischer, the boxing authority, summed up the spirit that prevailed in Yankee Stadium that night: "The heavyweight championship of the world remained in America . . . the barrage that swept Schmeling to such swift disaster [enabled] an American youth to retain for his country the heavyweight title."

8. "AIN'T FIGHTIN' FOR NOTHIN'"

But there were other fights for other causes. The rehabilitation of Louis' self-esteem, though it uplifted other Negroes too, was not enough. As a professional boxer, he was proud to be champion; as a man, he was frustrated by the very real inadequacies that kept his personality half submerged. He hired a tutor. He tried to master the mysteries of grammatical speech. He tried to build a satisfactory family life—and failed.

As a Negro, he was troubled. Establishing a fund for the Federal

Council of Churches of Christ in America, he wrote, "Before I retire, I want to put up one more fight—the best of my career—to help my people." In 1940, though scarcely prepared for it intellectually, he campaigned for Wendell Willkie, delivering practically the same speech to Negroes in a dozen cities. "I am a fighter, not a politician. This country has been good to me, and has given me everything I have, and I want it to be good to you and give you everything you need. I am for Willkie because I think he will help my people. I think my people ought to be for him too."

On January 9, 1942, he defended his title against Buddy Baer and turned his purse over to the Navy Relief Fund. Before the fight, when a reporter asked him how it felt to be "fighting for nothing," Louis shot back, "Ain't fightin' for nothin'. Fightin' for my country." Willkie spoke briefly from the ring: "Thank you, Joe Louis, in the name of the United States Navy and the American people. Thank you for your magnificent contribution and generosity in risking for nothing a title you have won through blood, sweat and toil."

Three days later—just five weeks after Pearl Harbor—Joe Louis enlisted as a private in the army, and Paul Gallico, who had once called Joe Louis Barrow "a mean, mean man . . . just emerging from the pit," was moved to write in *Liberty* magazine: "Citizen Barrow has set us a lesson. Can we learn it, we are saved. Should we ignore it, we shall reap what we deserve."

PART FOUR

And Long Endure

CHAPTER TEN

"You Can't Tell Which of Them Joes"

AMERICA HAD already fought this war longer than she had fought any war against a foreign foe. It had started in December 1941, and many men had died on alien seas, in strange lands where they had never thought to be, and in the screaming air. Now it was early spring of 1945, and the only sure thing was that, though the fighting and the dying would go on, the things for which the war was being fought could not be won in blood alone. This was the one solid, unshakable certainty in a war in which nothing else—neither its shape nor its dimensions, its tactics nor its weapons—remained for long the same.

This war had a genius of its own, and that genius not only wrought changes in the current of each battle, but in contingency after grave contingency and the shifting alterations of the mind to meet them, it changed rules and customs and, sometimes, the stubborn heritage of men's home-grown thoughts. Yet the decisions and the acts that marked these changes were for the most part so strangely low-keyed when they came as to make them seem almost the normal course of things, and to indicate perhaps that, for all the hard necessity of them, a conscience and a will had gone before.

Only after decisions had been made and acts fulfilled did men look back and recognize the strangeness—and not always then.

Thus the *Stars and Stripes*, an army newspaper, reported with great casualness, "The plan of mixing white and colored troops in fighting units, a departure from previous U. S. Army practice, is operating successfully." This was printed on April 6, 1945, four full months after General George Patton had packed white troops on Negro-manned tanks and rushed them to the Ardennes to fight and die together. It was a month after the fight at Remagen where, fighting in mixed companies of armored infantry, eight hundred men had died. And it was two weeks after an incident in a woods near a German town called Wessel.

The Germans were in the blasted woods. The trees were mostly naked of branches, and the trunks of the trees were barked and splintered, and the floor of the woods was knee-high in the debris from the trees. A road divided the woods. It was a dirt road, pocked with small craters, and though it had once had real military value, it had little now. Indeed, when the main striking force of the American Third Army drove north in February and early March, this road had not been used. It simply went north to Wessel, a town taken by elements of the 17th Airborne, who had dropped from the sky, and the town where K Company of the 349th Infantry Regiment was headed on March 24 when it was stopped by the Germans who held the woods. K Company was scheduled to be re-equipped in Wessel and trucked from there to join the regiment farther north.

There should have been no battle. It was an accident, and it had no bearing on the big pattern of the war. The real fighting was going on way north of Wessel, and Wessel itself was four miles from the woods. With a small exception, this was Allied territory for thirty miles around.

The exception was the woods, and the Germans had no business in it, and no one either then or afterward had any clear idea of why they were in it, or what some of them were doing dressed in American uniforms, or why it should be that of the eighteen who were finally captured at least a half dozen spoke English with no trace of accent. Undoubtedly they were saboteurs who had been dropped behind the lines. But why in that place? What was there to sabotage?

K Company, commanded by a temporary major and consisting of three platoons, came down the road at about ten o'clock in the morning. The weather was unusually fine for the time of year, and the men were relaxed, tramping along in lines of four at an unsoldierly eighty-five paces a minute—there was no hurry—and taking a civilian-like care to avoid the muddy holes in the road. K was one of those companies newly reorganized on the new integrated basis, and it had a platoon of Negroes mixed in with two platoons of whites. Most of the Negroes had been service-of-supply troops—ordnance men, truckers, engineers, and signalers—eight weeks before, but when the new policy was handed down they were among the many thousands of Negroes who had applied for transfer to combat. So many had applied that to take all of them would have disrupted the vital functions of supply, and the number taken was finally limited to three thousand. These were some of them. They were as proud as they could be, but they felt that they were on trial, and they could not wait to join the regiment and get into combat.

The last lines of the company had passed two or three hundred yards into the shade cast on the road by the woods when one of the Negro GIs said to the sergeant walking beside him, "I seen something move in them woods," and pointed to the left. The sergeant was not impressed. "I tell you, Sarge, I seen something move." "Okay," the sergeant said, "you got my permission to go see."

The men who heard this exchange laughed, and all the nearest men slowed down and watched the soldier who had seen something move cross the road, jump the ditch, and scramble up the steep bank on the other side. A shot whanged out. The soldier tumbled forward and out of sight. Before the men in the road could recover from their surprise, machine-gun and rifle fire came pouring out of the woods on both sides. Some men broke back along the road clear of the woods, but most hit and hugged the ground. The sergeant shouted, "Goddamn, there is something in them woods! Men with guns!" The steel kept zinging back and forth over their heads and into the trees. Up forward, the major, prone with the rest, raised himself to a low crouch and looked around.

There were three things they could do. They could make a dash for the clear road more than a tenth of a mile ahead; they could make a dash for the clear road several hundred yards behind; they could stay where they were until darkness came.

There was an alternative that the major refused to consider, for the last thing he wanted was a fight. The heaviest weapons his men had were Browning automatic rifles, and there were only eight of them. The stuff that was coming at them—harmlessly enough so long as they stayed down—seemed no heavier, but there was no way of knowing how many of the enemy there were to send it. Also, the Negroes were a question. They were new to his command. He had never seen them in combat, and, though he considered himself a man without prejudice, the major half believed what he had heard. He just did not know what kind of soldiers they would make. He just did not know what kind of *men* they were.

Crouching, the major looked up and down the road. The men had hurled themselves down just as they were, in lines of four, but now they were separating, crawling on their bellies, some toward the ditch on one side and some toward the ditch on the other side of the road. No one was in panic. The men crawled a few feet and then lay quietly awhile and crawled again, cursing the unseen enemy in the woods and waiting for the major to make up his mind.

But it was not entirely up to the major to decide how the situation was to be met, for even as he tried to estimate it the men became targets for a new, more intense burst of fire. Some of the enemy on the left had made their way to the embankment and, protected behind it, were firing down on the road. The Americans returned the fire blindly. The most they hoped for was to prevent the Germans from getting pot shots at them. The major shouted, "Watch the right too! Watch the right!" Some of the men swung round on their bellies and watched the right.

Meanwhile a lieutenant, who with about a dozen men had sprinted clear of the woods with the first burst of fire, had an idea.

He told the men who were with him about it, and then he sent a soldier forward to tell the major. The lieutenant and his men would leave the road, skirt the woods on the right for a likely distance, and then go into the woods to see what they could see.

When the major sent back word to try it, the lieutenant ordered his men to fix bayonets, and they went into the field at the edge of the woods, which, bending sharply outward here, stretched for a quarter of a mile. At three or four hundred yards, pausing to get some sense of the enemy's location by the sound of his fire, they ventured in. Underbrush and debris made the going difficult. The men spread out, but kept each other in sight among the trees, and went as quietly as they could. They must have effected a measure of surprise, for well back from the road they came upon five Germans huddled over a spring in a small clearing. Apparently they had left their weapons up on the line. They surrendered at once. One of the Negroes in the lieutenant's command shouted jubilantly, "We got us some Krauts!" That was the end of surprise. Germans could be heard crashing toward them from the direction of the road. The Americans had to fight a retreat through the trees. One of the prisoners escaped.

When they got back to the road an American lay dead in the road and the others were fighting from the ditches. A few grenades on either side would have made a great difference. The men in the ditch on the right were firing over the heads of their own men in the ditch on the left, and vice versa, and each of these lines had its back to the Germans who were firing on it. As a military matter, the situation was completely ridiculous. The stalemate was so thorough that the major could leave the ditch without great risk and go down the road to the edge of the woods to question the scouting party.

It did not occur to him to question the prisoners. He himself did not speak German. Schooled as he was in the ordinary ways of his National Guard, civilian-insurance-broker background, it did not cross his mind that an ordinary German might speak English. That he did question the prisoners was an accident of his emotions. When he got from the lieutenant nothing as to the number and disposition of the enemy, nothing more valuable than the bare report of the skirmish in the woods, the major looked at the prisoners and re-marked with evident annoyance, "Well, it's a sure thing these s.o.b.'s won't escape."

The reaction was immediate. Two of the prisoners, not under-standing and perhaps thinking themselves addressed, stiffened; the third drew his elbows in and spread his hands; and the fourth, grinning, said, "But Captain, we do not wish to escape." His English was perfect.

The major stared at him, and at all of them, really seeing them for the first time. They were not the "syphilitic old bastards" from the bottom of the barrel the Germans were supposed to be using now. They were younger than he, and he had just turned thirty. Sud-denly he saw them as persons, and a feeling of human comradeship might have stirred in the major under other circumstances. He was that kind of man. But the man was submerged in the soldier, and the soldier was intent on his military problem. The major's youthful face grew rigid with responsibility. He questioned the English-speaking prisoner closely.

How many Germans were in the woods? A handful on one side, fewer on the other. What did he call a handful? Perhaps twenty-five or thirty on the left, not so many on the right—that morning some had been sent out to reconnoiter for a route to rejoin other German forces. Didn't they know there were no other German forces within fifty miles? A shrug. Well, what weapons did they have there in the woods? Rifles and perhaps five machine guns and two mortars. The mortars and three of the machine guns were on the left. Since they were badly outnumbered, would they surrender? Those on the right probably, but those on the left—no; they were SS; they were Nazi.

"You're not Nazi?"

The spokesman prisoner looked at the hand-spreading prisoner, and they both grinned. The major searched them for identification. They had none.

On the basis of this information the major decided to try to clear the woods. The word was passed along. Both sides of the woods would have to be cleared simultaneously, and the major meant to drive in front and rear. He divided and disposed his men for this purpose. A quarter of them were sent across the open field along the edge of the woods on the right, and another quarter skirted the woods on the left. At a given signal they were to go in with the object of getting behind the enemy. The rest of the men, facing the Germans from the road, were to go in after the enemy was engaged in the woods.

It sounded like a cinch, but it was not. There could be no secrecy in the preparations, and what the Germans could not see happening they could make intelligent guesses about, and when the attack came they were ready—especially those on the left. The Americans had to come to them. They had to tunnel through underbrush, climb over fallen trees. The shouts they raised as they went in, like Arkansas farmers on a rat hunt, soon turned to curses of rage and frustration. They lost contact with one another, and it was each man for himself. Machine-gun and rifle fire streaked through the trees; mortar bursts sent debris flying. There may have been only twenty-five or thirty of the enemy, but it seemed at least a hundred—and all hidden, all firing without showing themselves. It was like fighting in the dark passages of an abandoned mine filled with rotting timbers and hung with the webs of monstrous steel-spinning spiders, and exploding on all sides with charges of powder. The woods pinged and hammered and roared.

The men on the right finished first, stumbled out to the road with eleven prisoners, collected themselves, and rushed in on the left. They managed to keep together pretty well and to fight effectively as a team. Coming to the rear of a mortar and some riflemen spread out in the underbrush before it, they killed several of the enemy and took two prisoners. It ended quickly after that. The firing diminished to single shots and then to silence. The men who were scattered all through the woods now began to shout, somewhat tremulously, inquiringly, to find one another. Gradually the shouts converged, and finally one hundred and thirty-seven Americans came out of the woods almost together.

They brought four prisoners with them, but they were too dazed to remark that the prisoners wore American battle jackets and helmets. Including the soldier who had seen something move and the one who had got it on the road, eleven of the company had been killed, but no one mentioned the fact; no one asked questions. They looked a mess. It was incredible that they should have got so ragged and grimed and smudged with dirt. Their emotions were in a state too. They were too stupefied from the shock of the crazy battle to do anything but stand there in the road and stare about with glazed eyes. They did not seem to know what to do with themselves, or with the prisoners, or with the dead man who lay sprawled down the road. They seemed to be waiting for something to happen, and nothing happened for a long time.

Then, suddenly, a Negro soldier was afflicted with laughter. He doubled over and stumbled drunkenly in the middle of the road in a paroxysm of laughter. He tried to smother it, but every time he got it under control his eyes would light instantly on someone's face and he was off again. In slowly gathering wonderment the men looked at him. The major was the first to recover. He took the soldier by the arm and shook him. "What are you laughing at, soldier? Hold it now," the major said. "Hold it, soldier," he repeated more sternly as the man looked at him and broke out again.

"You too, Major," the Negro said, tears streaming. "Major, sir," he said, his voice beginning to whoop again, "I swear to God an' hope to die if you can tell which of them Joes is white and which is colored! Look at 'em, Major. I swear to God . . ."

Grinning sheepishly, the men looked at each other, and some began to laugh. The major laughed, the men laughed, and even some of the prisoners laughed. The road rang with the sound of it rising, rippling, and gathering to a hilarious roar. When it had spent itself the major, frowning, said, "Okay. Okay, soldiers. We've still got work to do. The war's not over yet."

CHAPTER ELEVEN

Morning Fair

1. STRATEGY

BACK HOME in America the Negro's political, economic, and social position was better than it had ever been before. It was far from ideal, but, among other things, the Supreme Court had ruled it unconstitutional to exclude him from white Democratic party primaries; his employment opportunities were greater; his wage differential had been practically eliminated; he was increasingly active in organized labor. Some of the bars to his advancement in the military were down.

Even the South seemed to realize that the physical struggle against fascism had subjected the traditional pattern of race relations and attitudes to considerable strain, and while some Southerners reacted to this in their accustomed ways, the best minds of the South moved to meet it. Liberals like Ralph McGill of Georgia and Virginius Dabney of Virginia, together with a handful of ministers and educators, took the initiative in a program of "new morality to give assurance [to Negroes] of our sincere goodwill and desire to cooperate."

If cynicism suggested that the manifestations of this "new mo-

rality" were compelled by the inexorable logic of history and a perception of America's new place in the world, rather than created
in the integrity of the hearts of men, so much the better. Perhaps
America had grown more realistic, even as the world had shrunk.
Good will had often in the past proved an uncertain commodity in
the market of race relations, and however much Negroes respected
it, they were no longer willing to depend upon it. The war had joined
their fate to that of minority and colonial peoples throughout the
world, and the new touchstones of race destiny and of the destiny
of all men were economic and political. If practical politics and economics were inspired by kindliness, well and good; but they should
first be informed by simple reason and a reasonable concern for the
safety of the world. Negroes believed with Lester Granger, head of
the Urban League: "The United States must hold to the elemental
principles of cooperation. . . . Back of all that is planned or
achieved is the fact that henceforth it is one world or none."

So it was not that Negroes rejected good will. It was never quite
worthless, and, in fact, it had brought about many a measure beneficial to them. The shocked mourning over the death of President
Roosevelt would have been less deep except that Negroes deeply felt
the loss of his humanitarian interest. They respected the good will
shown by the Department of State when it accredited several Negroes to the organizational meeting of the United Nations, and they
applauded the Preamble and Article I of the UN Charter, which
reaffirmed a belief in human rights and "fundamental freedom for
all without distinction as to race. . . ."

But Negroes knew that if the charter meant what it said, that
if democracy would be fulfilled—and, indeed, if it would be saved—
then the instruments of democratic government—the executive, the
legislative, and the judicial—must join an attack on the inequities
inherent in racial segregation. As they approached the halfway
mark of the twentieth century Negroes by and large looked beyond
solicitude to strength, beyond men to the measures they proposed,
beyond messiahs to machinery, and beyond good will to strategy.

The strategy was scarcely new: the NAACP had devised it long

ago. It was simply applied on a new and broader front and directed
by a new, rigidly disciplined and yet resilient mind.

2. NOBODY'S FOOL

Until he was twenty-one Thoroughgood Marshall
had no idea of becoming a lawyer. Entirely without self-conscious-
ness before that time, he gave little thought to *becoming* anything.
He simply was. And what he was amounted to a yeasty mixture of
brash assertiveness, a sharp and sportive sense of humor, an instinct
for people, an amused irreverence for the "solemn finer things of
life," and mercenary ambitiousness. At forty-five he retained his
sense of humor and his gregariousness, but all else had changed. At
forty-five he had defended in a hundred courts of law the finest
concepts of human dignity and equality of civil rights, had won
twelve of fourteen cases on these issues before the highest court in
the land, and was everywhere acknowledged to be the leading civil
rights lawyer of his time. The transformation was less accidental
than providential.

Marshall was born in Baltimore in 1908—that prophetic year
when a group of deeply troubled whites conceived the idea of the
NAACP—and into a class that was then still making a slow and
sometimes painful transition from staid color-conscious mulatto
aristocrats to race-conscious bourgeoisie. His mother was a public-
school teacher; his father chief steward of a country club. Both—as
such things are calculated—were at least half white. The census
takers never knew what to make of Marshall's paternal grandmother. Was she white or colored? Her answer was that she could
not say. She had been raised in a Negro home in Virginia, and that
was all she knew.

On both sides of the Marshall family there was a tradition of
rebellion, but personal achievement and family position had attenu-
ated it long before Thoroughgood reached the age of discovery. During his boyhood it showed up chiefly in his father's disputatiousness.
William Marshall argued about everything and anything, but he did

not bluster. He believed in facts. Much of his leisure time was spent looking them up and cramming them in and using them to challenge the logic of even the most commonly accepted ideas. There was not much that he would take for granted. Thoroughgood, his younger son, inherited his disputatious bent and his loud, commanding voice. Often the strangers who passed along the street where the Marshalls lived must have wondered what such loud-mouthed Negroes were doing in such an obviously genteel Negro neighborhood.

The Marshalls lived a happy, comfortable life. Compared to the lives of Negroes in neighborhoods south and east of them, it was very comfortable indeed. But in the years just before and after the First World War few Negroes on Druid Hill Avenue bothered to compare—except perhaps to confirm the general opinion that poverty, disease, and crime were due to shiftlessness. Apparently even William Marshall took this for granted. For fear that improvidence was not demonstrably an inborn trait, it was his idea that his boys should avoid contact with it in all its forms. Thoroughgood was sent to the school where his mother taught, where she could keep an eye on him. Since he was endowed with more than the normal supply of intellectual curiosity, he galloped through his studies, especially those he liked. At home he did his share of chores. But curiosity and gregariousness are a hard combination to control, and now and then he slipped away and prowled the east and south side's bitter streets, where, probably, he mistook the visible insignias of despair for something else again. He had still to reach the age of discovery.

He graduated from high school and entered college in 1926. Lincoln University, in Pennsylvania, was one of the half dozen really choice colleges for Negroes. Its students and alumni called it the "black Princeton." It had been founded by a Princeton graduate, it sported Princeton's colors as its own, and its faculty was staffed almost exclusively with Princeton men. It was a good school, more strict for learning than most, but very loose on social control, and completely indifferent to falderal and academic glitter.

Its students came from everywhere, including Asia and Africa, and represented the economic classes from laboring poor to semi-idle rich. Though Lincoln men talked a great deal about making "big money" (it was a period of financial boom), and though the educational ambitions of most of them were geared to one or another of the independent professions (called rackets) that seemed to guarantee this end, a display of wealth brought a man no more respect than poverty brought scorn. "Don't tell us who your daddy is," incoming freshmen were told, "show us what you are."

Nearly everybody worked. Rich and poor competed not only for academic honors but for summer jobs as waiters, kitchen help, and bellhops at resorts along the Eastern coast. Lincoln men were as boisterous as gamins, as ebullient as fizz, and as alert as startled foxes.

In this raucous community of three hundred, young Marshall quickly found his place. He could "kid" and "crack wise" as effectively as any. He was louder and brasher than most.

By the middle of his sophomore year he began to discover things other than the raw pleasures of late adolescence, the thrill of learning under competent instructors, and—as a member of the Forensic Society—the challenge of debate. Beneath the crude manners, which Lincoln men made a point of flaunting like flags, and the blatant cynicism in their talk of the big money, beneath the selfish ambitions projected in their boastful dreams blazed a furious zeal for the concept of racial equality, burned a bitter hatred of injustice, smoldered a lava flow of race consciousness that alternately anguished and exalted them. Never in the presence of their white instructors— for these feelings were confused by pride and shame as well, and must never be exposed to whites—but in nightly bull sessions they expressed themselves without restraint or pretense.

It was the era of the "new Negro." The Harlem renaissance was at its height, and Lincoln men were extravagantly proud of the successes of Paul Robeson, the literary acclaim of the new, young Negro poets and writers, the musical-comedy renown of Florence Mills. But Garvey's release from prison and his deportation in 1927 was an occasion for the white press to review his amazing exploits in a vein of comic scorn, and Lincoln bull sessions were often bitter with denunciations of "niggers who cut the hog." Many a bull session lasted all night.

Marshall began to discover who and what he was. Race consciousness grew to bud. He read all the books by or about Negroes he could lay his hands on. Sociology, history, fiction, and poetry were pouring from the press in unbelievable quantity. He read Julia Peterkin and Carl Van Vechten and was skeptical. He read Jerome Dowd's *The American Negro* and felt challenged. He read Carter Woodson's *The Negro in American History* and was uplifted. He read Du Bois. "To be sure," he read, "behind the thought lurks the afterthought—suppose, after all, the World is right and we are less than men?" Marshall was troubled, and his private war of impulses raged.

But his high-spirited sense of life could not be dampened for long. Once he began to discover himself, a fundamental integrity fixed the abiding elements of his character in a pattern which, though still incomplete—and for all the surface that overlay it—could scarcely be mistaken. "Don't let his loud mouth fool you," Marshall's acquaintances said; "he's nobody's fool." He was not only honest but frank to the point of insult. His temper was volatile. He hated sham. He had a natural affinity for the underdog, for arguing the unpopular side ("just to exercise his brains"), and for fighting against the odds. He would one day be satisfied with nothing less than complete dedication. Without willing it or intending it, he would one day find composed within himself a pride and passion of race and a shame and hatred of racial inequality that marked him a "new Negro." At twenty-one the most he lacked was self-discipline and the proper channel for his energies. Before another year had passed, he was on his way to both.

Marshall was graduated cum laude from Lincoln in 1930, and in the fall of that year enrolled in the law school at Howard University. He had by this time married a bright young coed from the University of Pennsylvania, and money, never plentiful at any time, was pitifully scarce. The young couple lived in Baltimore, where everything was a shade cheaper than in Washington, and Marshall commuted to the university. He was up every morning at five for the long day ahead. Classes and study occupied most of it, but there was a wife to provide for and tuition to pay. He worked in the law library at night, and he squeezed in odd jobs when he could. Frequently it was long after midnight when he got home. It was not an easy life, but it was an absorbing one.

Howard University was experiencing a regeneration. Its first Negro president, Mordecai Johnson, had set out willfully to destroy the reputation for social glamor that, while it brought the university a kind of prestige, had sapped its intellectual and spiritual vitality for half a century. A man of vision and tremendous drive, Dr. Johnson was one of those Negroes who believed that the ferment of the times, the shifting patterns of thought and behavior, the skeptical inquiry and rebellion of the middle-class intellectual against old dogmas, the loosening of conventions, the to-hell-with-it disillusionment of the masses—in short, the change, the doubt, the fear and chaos that characterized the great depression—presented an opportunity for the social reparation of the Negro, if only the Negro would seize it. Johnson believed that the business of education was to incite beneficial change and to help solve the problems that change brings. An institution of learning, while it protected the good and valuable in older traditions, must at the same time encourage that "higher individualism" that constantly makes for new and greater values.

He had attracted to the university men of similar thought and of undeniable intellectual stature. Their ideas and their learning flowed back and forth through the university like the waves of an alluvial tide. Alain Locke, the spiritual father of the Negro renaissance, was there in philosophy, E. E. Just in the natural sciences, Franklin Frazier in sociology, Charles Burch and Sterling Brown in literature, Rayford Logan in history, and Ralph Bunche in government and politics. But especially significant for the direct influence they had on Thurgood Marshall (he had legalized the diminutive by this time) were Charles Houston, dean of the law school, and William Hastie and James Nabrit. In two years Houston converted Howard Law from a second- or third-rate school into a first-rate school of a very special kind.

While not exclusively committed to a narrow specialization, the law school was thoroughly dedicated to the enlargement of the Negro's civil rights. Houston himself frequently represented the NAACP in cases involving these rights, and so did Nabrit, and so did Hastie, a former editor of the *Harvard Law Review*, who joined the faculty in 1930. Howard Law had become a kind of legal laboratory, where officials of the NAACP met with the faculty and some of the brighter advanced students to plan offensive strategies against racial inequalities, especially in education. In the first case tried in Virginia in 1932–33, court action by day was followed by planning at night in the Howard Law Library. It was during this time that Thurgood Marshall came to the attention of Walter White, chief executive of the NAACP. White wrote in his autobiography of:

". . . a lanky, brash young senior law student who was always present. I used to wonder at his presence and sometimes was amazed at his assertiveness in challenging positions [taken] by Charlie [Houston] and the other lawyers. But I soon learned of his great value to the case in doing everything he was asked, from research on obscure legal opinions to foraging for coffee and sandwiches. This law student was Thurgood Marshall who later became special counsel of the Association and one whose arguments were listened to with respect by the U. S. Supreme Court."

But before he became special counsel for the NAACP, Marshall went into private practice in Baltimore. He did not expect to make much money, but he did hope to provide a modest living for his wife. He barely managed. His clients were poor in everything except frustrated rage at the injustices of dispossessions, evictions, police brutality, and excessive penalties for slight offenses. Marshall, who had "learned what rights were," threw himself into these cases with a zeal that the prospect of large fees could not possibly have stimulated. He took many of them without the slightest expectation of a fee. He became known in Baltimore and the surrounding county as the "little man's lawyer." He became known as a crusader in the war for human rights.

It was a war for more than the rights of Negroes (for as a matter of fact some of his clients were white, though usually alien and poor). "What's at stake here is more than the rights of my client," he argued in his first important case, brought to compel the University of Maryland to admit a Negro student. "What's at stake is the moral commitment stated in our country's creed."

This was no shot in the legal dark. It was just beginning to dawn on him—and he had not yet put it into words—that the test of democracy, no less than of the moral power of justice, lay in the people's will to accept the equal application of the laws. He was just beginning to take on with certitude and passion his race's role as the catalyst in the slow-working moral chemistry of America.

When Charles Houston turned Howard Law School over to the capable direction of William Hastie and became special counsel of the NAACP in 1935, he invited Thurgood Marshall to become his assistant. It meant for Marshall a regular though penny-pinching salary. But it also meant devoting all of his time and intelligence to the kind of legal work he loved and joining an organized, co-operative effort to attain ends which, he felt, must no longer be compromised. Houston was too frank not to confess that it would also mean exhausted patience, discouragement, privation, and even physical danger. Marshall accepted with alacrity. In 1938, his health severely strained, Houston resigned, and Thurgood Marshall succeeded him. Special counsel for the NAACP had never been a sinecure. In the 1930s it was probably the most demanding legal post in the country.

3. BRIDGEHEADS

As we have seen, the Administration of President Roosevelt greatly stimulated the new growth of the old idea of social reform. The decade of the thirties was the decade of the rehabilitation of the "common man," and especially of that "one third" of the American common men who were "ill-fed, ill-housed and ill-clothed." The federal housing program got under way, the federal government in the role of social welfare agent came to be the accepted thing, and the Congress voted, for purposes of relief, vast programs of public works. Security was the word for all this, and the bringers of the word differed from one another as radically as Upton Sinclair, Francis Townsend, and Huey Long. Reflected even in the shallow surface of popular entertainment, and apparently affecting everyone, reform was in the air.

True, its periodic resurrection was as much a part of America's history as the Fourth of July, but heretofore social reform had been thought of in terms of charitable, voluntary action. Now it was thought of in terms of governmental and legal action. The NAACP saw an advantage. In the seventy-fifth anniversary year of the Emancipation it undertook a great and arduous offensive against racially discriminatory practices and laws.

The very first brief Marshall prepared in his new job was in a suit brought against the University of Missouri to admit a Negro to the law school. The suit differed radically from the Maryland case, and it had far greater significance. When Lloyd Gaines, the plaintiff, applied for admission to the university he was denied on the grounds that a state provision to finance the graduate and professional training of Negroes in schools outside the state constituted equality. Many Southern states had a similar provision, and Negroes had taken advantage of it, and no one had questioned the constitutionality of it. The lower courts upheld the state's contention that it was "contrary to the constitution, laws and public policy of the State to admit a Negro as a student in the University of Missouri." The NAACP carried the case to the Supreme Court.

Marshall based his argument squarely on that clause in the Fourteenth Amendment which forbids the state to deny any person under its jurisdiction the equal protection of the laws. The United States Supreme Court was asked to decide on the applicability of this clause to the case at hand. On December 12, 1938, it ruled six to two that "equality of education must be provided within the borders of the State." It was a broad decision that not only reaffirmed an earlier opinion that "separation [of the races] is legal only when it provides equality between the races," but opened the way for legal action to compel the equalization of school funds, teachers' salaries, and school facilities of all kinds.

If many thought the decision was broad enough to sweep away discrimination in education all over the South, Marshall himself had no such illusion. Two years with the NAACP had given him some experience of the South's fanatic will to resist. He knew that the struggle had only started, and that each strong point must be stormed in a separate action. The most he hoped for at that time was that legal assault after assault (he was prepared "to fight till doomsday") would so burden the South with the expense of providing separate but truly equal education as to weaken her resistance. He had not yet begun his brooding absorption in the abstract meanings of democracy. He was still committed only to the concrete measures of democracy and to the legal steps that would make these measures full. And these quite aside, there were fronts of elemental civil rights and justice still to defend.

There was, for instance, the right of Negroes to serve on juries. In 1940, when a Negro physician of Dallas, Texas, dared to presume that a summons to jury duty addressed to him was really meant for him, he was kicked down the courthouse steps. Marshall flew to Texas. He had at least an assault case, if he cared to prosecute it. But he was after something more. He lingered in Dallas only long enough to learn the facts and to marvel at the tensions that the kicking incident had caused, and then he went on to Austin. Unannounced until his actual arrival at the capital itself, he presented himself for a conference with Governor James Allred.

The governor at first seemed offended by such brashness, but he soon got over it. Marshall neither looked nor sounded like an agitator. He talked to the governor with quiet sincerity. His whole, somewhat easygoing manner bespoke the belief that a reasonable man will be moved by reason. Within the hour Allred "ordered out the Texas Rangers to defend the right of Negroes to jury service."

But that right had to be protected time after time in state after state until at last, in 1943, Marshall won certification of it in a Supreme Court decision that held the exclusion of Negroes from jury rolls in violation of the due-process clause, and therefore unconstitutional.

Other and earlier struggles, in Texas and elsewhere, were proving less decisive, and Marshall had to fight some of his predecessors' battles all over again—again to win victories that were incomplete. In 1917 the Supreme Court had voided ordinances restricting Negro residence to specified sections of cities, but private restrictive covenants had kept Negroes in ghettos and slums. The Supreme Court did not frown upon such covenants until the 1940s. The "grandfather clauses," too, were repugnant to the Constitution, and had been so declared in 1915, but the white Democratic primary was an effective bar to the Southern Negro's exercise of the franchise. Not until 1944 did Marshall win a victory over it. And in some places even then, the whites' threats of violence and economic reprisal—and where not these, then the Negro's force-grown lethargy and ignorance—effected what was no longer legally allowed.

But the sulphur and brimstone reek of violence was not unknown to Thurgood Marshall. The town of Hugo, Oklahoma, smoked with it for a time in 1941, when Marshall went there to fight for the cause of simple justice. A Negro odd-jobs man named Lyons had been charged with the murder of a white family of four and with setting fire to their house to hide his crime. All the evidence seemed to indicate the guilt of another person or persons. The Negroes of the town thought so anyway. "Because Lyons is colored and defenseless, he's been framed like a picture," they told the NAACP. Marshall was sent to defend him.

When he arrived the hostility of the whites had aroused such fear in Negroes that many of them had smuggled in arms from Tulsa and Oklahoma City. They had taken elaborate precautions for Marshall's safety. He was to have a protective guard; a different sleeping place was arranged for each night. But Marshall, six feet tall and weighing close to two hundred pounds, was next to impos-

sible to hide in a town so small, and, if the whites were determined
to harm him, quite impossible to protect by such means as the Negroes had. He was gregarious, he was inquisitive. He had his client
to see, questions to ask, prospective witnesses—whites among them
—to interview. He dismissed his bodyguard. For almost a week he
moved about the county-seat town as though he were completely
ignorant of its subterranean passions.

By the time the trial opened all the townspeople knew who Marshall was and what he was doing there. They packed the courtroom.
They seemed as curious as hostile. Marshall's preliminary presenta-
tion of the case seemed to melt the town's icy conviction of the
defendant's guilt. He was a model of quiet dignity, easy decorum,
and courtesy in the courtroom. He did not rant and rave. He did not
browbeat witnesses. But he did not pull his legal punches either.

His main defense hinged on the fact that his client had been in-
timidated, but he developed testimony that strongly implied the
guilt of others, including powerful local white members of a state-
wide bootleg ring. He hinted at the venal corruption of some local
officials. He proved that Lyons had been beaten after his arrest, and
Marshall called this "police brutality." He drew an admission that
the scorched and bloody bones of the victims had been piled on the
body of the accused in an effort to make him confess, and Marshall
called this "sadism" and "torture." But far from increasing hostility,
he coaxed the townspeople and the jury toward an awareness of
pride and beauty in doing justice. He believed, and was later to say,
that "even in the most prejudiced communities, the majority of the
people have some respect for truth and some sense of justice, no
matter how deeply hidden it is at times." On the last day of the
trial the superintendent of schools, who had been in constant at-
tendance, dismissed classes for half a day so that the white high
school students could go and "hear that Nigrah lawyer" sum up.

Marshall did not get an acquittal. The jury and the town could
not so abruptly sever all the complex emotional ties that bound
them to the unforbearing past, nor quite yet admit of a complete
victory of conscience over ancient consciousness and custom. But

he won a partial victory for justice. The accused was sentenced to
life imprisonment rather than to death—as he surely would have
been had the jury and the town believed him guilty.

One townsman, however, did break with the past. The father of
the woman allegedly slain by Lyons took up the fight for the Negro's freedom. The fight was lost, but an attitude was won. Four
years later, in 1945, the slain woman's father, white native of Oklahoma, became president of the local branch of the NAACP.

4. THE CONSCIENCE OF THE COUNTRY

After nearly two hundred and fifty years of dubious
battle in the fields of conscience, an attitude seemed generally to
have been won and a change seemed generally to be coming to the
moral climate of America. Both the attitude and the change "were
marked," said Frederick Lewis Allen, "by a broader and broader answer" to the question, " 'Who is my neighbor?' " They were marked
by an increasing regard for human needs, by a strengthening conviction of the interdependence of peoples, by a growing prevalence
of the one-world idea, and, again to quote Allen, "by an expanding
acceptance in America . . . of 'the commitment to equality.' "

Nineteen forty-five was the year when integration was begun in
the army and seemed assured in the future of other branches of
the armed services. It was the year when New York and Massachusetts, soon to be followed by Wisconsin and Oregon, set up Fair
Employment Practices agencies; the year a Negro became a vice-
president of an international union in CIO; and the year a Negro
was first mentioned (and a few months later chosen) as governor
of the Virgin Islands. It was the year of the organization of the
United Nations.

Few men in American public life reacted so directly to all this as
the secretary and the special counsel of the NAACP. Probably no
two men in America felt it to be so direct a challenge to the democratic ideal. Both Walter White and Thurgood Marshall had long
since anchored the program of the NAACP in the proposition that

democracy is capable of infinite improvement; both had anchored their belief in the thesis that the Negro's very presence in America had helped to quicken and extend the American idea of democracy. The changed attitude and the changing moral climate, then, were a challenge to more than the abstract principle. They were a challenge to the work to which White and Marshall had devoted their lives. They moved to confront the challenge with a new, bold idea: the idea that racial segregation is abhorrent to the concept and the ideal structure of democracy.

As a social idea, this was easy to credit; as a legal principle, it would be difficult to affirm. As a social proposition, all history proved it, and its truth was reflected in all the indices—education, employment, politics, health, housing, and crime—one cared to cite. As a doctrine of American law, all legal precedent was against it.

But Marshall had not had a dozen matchless years of experience in civil law for nothing. He believed that the equalitarian concepts embodied in the Declaration of Independence and the constitutional proscription of distinctions based on race and color should be made to apply. If as a matter of law it could be proved that segregation per se is inequality, constitutional guarantees would take care of the rest. He believed it could be proved. He had not, as he said, been a Negro all his life for nothing either.

So there began five years of intensive preparation. This included not only lower-court hearings attacking inequalities in the salaries of Negro teachers, in educational opportunities, in employment, in travel accommodations, and in the exercise of the ballot—thus establishing precedents and erecting a body of confirmable opinion item by item; but it also included periodic conclaves the likes of which had never before been convened for such purposes.

For days at a time, year after year, social scientists, psychologists, historians, legal experts, and educators—white and colored, and all volunteers—met in New York to wrestle with every aspect of the problem that Marshall and his staff thought likely to be raised in a court of law. Less frequently, in the days just before an actual hearing, the staff of NAACP lawyers—most of them, too, volunteers—would hold moot court in the Howard Law School library, with faculty members acting as judges. "They're going to try everything in the book," Marshall said, referring to the opposition. "Our job is to stay ahead of them."

But even keeping up with "them" required tremendous emotional, intellectual, and sheer physical energy. The "commitment to equality" was not so evident in the South. That it was there, especially among white college and university students, was indicated in various opinion polls, but the South's most powerful and vociferous leaders professed to see any breach in the legal wall protecting "immemorial custom" as threatening the South with an "inundating black tide" that would "destroy the South's precious way of life."

Though Marshall laughed without noticeable bitterness at such immoderate outbursts, he knew the complex snarl of emotions they revealed. He knew his own emotional involvement, hide it as he might from all but his closest associates. He appreciated the fact that if he was amazed and revolted by the opposition's grim focus on racial prejudice, the opposition could not be expected to sympathize with his equally grim focus on destroying the interpretations of the law that supported it. In one Southern court after another, local, state and federal—thirteen times in five years—he argued that "injury results to the human personality subjecting or subjected to" civil inequalities. But the argument was still tangential. He did not try to prove it yet. He was content for the time merely to prove that inequalities existed. He worked eighteen and twenty hours a day. He traveled fifty thousand miles a year. In 1950 he was able to establish the legal bridgehead from which to launch the offensive against segregation itself.

The bridgehead was established on two cases: Sweatt vs. Painter, and McLaurin vs. Oklahoma State Regents. In the first, the state of Texas had responded to a Negro's application to the state law school by hastily founding a separate law school for Negroes under the "separate but equal" doctrine. Arguing the case before the United States Supreme Court, Marshall took the position that not only the "quantitative differences between the white and Negro law schools with respect to such matters as the number of faculty members, the size of the library and the scope of the curricula," but those "more important factors, incapable of objective measurement"— the reputation of the faculty, the experience of the administration, "the status and influence of the alumni"—proved the inequality of the Negro law school. Sweatt, Marshall argued, was entitled to his "full constitutional rights," to a legal education equal in every way to that "offered by the State to students of other races."

The Supreme Court agreed with him and ordered Sweatt admitted to the university.

In the second case another, broader, and more salient point was at issue. The plaintiff McLaurin had been admitted to the University of Oklahoma, so there was no question of the equality of faculty, facilities, and curricula. But McLaurin had been forced to sit apart from other students in classroom and library, and generally to study and live on a segregated basis. The point was whether such "State-imposed segregation destroys equality of educational benefits."

The Supreme Court held that it did.

CHAPTER TWELVE

Mr. Smith Goes to Washington

On Sunday, May 16, 1954, Negroes singly and in
groups began arriving in Washington. There were
not enough of them to be particularly conspicuous, but still there
were a great many, most of them strangers to the capital. Although
newspapers throughout the country had been speculating on the
likelihood, no one except the justices of the Supreme Court really
knew that Monday, May 17, was to be the day when what had been
called "the noblest prerogative of democracy" either would be forsworn for the immediate present or assumed for all time. Except
the justices, no one knew that Monday would bring the decision as
to whether "segregation and a determination to hold some men inherently unequal to others" would prevail or be destroyed in law.
Yet on Sunday a thousand or more Negroes from all parts of the
country streamed toward the place of decision as if drawn there by
instinct.

Some of the lawyers who represented them had been in Washington for nearly a week. They had calculated on the last Monday of the
Court's present session, and tomorrow was it. In their six-room headquarters suite of the Wardman-Park Hotel, where none of them ex-

cept Greenberg, Pinsky, and Weinstein, who were Jews, and Ming and Robinson, who were fair-complexioned enough to pass for white, could have stayed during the first hearing in 1952, they spent their time rehashing all the arguments. One moment they would decide that the decision would be rendered for them, and the very next that it would be rendered against them.

They tried to divert themselves with penny-ante poker, and with talk about the baseball season just getting under way. Thurgood Marshall told some of his longest, funniest stories. But nothing diverted them for long. Somebody would remember a precedent that might possibly have been pushed in argument, and somebody else would mention an authority who might have been more extensively cited. But in fact the brief that had been prepared for the second hearing, now ten months in the past, was as thorough as the great learning of two dozen scholars and the legal knowledge of as many lawyers could make it. It ran to two hundred and thirty-five close-printed pages, and it had cited all the pertinent precedents and quoted all the relevant authorities. The truth of the matter was that the lawyers were as nervous as cats.

Their clients were much less nervous. They were less sophisticated and far less knowledgeable than the lawyers. The nice and tricky questions of constitutionality and legal precedents scarcely troubled them. Indeed, most of them were so artless that the warnings of their leaders and even the unhappy past had not prepared them really to credit the fact that what the world knew to be morally wrong might be declared legally right. They had, Marshall had said, "no conception of a *legal* means of denying them what is theirs of right."

Most of those who arrived on Sunday—a clear, fine day—were more curious than troubled. Many of them did not know where the Supreme Court was, though they intended to be there when the time came. Many of them had no place to stay. Some—and probably a majority—did not know that Washington had lately been made an "open city" and that its places of public accommodation were available to all alike. They sought out other Negroes and inquired where the "colored" section and "colored" restaurants and "places where the colored stayed" were. There was a run-down Negro motel a mile or two south across the Virginia line, and some went there. There was a better motel "for colored" north across the Maryland line, and some went there. Some spent Sunday night in the railroad station; some in the bus station. A group of seven from South Carolina were especially lucky. They met a minister formerly of their state, and he invited them to his evening church service and got members of his church to take them in for the night.

The first man to reach the Supreme Court building on Monday morning arrived there at one o'clock. He was Arthur Smith, a Negro aged seventy-six, and he had come down on the midnight train from his home in Baltimore. He was no stranger to the city. For forty-one years he had commuted to his job as a messenger in the State Department, and he knew his way about. He realized that he could not get into the building until the doors opened at nine o'clock, or into the courtroom itself until eleven, but he had come for the first hearing in 1952, and for the reargument in 1953, and both times he had come too late. He did not intend to be late this time. He carried a cushion under his arm and two fat sandwiches in his sagging topcoat pocket.

He walked up and down in front of the building and along East Capitol Street for a while. He wondered how long it would be before he would be able to discern the first faint glimmer of dawn. He had some notion of watching it come up. Finally he grew tired of walking and climbed the courthouse steps, placed his cushion in the shadow of a balustrade, and sat down. In a moment he was asleep. At just before three he was awakened by a guard shining a light in his face and inquiring what he was doing there. Smith told him. Proud but deferential, he showed the guard his twenty-five-year service pin and the inscription on the gold watch his fellow employees had given him when he retired. He talked at some length. Satisfied, the guard moved on.

Shortly after that Mr. Smith had a companion in his vigil, who told him his name was Crosby Ewing. He had been in the city since

evening of the day before, but "the darnedest thing," he told Mr.
Smith, "after all the trouble of finding a place to sleep, doggone if
I didn't wake up in the middle of the night worrying that I'd miss
what I came for."

The two men talked. Mr. Smith was garrulous, and he boasted a
little. He said he had once lived on the same street in Baltimore
where the "head lawyer's" mother now lived. He said he must have
seen the head lawyer many a time without ever suspecting "that
little ol' boy in knee pants would some day be a great leader of our
people." After it was over today, he said, if he got a chance he was
going to make himself known to Thurgood Marshall and congratu-
late him. Ewing asked Mr. Smith if he would do this no matter how
it turned out, "even if we lose?" Mr. Smith said he would. They were
silent for a while.

"But suppose we do lose? What'll we colored do then? Just suppose now," Ewing warned, as if he dared Mr. Smith to think that
such a supposition could possibly be true.

"We'll endure it," Mr. Smith said casually, pulling out the sandwiches and offering his companion one. He took the wax paper from
the top half of his sandwich and then he said, "Then we'll come
back as many times as we have to. It ain't going to be forever.
That's the thing about it. A time'll come when we won't have to
endure no more." Then he bit into his sandwich.

"You sound mighty sure," Crosby Ewing said.

"Ain't you?" Mr. Smith replied.

Long before eight o'clock there was a sprinkling of people on the
courthouse steps and standing among the columns of the marble
portico. When the hour struck the first queue formed, and when
the doors slid back at nine o'clock there were five long queues. Black
and white, young and old shuffled into the great main hall. Here
for two hours more they waited, mostly in silence, for the splendid
hall awed them. Then the courtroom doors themselves were opened
and the courtroom filled up. The two sections of seats, the side aisles,
and the Ionic colonnade were filled in a twinkling.

At eleven forty-five some of the lawyers for both sides came in and took the front benches on the left. There was an instant craning of necks and a hushed sibilance of whispering as the audience recognized this face or that. There were states' attorneys general with members of their staffs, some private lawyers, and the Negro lawyers, undifferentiated as to seating, and, so far as a disinterested visitor might discover at sight, undivided. Thurgood Marshall was there, big, rumpled, restlessly turning his head right and left.

Promptly at noon the red velvet curtains parted behind the nine chairs on the dais, the sitting audience rose at once, and the Chief Justice of the United States, followed by eight black-robed associate justices, filed in. They sat down. The audience sat. One of the justices began to read from a sheaf of papers on the long desk before him. When he had finished, another read from another sheaf of papers. Three decisions were read before the Chief Justice himself began to read in a rather high-pitched voice. Just as he uttered the first words there was a discreet rush from somewhere, and a half dozen reporters, who had been taken by surprise in the pressroom below, scrambled to the press tables next the aisles. The Chief Justice went on reading. He finished at one-five in the afternoon.

As the audience rose to leave in hushed silence, there was not a Negro among them who did not feel his allegiance to democracy strengthened and his faith in the American dream renewed.

Mr. Smith did not have the opportunity to see Thurgood Marshall afterward, but at the end of the week he clipped an editorial from a Negro paper, added a single word of his own, and addressed both to the NAACP. The editorial said, "The conscience of America has spoken through its constitutional voice. . . ." The word Mr. Smith added was "Amen."

Thurgood Marshall said, "The war's not over yet. We've still got work to do."

A Note of Thanks
and a Partial List of Sources

No ONE who undertakes a book of this kind could ever even
initially suppose himself completely independent of the assistance and co-operation of others. His debt grows as his work proceeds, and
my debt is substantial. I wish to acknowledge how much I owe to the dozens
of people who, like Ralph Bunche, Greene Buster, Thurgood Marshall, and
A. Philip Randolph, took time to answer numerous letters, to talk and in
general to bear with my importunities.

In the Congressional Library in Washington, the Founders Library at Howard University, the Free Library in Wilmington, Delaware, and in the distinguished Schomburg Collection in New York I had the generous help of
the librarians. But I am especially indebted to the entire staff of the Huntington Library at Hampton Institute, where I was given private space and where
most of this work was done. The reference and research librarians, Mrs.
Addie Cross and Miss Yvette Cameron, were particularly helpful by finding
obscure references and unearthing mines of material which certainly broadened my knowledge and deepened, I trust, my perception of American history and Negro life in America.

Though I followed my own bent, the discerning criticisms of Mr. Lewis
Gannett and Mr. George Shively saved me from many errors of thought
and expression. They could not save me from all. Such errors as remain are
entirely mine.

Finally, without time and freedom from committee and other assignments
that take so much of the energy of college teachers these days, this book
would have been much longer in the writing and, conceivably, might not

have been written at all. President Alonzo G. Moron and Dean William H.
Martin, of Hampton Institute, have my grateful thanks.

A list of sources that were especially helpful follows:

Adams, James Truslow. *The March of Democracy: The Rise of the Union.*
New York, 1932.

Allen, Frederick Lewis. *The Big Change: America Transforms Itself 1900–
'50.* New York, 1952.

———. *Since Yesterday: The Nineteen-Thirties in America.* New York, 1940.

Allen, James S. *Reconstruction: The Battle for Democracy.* New York, 1937.

Aptheker, Herbert. *American Negro Slave Revolts.* New York, 1943.

———. *Essays in the History of the American Negro.* New York, 1945.

———. *The Negro in the Civil War.* New York, 1938.

———. *To Be Free.* New York, 1948.

Baker, Ray Stannard. *Following the Color Line.* New York, 1908.

Beard, Charles A., and Mary R. *The Rise of American Civilization.* 2 vols.
New York, 1933.

Blesh, Rudie, and Janis, Harriet. *They All Played Ragtime.* New York, 1950.

Bontemps, Arna, and Conroy, Jack. *They Seek a City.* New York, 1945.

Bowers, Claude G. *The Tragic Era.* New York, 1929.

Brawley, Benjamin. *The Negro Genius.* New York, 1937.

———. *A Social History of the Negro.* New York, 1921.

Brazeal, Brailsford R. *The Brotherhood of Sleeping Car Porters.* New York,
1946.

Brown, Hallie Q. *Pen Pictures of Pioneers of Wilberforce.* Xenia (Ohio),
1937.

Buckler, Helen. *Doctor Dan: Pioneer in American Surgery.* Boston, 1954.

Buckmaster, Henrietta. *Let My People Go.* New York, 1941.

Butcher, Margaret Just. *The Negro in American Culture.* New York, 1956.

Cash, W. J. *The Mind of the South.* New York, 1941.

Coan, Josephus Alexander. *Daniel Payne, Christian Educator.* Philadelphia,
1935.

Conrad, Earl. *Harriet Tubman.* Washington, 1943.

Cronon, Edmund David. *Black Moses: The Story of Marcus Garvey.* Madison, 1955.

Curti, Merle. *The Growth of American Thought.* New York, 1943.

Dabney, Virginius. *Liberalism in the South.* Chapel Hill, 1932.

Detweiler, Frederick G. *The Negro Press in the United States.* Chicago, 1922.

Drake, St. Clair, and Cayton, Horace. *Black Metropolis.* New York, 1945.

Du Bois, W. E. Burghardt. *Black Reconstruction in America.* New York,
1935.

————. *Color and Democracy*. New York, 1945.

————. *Darkwater*. New York, 1920.

————. *Dusk of Dawn*. New York, 1940.

————. *The Negro Church*. Atlanta, 1903.

————. *The Philadelphia Negro*. Philadelphia, 1899.

————. *The Souls of Black Folk*. Chicago, 1903.

Dumond, Dwight Lowell. *America in Our Time, 1896–1946*. New York, 1947.

Eaton, Clement. *Freedom of Thought in the Old South*. Durham, 1940.

Embree, Edwin. *American Negroes: A Handbook*. New York, 1942.

————. *Brown Americans*. New York, 1944.

————. *13 Against the Odds*. New York, 1945.

Fauset, Arthur Huff. *For Freedom*. Philadelphia, 1937.

————. *Sojourner Truth: God's Faithful Pilgrim*. Chapel Hill, 1938.

Fite, Emerson David. *Social and Industrial Conditions During the Civil War*. New York, 1910.

Fleischer, Nat. *Black Dynamite*. Vol. 2. New York, 1938.

Fleming, Walter L. "'Pap' Singleton, The Moses of the Colored Exodus." *The American Journal of Sociology*, July, 1909.

Foner, Philip S. *The Life and Writings of Frederick Douglass*. 3 vols. New York, 1954.

Frazier, E. Franklin. *The Negro Family in the United States*. Chicago, 1939.

Furr, Arthur. *Democracy's Negroes*. Boston, 1947.

Gallagher, Buell G. *American Caste and the Negro College*. New York, 1938.

Ginzberg, Eli, et al. *The Negro Potential*. New York, 1956.

Graham, Shirley. *Paul Robeson: Citizen of the World*. New York, 1946.

————. *There Was Once a Slave: The Heroic Story of Frederick Douglass*. New York, 1947.

Hawk, Emory. *Economic History of the South*. New York, 1934.

Hesseltine, William B. *The South in American History*. New York, 1943.

Ingersoll, Ralph. *Top Secret*. New York, 1946.

Jenkins, William Sumner. *Pro-Slavery Thought in the Old South*. Chapel Hill, 1935.

Johnson, Charles S. *Growing Up in the Black Belt*. Washington, 1941.

————. *The Negro College Graduate*. Chapel Hill, 1938.

Johnson, James Weldon. *Along This Way*. New York, 1933.

————. *Black Manhattan*. New York, 1930.

Kardiner, Abram, and Ovesey, Lionel. *The Mark of Oppression*. New York, 1951.

Karsner, David. *John Brown: Terrible 'Saint.'* New York, 1934.

Kennedy, Louise Venable. *The Negro Peasant Turns Cityward*. New York, 1930.

Kerlin, Robert T. *Voice of the Negro*. New York, 1920.

Little, Arthur W. *From Harlem to the Rhine*. New York, 1936.

Logan, Rayford. *The Negro in American Life and Thought*. New York, 1954.

———. *The Negro and the Post-War World*. Washington, 1945.

Mandelbaum, David G. *Soldier Groups and Negro Soldiers*. Berkeley, 1952.

McGinnis, Frederick A. *A History of Wilberforce University*. Wilberforce (Ohio), 1941.

McKay, Claude. *A Long Way From Home*. New York, 1937.

McKay, Martha Nicholson. *When the Tide Turned in the Civil War*. Indianapolis, 1929.

Morrison, Samuel Eliot, and Commager, Henry Steele. *The Growth of the American Republic*. New York, 1930.

Moton, Robert Russa. *What the Negro Thinks*. New York, 1929.

The Negro in Virginia. (WPA Writers Project.) New York, 1940.

Nichols, Lee. *Breakthrough on the Color Front*. New York, 1954.

Ottley, Roi. *The Lonely Warrior*. Chicago, 1955.

———. *New World A-Coming*. Boston, 1943.

Ovington, Mary White. *The Walls Came Tumbling Down*. New York, 1947.

Page, Thomas Nelson. *The Old South*. New York, 1892.

Powdermaker, Hortense. *After Freedom*. New York, 1939.

Pyle, Ernie. *Brave Men*. New York, 1943.

Quarles, Benjamin. *Frederick Douglass*. Washington, 1948.

———. *The Negro in the Civil War*. Boston, 1954.

Reid, Ira DeA. *In a Minor Key*. Washington, 1940.

Reuter, Edward Byron. *The American Race Problem*. New York, 1927.

Richardson, Benjamin. *Great American Negroes*. New York, 1945.

Richardson, Clement (ed.). *The National Cyclopedia of the Colored Race*. Montgomery (Alabama), 1919.

Robeson, Eslanda Goode. *Paul Robeson, Negro*. New York, 1930.

Rogers, J. A. *World's Great Men of Color*. 2 vols. New York, 1947.

Rollin, Frank A. *Martin R. Delany*. Boston, 1868.

Rose, Arnold. *The Negro in America*. New York, 1944.

Schlesinger, Arthur M., Jr. *The Age of Jackson*. Boston, 1946.

Schoenfeld, Seymour J. *The Negro in the Armed Forces*. Washington, 1945.

Scott, Emmett J. *The American Negro in the World War*. Washington, 1919.

———. *Booker T. Washington*. New York, 1916.

Shulman, Milton. *Defeat in the West*. New York, 1948.

Silvera, John D. *The Negro in World War II.* New York, 1949.

Soper, Edmund Davison. *Racism: A World Issue.* New York, 1947.

Spero, Sterling D., and Harris, Abram L. *The Black Worker: The Negro and the Labor Movement.* New York, 1931.

Sterner, Richard, et al. *The Negro's Share.* New York, 1943.

Tannenbaum, Frank. *Darker Phases of the South.* New York, 1924.

This Is Our War. (Dispatches from Negro War Correspondents in World War II.) Baltimore, 1945.

Tyler, Alice Felt. *Freedom's Ferment.* Minneapolis, 1944.

Washington, Booker T. *The Negro in Business.* Boston, 1907.

———. *The Negro in the South.* Philadelphia, 1907.

———. *Up From Slavery.* New York, 1901.

Weaver, Robert C. *Negro Labor.* New York, 1946.

Weinberg, Albert K. *Manifest Destiny: A Study of Nationalist Expansion in American History.* Baltimore, 1935.

Wesley, Charles H. *Richard Allen: Apostle of Freedom.* Washington, 1935.

Wharton, Vernon Lane. *The Negro in Mississippi, 1865–1890.* Chapel Hill, 1938.

White, Walter. *A Man Called White.* New York, 1948.

———. *A Rising Wind.* New York, 1945.

Williams, Charles H. *Sidelights on Negro Soldiers.* Boston, 1923.

Williams, George W. *Negro Troops in the Rebellion: 1861–1865.* New York, 1888.

Wilson, Joseph T. *The Black Phalanx: A History of the Negro Soldiers of the U.S. in the Wars of 1775–1812, 1861–1865.* Hartford, 1888.

Woodson, Carter G. *A Century of Negro Migration.* Washington, 1918.

———. *The Education of the Negro Prior to 1861.* Washington, 1919.

———. *History of the Negro Church.* Washington, 1921.

———. *The Mind of the Negro As Reflected in Letters Written During the Crisis 1800–1860.* Washington, 1926.

———. *The Negro in Our History.* Washington, 1921.

———. *The Negro Professional Man and the Community.* Washington, 1934.

Woodward, C. Vann. *The Strange Career of Jim Crow.* New York, 1955.

Yank–The G I Story of the War. (Dispatches from *Yank* correspondents.) New York, 1947.

NEWSPAPERS, MAGAZINES & SPECIAL SOURCES

Afro-American Newspaper. Baltimore.

Century Magazine.

Chicago *Bee*.
Chicago *Defender*.
Chicago *Whip*.
Crisis Magazine.
Crusader. Chicago.
Journal & Guide. Norfolk.
Journal of Negro History.
Messenger Magazine.
Negro World.
New Masses.
New Republic.
New York Age.
Opportunity Magazine.
Pittsburgh *Courier*.
Report of the Gillem Board, War Department. November, 1945.
Small Unit Actions. Historical Division, U. S. War Department.
Study of the Negro in Military Service, by Jean Byers. (Mimeographed copy
    for "departmental use.") January, 1950.
Survey Graphic.

INDEX

Abbott, Flora, 190
Abbott, Robert Sengstacke, 156, 183, 188, 191–96, 204–8, 211, 213, 214, 217, 219
Abbott, Tom, 189
Abolitionism, 35, 41, 45, 59, 73; midwestern violence against, 76–77
Addams, Jane, 199
AFL. *See* American Federation of Labor
Africa, 24, 52, 228, 235
Africana, 243
African Free School, 69
African Grove, 68
African Methodist Episcopal Church, 27, 32, 45, 52–53, 74, 80, 128, 152, 249
African Orthodox Church, 236
African Zion Church, 73, 152
Africa Times and Orient Review, 230
Agricultural Adjustment Administration, 267
Alabama, 23, 52, 67, 208, 274
Alcorn, J. L., 106
Alexander, W. W., 269
Allen, Frederick Lewis, 285–86, 326
All God's Chillun Got Wings, 243, 277, 278–79
Allred, James, 323
Amalgamated Clothing Workers, 256

Amenia (N.Y.) conference, 213
America: imperialist expansion, 86; society in 1830's, 41; way of life, 41
American College of Surgeons, 177
American Federation of Labor, 256, 259, 264
American Mercury, 242
American Missionary Society, 191
American Negro Labor Congress, 241, 247, 248
American Negro, The, 318
American party, 59
American Revolution, 22, 26
American Sentinel, 41
American "way of life," 41
Anderson, Harry, 131–32, 133
Anderson, Louis B., 195
Andrews, Dr. J. Wyllys, 173
Anglo-Saxon Clubs of America, 237
Anglo-Saxon League, 247
Anne, 84
Antietam, battle of, 17
Anti-Slavery Bugle, 78
Armour family, 141
Armstrong, Samuel Chapman, 121
Ashwood, Amy, 229
Associated Press, 213
Association of Railroad Executives, 256
Atchison, David, 60
Atlanta, Ga., 162, 247
Atlanta *Constitution*, 212

Atlanta Cotton States Exposition, 124
Atlanta *Journal*, 92
Atlanta Life Insurance Co., 241
Atlanta University, 197
"Atlanta University Studies," 197
Atlantic Monthly, 79, 149
Atrocities, 218. *See also* Lynchings
Auld, Thomas, 47
Austria, 226, 299
Austria-Hungary, 188
Autobiography of an Ex-Coloured Man, The, 242

Babson, Roger W., 244
Bagnall, Rev. Dr. Robert, 239
Bailey, Frederick Augustus Washington. *See* Johnson, Frederick
Baker, Josephine, 243
Baker, Ray Stannard, 212
Baldwin, Mrs. W. H., 201
Ballou, C. C., 217, 218
Baltimore, Md., 318–19
Bandera, Quintín, 126
Banks, Sammy, 80
Baptists, 77
Barnburners, 50
Barrow, Monroe, 288–89
"Baumfree," 65
Beach Institute, 191, 192
Beaumont (Tex.) *Enterprise*, 201
Beecher, Henry Ward, 56, 131
Beethoven, Ludwig van, 232
Bennett, James Gordon, 22
Benson, George, 75
Bentley, Dr. Charles, 140, 162, 166
Benton, 95
Berea College, 36
Berlin, University of, 187
Bernadotte, Jean Baptiste, 232
Bethune, Mary McLeod, 270, 274
Beveridge, Albert J., 86, 126
Big Four Brotherhoods, 252, 256
Billings, Dr. Frank, 140–41
Birds, The, 186
Birney, James, 76
Birth of a Nation, The, 212
Black, Julian, 291–93, 296
Black Codes, 98–99, 102, 103

Black Cross Line, 240
Blacker the Berry, The, 277
Blackever, James, 156
Black Star Line, 235–36, 238
Black Worker, 262–63
Blease, Cole, 208
Bolivar County colony, 114–16, 117, 118
Bolshevism, 233–34
Bonneau, Thomas, 32
Bonus march on Washington, 272
Book of Negro Spirituals, 242
Booze, Edmund, 125
Bordeaux, Sarah, 32
Boston, Mass., 37, 40, 42, 43, 53
Boston Harbor, 15
Bourbon system, 106
Bowdoin College, 69
Boyd, Henry, 96
Bribeck College, 230
Brief Exposition of the Practice of the Times, A, 76
Brierfield Plantation, 95, 97, 110
British Museum, 230
British West Indies, 228, 229
Broad Ax (Chicago), 169, 196, 202
Broadway, 243, 244
Brotherhood of Sleeping Car Porters, 254–55, 256, 257, 262, 264, 272. *See also* Pullman porters, unionization
Brown, Edgar G., 286
Brown, Rev. John, 34, 48, 53, 59–60, 61–62, 78, 81
Brown, Morris, 29, 32
Brown, Sterling, 319
Brown, William Wells, 55
Brown Fellowship Society, 27, 28, 33
Browning, Robert, 232
Brownsville, Texas, 198
Bruce, Blanche K., 105, 107, 114
Bruce, John, 231
Bryan, William Jennings, 163
Bryant, William Cullen, 41
Buchanan, James, 62, 81
Buffalo, N.Y., 50
Buford, Dr. Coleman, 178
Bull Run, battles of, 13, 21
Bunche, Ralph, 270, 319

Bunker Hill, 25
Burch, Charles, 319
Burnet, Jacob, 76
Butler, Flora, 189
Byford, Dr. H. T., 140
Byrnes, James F., 214, 233, 234, 269
Byron, Lord, 182

Calhoun, John C., 34–35, 51, 94
California, 49, 51, 52
Calverton, V. F., 243
Cambridge University, 69
Camden Town, 283
Camp, Walter, 275
Canada, 52, 53, 62
Cane, 243
Capers, Bishop William, 35–36
Carnegie, Andrew, 168
Cass, Lewis, 50
Catholics, 247
Central America, 229, 231
Century of Negro Migration, A, 242
Cervera, Topete, 91
Chambersburg, Pa., 61
Chancellorsville, battle of, 13, 21
Charles XIV, King of Sweden, 232
Charleston (dance), 243
Charleston, S.C., 18, 27–28, 33, 38, 62, 68; Negro rebellion (1822), 29–30; reprisals after rebellion, 31–32
Charleston Harbor, 31
Chase, Salmon P., 60
Chestnutt, Charles, 149–50
Chicago, 127, 165, 247; Negroes in, 133–34, 138–39, 143, 166, 194, 195–96; Negro papers in, 196
Chicago, University of, 242
Chicago Art Institute, 152
Chicago *Bee*, 175
Chicago Commission on Race Relations, 205
Chicago *Defender*. See *Defender*
Chicago Medical College, 128, 134, 140, 143, 145
Chicago Medical Journal, 167
Chicago Medical Society, 167
Chicago Urban League, 261
Chicago *Whip*, 261, 262

Chicago World's Fair, 144, 145, 150, 193
Chickamauga Park, Ga., 85
Chocolate Dandies, 243
Cincinnati, O., 40, 41, 76, 95, 130, 133; Negroes in, 96
Cincinnati Conservatory, 130
Cincinnati Exposition, 97
City College (N.Y.), 250
City of Washington, 83
City Railway Company (Chicago), 136, 139
Civilian Conservation Corps (CCC), 269
Civilian Defense, 273
Civil rights, 320, 322–36. See also Integration
Civil War, 61, 62, 93, 95, 129
Claflin University, 192
Clark, Charles, 100
Clarke, Edward Young, 237
Clay, Henry, 51
Cleveland, Grover, 119, 123, 125, 153, 154
Cleveland, O., 22
Coffin, William, 45
Collins, John, 45
Colonel's Dream, The, 149
Colonization Society, 30
Color, 243
Colored American, 156
Colored Convention, 55
Colored Farmers' Alliance and Co-operative Union, 114
Colored Housewives' League, 241
Colored Merchants' Association, 241
Colored Methodist Church, 152
Columbian Orator, 34
Columbia University, 242, 275
Comal, 83–84
Committee of Eight, 239
Communal living experiment, 71
Communism, 234, 247, 280–81, 284, 285, 286
Compromise of 1850, 58, 81
Concha, 84, 85
Confederacy, capital of, 94
Confederate Army, 23
Confederate Congress, 18, 23

Confederates, 16, 20
Congregational Ministers Union (Chicago), 263
Connelly, Marc, 243
Conservator (Chicago), 175, 196, 202
Continental Army, 25
Convention of 1863, 24
Convict laborers, 111, 114
Cookman Institute, 249
Coolidge, Calvin, 240, 257, 258
Council of African Affairs, 285
Court of Ethiopia, 236
Cow Town, 158
Cox, Earnest S., 237
Coxey, Jake, 272
Craft, Henry, 272
Crescent City, Fla., 249
Crime (Negro), 43–44
Crisis (Chicago), 200, 202–3, 213, 214, 231, 235, 247
Croix de Guerre, 221, 227
Croly, Herbert, 186
Crosswaith, Frank, 272, 274
Crummell, Alexander, 69
Crusader (Chicago), 144–45
Culbertson, Dr. Cary, 178
Cullen, Countee, 243, 245
Cumberland Church Mission, 36
Cumming's Point, 18, 19, 20
Cunningham, Bill, 294–95
Czechoslovakia, 188

Dabney, Virginius, 313
Daiquiri, Cuba, 84, 85
Danzig, Allison, 294–95, 298
Darkwater, 242
Daugherty, Harry M., 239
Davis, Cushman K., 126
Davis, Gussie L., 130
Davis, Jefferson, 23, 93, 94, 95, 105
Davis, Mrs. Jefferson, 112
Davis, Joseph, 93, 94, 95, 97, 100, 111
Dayton, O., 150
Defender (Chicago), 196, 197, 204, 205, 206–7, 210–11, 213, 214, 231, 255
Delany, Martin, 52

Delaware, 53
Democratic party, 50, 81, 203. *See also* New Deal
De Molay, 15
Denmark, 188
Depressions: (1893), 144; (1894–95), 163; (1930's), 246–47, 280; effect on Negro, 246–49
De Priest, Oscar, 261–62
Dermott, Harold, 114
Dewey, John, 199
Dialectical materialism, 280–81
Discrimination, 247, 273–75. *See also* Black Codes
Disfranchisement, 197. *See also* Negro vote
District of Columbia, 35, 145
Dixie to Broadway, 243
Dixon, Thomas, 149
Dorr constitution, 46
Dos Passos, John, 244
Douglas, Stephen A., 58
Douglass, Charles, 15
Douglass, Frederick, 14, 15, 34, 44–62, 63, 68, 74, 81–82, 114, 124, 134, 145, 159, 162; *My Bondage and My Freedom*, 55
Douglass, Lewis, 15–16, 20–21
Dowd, Jerome, 318
Dred Scott decision, 60–61, 81
Dreiser, Theodore, 277
DuBois, Alexander, 184
DuBois, W. E. B., 93, 183–88, 197–204, 207–8, 208–9, 211, 213, 215, 217, 219, 235, 242, 318
Dumas, Alexander, 232
Dumont, John, 65, 66, 67
Dumont family, 65
Dun and Bradstreet, 241
Dunbar, Paul L., 150–51, 158, 165; *Lyrics of Lowly Life*, 151; *Majors and Minors*, 151
Dunbar Theatre Corporation, 241

Eason, James W. H., 238
East, slavery in, 76
Eastman, Max, 277, 282
East St. Louis, Ill., 214
Ebersole, Sarah, 160, 164

Edgerton, Wis., 131
Egypt, 230
Election (1866), 102–4
Elliott, John M., 213
Emancipation, 22, 26, 68
Emancipation Proclamation, 22
Embargo Act, 27
Emerson, Ralph Waldo, 52, 60
Emigrant Aid Society, 59
Emilio, Luis, 20, 21
Emperor Jones, The, 243, 277, 279
England, 41, 47, 52, 54, 56, 62, 81,
    188, 230, 240, 245, 279, 282
Equal Rights League, 129, 135
Ethiopia, 284, 287
Europe, 14, 152, 153, 187, 188, 280,
    282, 284
Evans, James, 270
Evrie, Charles Van, 39
Executive Order 8802, 273–74
Ezediel, Moses Jacob, 164

Fair Employment Practices agen-
    cies, 326
Fair Employment Practices Com-
    mittee, 274
Fascism, 283–84, 313
Father Divine, 248; Peace Move-
    ment, 248
Federal Election Bill, 153
Federal Council of Churches of
    Christ in America, 263, 300–1
Federal Housing Authority (FHA),
    269, 270
Fee, John G., 36
Feminist movement, 55, 68
Fenger, Dr. Christian, 141, 155
Ferber, Edna, 280
Ferris, William, 231
Field, Marshall, 141, 147
Fifteenth Amendment, 105
15th New York Infantry, 218
Fifth Army Corps, 85
54th Massachusetts Regiment, 13,
    14, 16, 17, 19, 20
Filipinos, 255, 256, 258
Finland, 284
Fire in the Flint, 243
Fisher, Rudolph, 243

Fisk Jubilee Singers, 181
Fisk University, 185, 186
Five Points House, 69
Flight, 243
Florida, 208
Foch, Marshal of France, 227
Folger, Benjamin, 71, 72
Force Bill, 116, 117
Ford, James, 281
Foreman, Clark, 269
Forrest, Nathan B., 108
Fort De Russey, 95
Fort Des Moines, 218
Fort Pillow, 108
Fort Robinson, 85
Fort Sumter, 19
Fort Wagner, 13, 16, 17, 18, 20, 21,
    22
Forten, George, 135
Foster, Stephen, 150
Fourteenth Amendment, 102, 104,
    130, 322
14th Infantry, 84
France, 152, 188, 245
Frank, Waldo, 243
Franklin, Benjamin, 76
Franklin Institute, 152
Frazier, Franklin, 319
Frederick Douglass's Paper. See
    North Star
Fredericksburg, battle of, 13, 21
Freedmen's Bureau, 102, 105, 107,
    109, 110, 130, 191
Freedmen's Hospital (Washington,
    D.C.), 150, 153, 154, 157, 158–
    61, 163–65, 168, 169, 170, 176
Freedom's Journal, 68
Free Enquirers, 68
Free Negroism, 39
Free Negroes, 39–44
Free Soil party, 52, 57–58, 81
Frémont, John C., 59
Friends of Negro Freedom, 241
Fugitive Slave Laws, 51, 52, 53, 81
Fuller, Dr. William, 178

Gage, Frances D., 78
Gaines, Lloyd, 322
Gallico, Paul, 297–98, 301

Garland Fund, 261, 262
Garnet, Rev. Henry H., 52, 74
Garrison, William Lloyd, 21, 37, 40,
    45, 46, 47, 48, 49, 52, 55, 57, 73,
    75–76
Garvey, Marcus, 227–31, 234–40,
    248–49, 254, 317–18
Gedney, Dr. James, 67
Gedney, Solomon, 67
George, J. Z., 117, 118
Georgia, 52, 188, 208, 214
Germans, 42, 43. *See also* Germany
Germany, 186, 188, 190, 284, 299;
    education methods, 186; World
    War I, 220–27
Gershwin, George, 244
Gettysburg Seminary, 68
Gide, André, 282
Gift of Black Folks, The, 242
Gillem, General, 110, 111
Gilmore, General, 17, 20
Glascow University, 69
Glaspell, Susan, 278
God's Trombones, 242
Goebbels, Josef, 299
Gold, Michael, 277, 285
Gómez, Máximo, 83
Grandfather clause, 200
Grand Gulf, battle of, 95
Granger, Lester, 249, 272, 274, 314
Grant, Ulysses S., 95, 104, 157–58
Gray, Edgar M., 238
Great Barrington, Mass., 184
Greeley, Horace, 14, 54
Green, Ben, 94, 95, 96, 97, 99, 100,
    108, 113, 114, 115, 120–21
Green, Paul, 243
Green, William, 259, 261, 263
Green Pastures, The, 244
Greenwich Village, 68–69
Greenwich Village Theater, 279
Gresham, Walter, 139, 154, 158, 162
Griffiths, Julia, 55
Griggs, Sutton, 149

Haiti, 145, 184, 212, 216
Hale, John P., 58
Hall, Dr. George, 143–44, 147, 155–

56, 162, 166, 171, 172–74, 175–
76, 195, 204
Hall, Theodocia, 172
Hamilton, Jones, 111, 114
Hamilton Club, 139
Hampton Institute, 121, 192, 193
Hampton Quarter, 193, 194
Hand, Augustus, 186
Hanna, Marcus A., 163
Hapgood, Norman, 186
Hardenberg family, 65
Harlem, 245, 250, 265, 277, 278,
    294; renaissance, 317–18
Harlem Labor Union, 272
Harlem Shadows, 243
Harper's Ferry, Va., 61–62, 81, 198
Harper's Weekly, 151
Harris, Abram, 270
Harris, Frank, 282
Harrison, Hubert H., 231
Hart, Albert Bushnell, 185
Harth, Mingo, 29
Harvard University, 149, 185–86,
    187, 188, 231
Hastie, William, 270, 320, 321
Hawaiian Islands, 86
Hayes, Garfield, 134, 187
Hayne, Robert, 28
Hayward, William, 219
Hearst, William Randolph, 287
Heggie's Scouts, 108
Heidelberg University, 69
Henry, Patrick, 26
Herder, Johann von, 41
Herrick, Robert, 186
Heyward, DuBose, 244
Higginson, Thomas Wentworth, 62
Hill, Jim, 113
Hill, Samuel, 75
Hitler, 284, 299, 300
Hitler-Stalin Pact, 284
Holland, 188
Hollidaysburg, Pa., 128
Hollis, Mack, 213
Holloway, Elizabeth, 28, 32
Home to Harlem, 277
Hoover, Herbert, 267–68
Hopkins, Pauline, 149
Horne, Frank, 270

Horton, George M., 81
House behind the Cedars, The, 149
Houston, Charles, 319–20, 321
Howard, Kate, 199
Howard, Perry W., 258
Howard, Robert, 37
Howard University, 157–58, 161, 198, 318; Law School, 319–20, 321, 328; Medical School, 178
Howe, Samuel, 62
Howells, William Dean, 150, 151, 199
Hughes, Langston, 242, 243, 244, 245
Humphreys, Benjamin, 98
Hurricane Plantation, 93, 95, 97, 110
Hyde Park (London), 230

Ickes, Harold, 269
Illinois, 42, 58, 60, 129
Illinois Idea, 196
Illinois State Board of Health, 128, 136, 139, 144
Immigration, 24, 42
Impressment, 23
In Abraham's Bosom, 243
Independent, 199
Indiana, 40, 42, 76
Indianapolis *Freeman*, 203
Indianola, 95
Industrial Defense Association, 256
Ingersoll, Robert, 131, 132
Integration, 326 ff.
International Congress of Races, 200
International Workers of the World, 233
Inter Ocean, 147
Interstate Commerce Commission, 256
Irish, 42, 43
Isabella, 65–67, 69, 71–74. *See also* Sojourner Truth
Italy, 62, 188, 245

Jackson, Andrew, 22
Jackson (Miss.) *Clarion-Ledger*, 108–9, 117
Jaggard, Dr. W. W., 140
Jamaica, 230

James, William, 185, 186
James Island, 13
Janesville, Wis., 131
Janesville *Gazette*, 132
Jay, William, 76
Jazz, 218, 243
Jazz Age, 244–45
Jenkins, Frederick, 54
Jews, 247, 299
Jim Crowism, 197, 204
Johns Hopkins University, 161
Johnson, Alice, 164–65
Johnson, Andrew, 98, 101, 102, 103, 104
Johnson, Campbell, 270
Johnson, Frederick. *See* Douglass, Frederick
Johnson, Henry, 221
Johnson, Rev. Hewlett, 282
Johnson, Jack, 292
Johnson, James Weldon, 242, 261, 262, 277
Johnson, Mordecai, 319
Joint Committee of Fifteen, 102, 104
Joint Committee on Un-American Activities, 286
Jones, Jenkin Lloyd, 132
Jones, John, 194
Jones, Robert Edmond, 278
Jones, Sissieretta, 152–53
Journal of Obstetrics, 167
Julian, George, 58
Just, E. E., 319

Kansas, 53, 58, 59–60, 76, 78, 79; exodus to, 182
Kansas-Nebraska Bill, 58, 81
Kansas Plaindealer, 195
Kemble, Fanny, 40
Kennedy, Dempsey, 73
Kennedy, John P., 149
Kent College of Law, 194
Kentucky, 51, 53
Keynes, John Maynard, 244, 266–67
Kilroe, Edwin P., 238
Knights of the Black Cross, 108
Knox, Frank, 271, 273
Knudsen, William S., 271

Kohlsaat, Herman, 147
Kohlsaat family, 141
Ku Klux Klan, 107, 108, 213, 232, 237, 247

Labor, and Negroes, 246–47. *See also* Pullman porters, unionization
Labor Mediation Board, 256–57, 258, 264–65
La Guardia, Fiorello, 273
La Nacionale, 230
Langston, John, 153, 165
La Prensa, 230
Las Guásimas, 85, 86
Laski, Harold, 282
Lawrence, Amos, 60
League for White Supremacy, 274
League of Nations, 287
Lee, Robert E., 62
Legislation: anti-Negro, 42, 100, 101, 208; slave enlistment, 23
Leopard's Spots, The, 149
Liberator, 37, 45, 277
Liberty party, 50, 51, 57, 59
"Libyan Sybil." *See* Isabella
Light, James, 278
Linares, General, 91
Lincoln, Abraham, 14, 22, 60, 81, 101, 102, 199, 273
Lincoln University, 316–17, 318
Literature, 242–43
Locke, Alain, 241, 242, 244, 245, 319
Lodge, Henry Cabot, 116
Logan, Rayford, 270, 272, 319
London, 230, 279
London *Daily Express*, 279
London *Daily Worker*, 283
London School of Economics, 282
London *Times*, 56
Long, Huey, 322
Longworth, Nicholas, 76
Louis, Joe, 286–301
Louisiana, anti-Negro legislatior. 100, 101
Lovejoy, Elijah, 76
Lowell, James Russell, 46, 50
Luxembourg, 152
Lynch, John R., 105, 106, 114, 117

Lynchings, 92, 148, 153, 197, 210, 218
Lyrics of Lowly Life, 151

McDuffie, George, 35
Maceo, Antonio, 126
McGill, Ralph, 313
MacGowan, Kenneth, 278
Mack, Julian, 239
McKay, Claude, 234, 243, 245, 277, 279, 282
McKinley, William, 91, 163, 174
McKinstrey, Willard E., 216
McLaurin *vs.* Oklahoma State Regents, 328–29
McPherson, Aimee Semple, 244
Magdalene Society, 69
Mahan, Asa, 76
Majors and Minors, 151
Mamba's Daughters, 244
Manifest destiny, 86
Manumission Society, 69
March-on-Washington movement, 272–73
Marne, 209
Marrow of Tradition, The, 149
Marrs, John, 73
Marshall, Dr. C. K., 110
Marshall, Thoroughgood, 315–29, 331, 334
Marx, Karl, 281
Marxism, 281, 286
Maryland, 28, 62
Massachusetts, 15; anti-Negro legislation, 42
Massachusetts Anti-Slavery Society, 45, 46, 47
Matthews, Robert. *See* Matthias
Matthias, 70–72, 79
Mayo, Dr. Willie, 178
Medico-Chirurgical Society, 161
Meharry Medical College, 176, 178
Mein Kampf, 299
Memphis, Tenn., 247
Memphis *Commercial Appeal*, 124
Memphis *News-Scimitar*, 218
Mencken, H. L., 243
Mercy Hospital (Chicago), 140
Mercy Hospital (Philadelphia), 178

Messenger, 238, 250–51, 256, 260

Methodist Federation for Social Science, 263

Methodists, 35

Metropolitan Museum of Art, 152

Meuse-Argonne, battle of, 221

Mexicans, 255, 256

Mexican War, 50, 94

Michigan, 42

Miller, Kelly, 198

Mills, Florence, 243, 317

Minor Moralist Society, 28, 33

Miscegenation, 25–26, 242

Mississippi, 23, 52, 96, 153, 104–5, 214; "An Act to Confer Civil Rights on Freedmen," 98; anti-Negro legislation, 100; Black Code, 98–99; Constitutional Convention (1890), 93, 117, 118; Negro in, 106–7; post-war Negro, 97–100

Mississippi Register, 112

Missouri, 60, 76

Missouri Compromise, 49, 60

Mitchell, Palmer, 233

Mixed society, 136–38, 143, 173

Modern Quarterly, 242

Modjeska, Helena, 132

Mohammed, Duse, 230

Mollin, C. W. M., 146

Monitor, 132

Montgomery, Benjamin, 99

Montgomery, Isaiah T., 93–100, 105–21, 125, 153

Montgomery, William, 113

Montgomery, Ala., 94

Montgomery *Advertiser*, 212

Morris, Edward, 194, 195

Morris Island, 14, 16, 19, 20

Morro Castle, 83, 84

Moton, Robert R., 201, 242

Mound Bayou. See Bolivar County colony

Mulattoes, 191, 206. See also Mixed society

Munich, Germany, 284, 299

Murray, Anna, 44

Murray, Pauli, 137; *Proud Shoes*, 137

Murray's *Primary Grammar*, 34

Music, 243. See also Jazz

Mussolini, Benito, 283–84

My Bondage and My Freedom, 55

NAACP. See National Association for the Advancement of Colored People

Nabrit, James, 320

Nantucket, 45

Narrative of the Life of Frederick Douglass, 47

Nashville (Tenn.) *Banner*, 210

Natchez (Miss.) *Democrat*, 110

Nation, The, 242, 264

National Advisory Committee, 271

National Association for the Advancement of Colored People, 178, 199, 200–1, 235, 247, 249, 261, 271, 314–15, 320, 321, 322, 323, 326–27, 334; Legal Redress Committee, 200

National Association of Colored Women, 152

National Association for Promotion of Labor Unionism among Negroes, 241

National Bureau of Labor, 123

National Farmers' Alliance, 114

National Federation for Constitutional Liberties (NFCL), 285

National government, Negroes in, 268

National Medical Association, 162, 171

National Negro Business League, 152

National Negro Congress, 285

National Urban League, 201, 235, 247, 248, 261, 271, 314

National Youth Administration, 269, 270, 273

Nazism, 284, 295, 299

Nebraska, 58

Negro: after World War I, 232–33, 240–45; after World War II, 313; aid to Confederate cause, 23; aristocracy, 96; attitude toward F. D. Roosevelt, 267–68; banks, 152; businesses, 152; caste system, 231;

church growth, 152, 262–63; concept of self, 150; crime, 43–44; culture, 277; and democracy, 234; economic conditions (New Deal), 267–75; education, 69, 80–81, 152; in 1890's, 148; fraternal orders, 152; identification, 22–23, 135–36, *see also* Mixed society; inferiority, 148–49, 167–68; income, 247; on labor market, 42–43; in medicine, *see* Dr. Daniel Hale Williams; migration North, 205; in mixed society, 135–38, 143, 173; place in American life, 119, 217, in the South, 122, 123, 125, in the North, 123–24, 125; press, 197; race concept, 43; recruitment, 14, 22, *see also* Negro soldiers; scientific calculation, 23; suicides, 137; sympathy for, 21–22. *See also* Discrimination; Lynchings; Mixed society; Unions

Negro Factories Corporation, 235–36

Negro in American History, The, 318

"Negro Mencken." *See* Owen, Chandler

Negro Seaman's Act, 31

Negro soldiers: Civil War, 13–21; officer training, 217–18; Spanish-American War, 84–91, 92. *See also* World War I and II

Negro suffrage, 104

Negro vote, 105, 118–19

Negro World, 231–32

Nell, William, 55

New Bedford, Mass., 42, 44, 68

New Deal, 267–75

New England Non-Resistance Society, 48

New Jersey, 41

New Masses, 242

New Mexico, 51

New Statesman, 283

New York (city), 22, 40, 42, 43, 74, 227, 247, 273, 274–75; Negro life in 1830's, 67–69

New York (state), 16, 22, 53, 67

New York, 84

New York *Age,* 122–23, 202, 203, 255–56

N.Y. *Commercial Advertiser,* 30

N.Y. *Daily Worker,* 285

N.Y. *Evening Post,* 197

N.Y. *Herald Tribune,* 22, 54, 236

N.Y. Stock Exchange, 76

N.Y. *Times,* 209, 286

New York University, 242

N.Y. Vigilance Committee, 44

Niagara Falls, Can., 197

Niagara Movement, 197, 198, 199

Nickelway, Rev. A. T., 92

Nigger Heaven, 277

Niles' Register, 40

9th Cavalry (Black Buffaloes), 85, 86

Non-Importation Acts, 27

North, 22; attitude toward Negro freedom, 22; Free Negroes threat, 40, 41–43; Negro exodus to (1915), 210–15; Negro place in, 123–24, 125, 148; sectionalism, 51

North Carolina, 23, 28, 62

North Carolina Medical Journal, 167–68

North Carolina Mutual Company, 241

North Carolina Record, 93

Northampton, Mass., 75

North Star, 49–52, 55

Northwestern University, 146, 151, 167

Norway, 188

NYA. *See* National Youth Administration

Oberlin College, 76

Office of Production Management, 270–71

Officer training, 217–18

Ohio, 42, 53, 78

Ohio Supreme Court, 76

Olmsted, Frederick, 32

Olympic Games (1936), 299

O'Neill, Eugene, 243, 277, 278–79

Opportunity, 256

Oregon, 51

Othello, 285

Ottley, Roi, 196, 298
Outlook, 92, 197
Ovington, Mary White, 169, 199
Owen, Chandler, 238–39, 241, 250
Owenites, 68

Page, Thomas Nelson, 149
Palmer, George Herbert, 185, 186
Palmer, Dr. Henry, 132–33
Pan-American Congress, 86
Panic of 1893, 163
Parker, Alton B., 175
Parker, Theodore, 54, 60, 62
Parrington, Vernon L., 130
Patton, George S., 306
Paul, William, 30
Payne, Daniel, 25, 26–29, 32–38,
    53, 61, 62, 68, 74, 80–81, 145
Payne, London, 25, 26–27
Pearl Harbor, 301
Pennington, J. W. C., 69
Pennsylvania, 42, 53
Pennsylvania, University of, 161,
    197, 318
Pershing, John J., 88
Peterkin, Julia, 318
Philadelphia, 40, 41, 42, 43, 44
Philadelphia Age, 22
Phillips, Wendell, 48–49
Pickens, William, 231
Pierce, Franklin, 22, 58
Pierson, Elijah, 69–70, 71
Pierson, Sarah, 69–70
Pillsbury, Parker, 75, 80
Pinckney, Charles, 35
Pittsburgh Courier, 261, 262
Poland, 188
Pomeroy, Samuel, 14
Populist revolt (1892), 163
Populists, 163
Porgy, 244, 277
Porter, David D., 95
Powell, Adam C., 268
Powell, John, 237
Princeton University, 316
Professor Haire's Academy, 132
Proud Shoes, 137
Provident Hospital and Training
    School (Chicago), 140, 141, 142,
    144, 145, 146, 147, 154, 155, 156,
    157, 160, 166, 167, 172, 176, 177,
    194
Provincetown Playhouse, 278
Pullman Company, 255, 256–65
Pullman Employee Representation
    Plan, 253
Pullman porters, unionization of,
    251–65
Purvis, Dr. Charles, 158, 160, 161,
    162, 163, 168
Purvis, Robert, 54–55

Quakers, 76–77

Race: duty, 137; prejudice, 207;
    pride, 241–42; problem, 209, 210,
    213–14; riots, 199, 232
Race relations officers, 270
Racial segregation, 274
Railroad Labor Board, 256
Railway Brotherhoods, 246
Railway Labor Act (1926), 257, 264
Railway Men's International Benev-
    olent Industrial Association, 253
Randolph, Asa Philip, 214, 235,
    238–39, 241, 249–65, 272, 273,
    274–75, 294
Rankin, Jeremiah, 164
Ransom, Rev. Reverdy, 167
Ray, Charles B., 73, 74
Reader's Digest, 297
Reconstruction, 92, 122, 130, 148,
    153, 208; problems, 101–4
Reconstruction Act (First), 104
Redmond, Charles, 54
Red River, 95
Red Rock, 149
Red Shirts, 92
Reid, Ira, 270
Republican party, 59, 81, 101–3,
    105, 130
Retrenchment Society, 69
Revels, Hiram, 105
Review of Reviews, 91–92
Reynolds, Rev. Louis, 128, 140, 143
"Rhapsody in Blue," 244
Rhode Island, 46
Rice, Grantland, 294–95

Richard Allen: Apostle of Freedom, 242
Richardson, Edmund, 111
Richmond *Planet*, 203, 209
Roberts, Dr. Carl, 176
Roberts, Needham, 221
Robeson, Eslanda, 276–77, 278, 282
Robeson, Paul, 245, 275–86, 317
Robeson, Rev. William Drew, 276
Robinson, Bojangles, 243
Robinson, Dr. Byron, 146
Robinson, Dr. F. B., 141
Robinson, Marius, 78
Rochester, N.Y., 49, 52, 53, 55
Rogers, J. A., 232
Roosevelt, Eleanor, 273, 285
Roosevelt, F. D., 265, 266–67, 271, 273, 274, 314, 321. *See also* New Deal
Roosevelt, Theodore, 174–75, 198, 202
Rope and Faggot: A Biography of Judge Lynch, 243
Rosenfeld, Paul, 243
Rosenwald, Julius, 188, 207
Rough Riders, 84, 85, 86, 87, 89, 174
Roxborough, John, 291–93, 294, 296
Royal Society of Surgeons, 146
Royce, Josiah, 186
Ruggles, David, 44
Runaway slaves, 53
Runnin' Wild, 243
Russell, Irwin, 150
Russia, 245, 277, 279, 282, 283, 284. *See also* Soviet Union
Russwurm, John, 69
Rutgers University, 275

Sabbatarians, 68
St. Ann's Bay, Jamaica, 229
St. Louis, Mo., 247
St. Louis *Argus*, 261, 262
St. Louis *Dispatch*, 79
St. Luke's Hospital (Chicago), 177
St. Simon's Island, 189
Sandiford, Ralph, 76; *A Brief Exposition of the Practice of the Times*, 76

Santayana, George, 185
Santiago, battle of, 86–91
Santiago Bay, Cuba, 83, 84
Santo Domingo, 29, 108
Savannah, color caste, 191
Savannah (Ga.) *Morning News*, 190
Say, Benjamin, 76–77
Scarborough, Catharine, 191–92, 193
Scarborough, Joseph, 191
Scarlet Sister Mary, 277
Schieffelin, W. T., 201
Schmeling, Max, 294–97, 299–300
Schurz, Carl, 14, 98
Schuyler, Daniel J., 262
Schuyler, George, 238
Scott, Dred, 60
Scott, Emmett, 170, 173
Scott, Walter, 182
Scribner's, 174
Scurvy sickness, 28
Secession, 35, 51, 52
2nd Massachusetts Regiment, 17
Sectionalism, 51, 94, 208
Self-Interpretating Bible, 34
Selika, Marie, 153
Sengstacke, Rev. John H. H., 189–91, 192, 194, 206
Separate but equal decisions, 123; doctrine, 148, 328
Seven Days, battle of, 13
Seward, William, 52, 78
Seymour, Horatio, 22
Shaw, Robert Gould, 17–18, 19, 20, 21
Show Boat, 280
Shuffle Along, 243
Siboney, 83, 84
Simon the Cyrenian, 278
Sinclair, Upton, 322
Singleton, Benjamin, 181–82
Sing Sing, N.Y., 71
Sissle, Noble, 218–19
6th Connecticut Regiment, 16
Slater fund, 186–87
Slavery, 66–67, 75–76, 98
Slave trade, 25–26, 45, 61
Smiley, Charles, 194
Smiley, J. Jockley, 204–5

Smith, Alfred E., 247
Smith, Gerrit, 50, 51, 60, 73, 74
Smith, Hoke, 154, 156
Smith, Dr. James McCune, 69
Smith, William, 53–54
Socialism, 250, 254
Social reform, 321–22. *See also* New Deal
Sojourner Truth, 74–75, 77–82. *See also* Isabella
South, 22; anomaly of Free Negroes, 39–40; attitude toward F. D. Roosevelt, 267; attitude toward Negro, 313–14; economic conditions after War of 1812, 27–28; enlistment legislation (Negro), 23; Negroes in, 201–2; Negroes in army, 23, (in 1890's) 148–49, (in 1915) 209–10, 211, 212; Negroes place in, 122, 123, 125; noblesse oblige, 122; political strength, 58; postwar, 129–30; sectionalism, 51; slavery in, 76; treatment of Negro, 124–25
South America, 24
South Carolina, 27, 28, 34–35, 39, 52, 62, 124, 214; anti-Negro legislation, 100; ban on Negro education, 38; Court of Appeals, 40; Supreme Court, 29
Southern Bell Telephone Company, 268
Soviet Union, 284–86. *See also* Russia
Spain, 14, 87, 125, 283, 284
Spanish-American War, 84–91, 126, 174, 198
Spartanburg, S.C., 218–19
Spencer, Oliver, 76
Spingarn, Arthur B., 200
Spingarn, Joel, 199, 216–17
Spirituals, 181–83, 185, 193, 242
Springfield, Ill., 199
Stanton, Elizabeth, 56
Stars and Stripes, 306
Stevens, Charles, 189
Stevens, Thaddeus, 101, 102
Stone, Lucy, 56, 57
Story, Moorfield, 199

Stowe, Harriet Beecher, 56–57, 70, 74, 78, 79
Strong, George C., 14–15, 16–17, 18, 19
Sturges, James, 73
Sullivan's Island, 18–19
Sumner, Charles, 14, 103
Surgery, 146
Survey Graphic, 256
Swallow Barn, 149
Sweatt *vs.* Painter, 328–29
Sweden, 188
Swisshelm, Jane, 56, 77

Taft, William Howard, 202
Talbot, John R., 92
Tanner, Henry, 152
Tappan, Arthur, 76
Tariff of Abominations (1828), 34
Tariffs: (1816) 34, (1824) 34, (1827) 34
Taylor, Zachary, 50
Tennessee, 23, 185, 213
Tenure of Office Act, 104
Terrorism, 92–93
Texas, 51, 104–5
Theatre Guild, 285
Third International, 234
Thompson, George, 48
Thoreau, Henry David, 60
369th New York Infantry, 220–27
Throckmorton, Cleon, 277–78
Tillman, Ben, 123, 193
Tocqueville, Alexis de, 41
Toomer, Jean, 243, 245
Topeka, 84
Torrence, Ridgely, 278
Totten, Ashley, 254
Townsend, Francis, 322
Treitschke, Heinrich von, 187
Truman, Harry S., 286
Tucker, George, 58
Turkey, 226
Turner, Nat, 37
Turner's Rebellion, 37
Tuskegee Institute, 121, 165–66, 168, 169, 170, 172, 173, 175, 201, 202
Tuskegee Student, 172–73, 201

25th Infantry, 84–85, 198–99
24th Infantry, 83, 215

Uncle Tom's Cabin, 56
Underground Railroad, 53, 59, 73, 77
Unemployment (1930's), 246–47
UNIA, 231, 235, 236, 238
Union Army, 22; Negro status in, 18
Unionization. *See* Pullman porters
Union League, 105
United Brotherhood Fraternal Insurance Company, 167
United Nations, 314
United States, 22
U.S. Army, 83, 232
U.S. Congress, 35, 51, 52, 58, 86, 102, 266; Negroes in, 105
U.S. Constitution, 47, 102, 103, 105, 197, 208
U.S. Employment Service, 271
U.S. Justice Department, 233, 250, 251
U.S. Marine, 212
U.S. Senate, 14, 43; Negroes in, 105
U.S. State Department, 270
U.S. Supreme Court, 313, 322–23, 324, 328–29, 330, 331, 332–34; Dred Scott decision, 60–61; separate but equal decision, 123, 148
U.S. Treasury Department, 270
U.S. War Department, 86, 215, 217, 219, 270
Unity Theatre Group, 283
Universal Negro Improvement and Conservation Association and African Communities League, 230–31. *See also* UNIA
Up from Slavery, 230
Urban League. *See* National Urban League
Utah, 51

Van Buren, Martin, 50
Van Vechten, Carl, 277, 318
Vesey, Denmark, 27, 29, 30, 32
Vicksburg, 95, 96
Victoria, Queen of England, 187
Vigilance Committee, 68

Villard, Oswald Garrison, 199
Vincent's Creek, 19
Virginia, 25–26, 28, 52, 61, 62, 104–5, 232; slavery in, 25–26; state constitution (1776), 26; Turner's Rebellion, 37
Virginia, University of, 58
Virgin Islands, 270

Waco, Tex., 212
Wade-Davis Bill, 101
Walker, David, 37; *Appeal,* 37
Wall, John, 20–21
Walling, William English, 199
Walls of Jericho, 243
Walrond, Eric, 231
Ward, Samuel R., 52
Warfield, Dr. William, 164, 168
War Labor Conference Board, 252
War Manpower Commission, 274
Warner, Richard, 238
War of 1812, 22, 27
Washington, Booker T., 55, 121–22, 124, 125, 129, 151, 165–66, 168–74, 175–76, 193, 198–99, 201, 202, 204, 208–9, 213, 230, 252, 253; Atlanta speech, 150, 162
Washington, D.C., 157–58, 330–34; bonus march on, 272; Negro march committee, 272–73
Washington *Bee,* 164
Waters, Ethel, 243
Watertown (N.Y.) *Times,* 216
Watson-Parker Bill, 256–57
Weary Blues, 243
Weaver, Robert, 270
Webster, Daniel, 51
Webster, Faith, 77
Wells, Ida B., 145
Wendell, Barrett, 185
Wescott, Glenway, 282
Wesley, Charles, 242
Wesley, John, 35
Wessel, Germany, 306
West: postwar for Negroes, 130; slavery in, 76
West Indies, 36
Weston, Samuel, 36, 37
West Point, 94, 215

What the Negro Thinks, 242

Wheeler, Joseph, 85, 88, 89, 91

Wheatley, Phillis, 43

Whigs, 50, 81

White, Walter, 243, 249, 272, 274, 320, 327

White House, 175, 266, 272

White supremacy, 118, 134, 237, 274

Wilberforce University, 80–81

Wilcox, Samuel, 96

Wilhelm II, Kaiser of Germany, 187

Williams, Aubrey, 269, 273

Williams, Daniel, 129, 135

Williams, Dr. Daniel Hale, 128–48, 149, 150, 154–78, 194

Williams, Fannie B., 122–23, 145

Williams, John Sharp, 149

Williams, Peter, 66, 67, 72, 73

Williams, Price, 129, 162

Williams, Sally, 131

Williams, Sarah Ann, 129, 162–63

Williams, Mrs. S. Laing, 169

Willkie, Wendell, 268–69, 301

Wilmot Proviso, 59

Wilson, Woodrow, 203, 208, 215–16

Winchester, battle of, 17

Wise, Henry, 59, 62

Women's rights, 77. *See also* Feminist movement

Wood, Leonard, 84

Wood, L. Hollingsworth, 201

Woodson, Carter G., 242, 318

Woofter, Thomas, 267

Woollcott, Alexander, 279, 283

World's Work, 212

World War I, 209; Negro participation in, 215–27

World War II, 285, 305; Negro participation in, 306–12

Wright, Caesar, 36, 37

Wright, Richard, 281

Yale University, 151

Yazoo-Mississippi Railroad, 114

Young, Charles, 215–16

Young, John D., Jr., 213

Young, Otto, 147

Zion Hill, 71, 72

THE MAINSTREAM OF AMERICA SERIES

PRESENTING the story of America in narrative form, this monumental series covers the entire sweep of this nation's history—from the earliest days of exploration to the recent days of turmoil and achievement. Books published in the series, for which Doubleday has received the Carey Thomas Award, are:

The Age of Fighting Sail by C. S. Forester

The Age of the Moguls by Stewart H. Holbrook

From Lexington to Liberty by Bruce Lancaster

Glory, God and Gold by Paul I. Wellman

The Land They Fought For by Clifford Dowdey

New Found World by Harold Lamb

Men to Match My Mountains by Irving Stone

The Men Who Made the Nation by John Dos Passos

This Hallowed Ground by Bruce Catton

Dreamers of the American Dream by Stewart H. Holbrook

The Lonesome Road by Saunders Redding

The Mainstream of America Series is edited by the distinguished critic and writer, Lewis Gannett. All books in the series are in print.